ADVANCED
EDUCATIONAL PSYCHOLOGY

ADVANCED
EDUCATIONAL PSYCHOLOGY

Advanced Educational Psychology

Seema Sharma

ANMOL PUBLICATIONS PVT. LTD.
NEW DELHI - 110 002 (INDIA)

ANMOL PUBLICATIONS PVT. LTD.
H.O.: 4374/4B, Ansari Road, Darya Ganj,
New Delhi-110 002 (India)
Ph.: 23278000, 23261597
B.O.: No. 1015, Ist Main Road, BSK IIIrd Stage
IIIrd Phase, IIIrd Block,
Bangalore - 560 085 (India)
Visit us at: www.anmolpublications.com

Advanced Educational Psychology

First Published, 2005
Reprint, 2008

PRINTED IN INDIA

Printed at Mehra Offset Press, Delhi.

Contents

Preface

Undoubtedly, psychology plays a significant role in the life of each and every humanbeing. But at the same time, it has its own diverse inherent facets too. To some, it proves to be positive, while for some as negative. It has left a wide impact on the life and career of man as a whole. As far as the role of psychology in education is concerned, it is really phenomenal. It has been the cause of construction and destruction, both. Starting from childhood, if it is utilised positively, it plays a vital role in the building up of a bright career of a child. But its negative application leaves the child stranded for the whole life. This is the reason that, a host of steps have been taken and are being taken, now more seriously, in the inception of the education of children. They are being shaped psychologically to measure the distance in education and life successfully.

Advanced educational psychology is the growing need for today's education system with matured perceptions. The modern society has taken a significant turn. The complexes of the people together with the complexes of society have also grown. The cultural and moral aspects find lesser importance in the society today. So, a dire liability falls on the shoulder of the teachers to shape the life of their disciples in such a way, that they are able to cope with the situations ahead. It is also the responsibility of the parents to educate and shape their children in such a way that they could become psychologically matured.

Psychology touches every part of life, while, the process of teaching contributes a lot in improving the standard of a child. The process of psychological learning also possesses the same significance in this regard. As far as Advanced Educational Psychology is concerned, the role of the educational psychologist should be considered potent to help the society in all ways.

The book, first of its kind, covers the whole spectrum of the discipline in a novel manner. Hopefully it would be recognised by all concerned — scholars, educationists, teachers, students and others.

Editor

1

Introduction

In a simple language, educational psychology implies the application of principles and practices of psychology to the various dimensions of education with a view to modify the behaviour of the learner in an educational environment so that he amicably adjusts himself with the society with maximum of satisfaction and security. Thus educational psychology is the applied branch of psychology in an educational setting.

Following definitions would enable us to understand the true meaning of educational psychology in its various facets.

In the words of Anderson, "While general psychology is a pure science, educational psychology is its application in the field of education with the aim of socialising an individual and modifying his behaviour".

E.A. Peel considers educational psychology as the 'science of education.'

Crow and Crow put it as, "Educational psychology describes and explains the learning experiences of an individual from birth through old age."

According to Skinner, "Educational psychology is that branch of psychology which deals with teaching and learning." He has also observed, "Educational psychology covers the entire range and behaviour of the personality as related to education."

Judd considers educational psychology as "the science which explains the changes that take place in the individuals as they pass through the various stages of development".

Stephen regards educational psychology as "the systematic study of the educational growth and development of a child."

The Encyclopaedia of Educational Research states, "Educational psychology is the study of the learner and of the learning-teaching process in its various (branches) directed towards helping the child come to terms with society with a maximum of security and satisfaction."

According to Walter B. Kolesnik, "Educational psychology is the study of those facts and principles of psychology which help to explain and improve the process of education."

In the words of Trow, "Educational psychology is the study of psychological aspects of educational situation."

A perusal of the above definitions would indicate that the definitions given by Anderson Kolesnik and 'The Encyclopaedia of Educational Research' provide the true meaning of educational psychology. Other definitions, by and large, put emphasis on 'Study' but do not emphatically state the ultimate aim of studying a subject. A mere study of the behaviour of the learner is not enough unless it is related to the modification of the behaviour towards desired ends.

From these it is concluded that educational psychology is that applied branch of psychology which studies the experiences and behaviours of the learners in relation to educational environment which is mainly provided by the teacher. Therefore, educational psychology becomes a psychology of teaching and learning. Teaching and learning are the main processes of education and the learner is a key figure in the process.

Meaning and Concept

Following points point out the nature of educational psychology. Some of the points overlap.

1. Educational psychology is an applied science.
2. Educational psychology is a social science.
3. Educational psychology is a positive science.
4. Educational psychology is a specific science.
5. Educational psychology is a developing and growing science.
6. Educational psychology is an academic discipline.
7. Educational psychology is not as exact as natural and physical sciences.

Scope of educational psychology is as vast as the scope of education itself. Gates and others have very aptly remarked, "The boundaries of educational psychology are uncertain and changing." The explosion of 'Information Technology '(IT) has been exercising a far-reaching influence on the scope of educational psychology. New and novel situations need new and novel approaches to educational matters. Nevertheless, we may mention the most significant areas of the scope of educational psychology. Here we are listing only the ways of classification.

Classification I: Broad Areas

1. Learner: Growth and Development
   - (a) Heredity and environment affecting the learner.
   - (b) General ,growth and development of the learner at different stages of education.
   - (c) Emotional, intellectual and social development of the learner.
   - (d) Individual differences of the learners.
   - (e) Learner's aptitudes, interests and intelligence.
2. Learning
   - (a) Concept of learning.
   - (b) Process of learning.
   - (c) Primary and concomitant learning.
   - (d) Domains of learning: Cognitive, Affective and Psychomotor.
   - (e) Learning process

(f) Factors affecting learning.

(g) Transfer of training.

(h) Learning situations.

3. Personality and Adjustment

(a) Emotions.

(b) Mental health of the learner.

(c) Mental health of the teacher.

(d) Character development.

(e) Social interaction.

4. Evaluation and Measurement

(a) Meaning of the concepts of evaluation and measurement.

(b) Basic principles of evaluation and measurement.

(c) Measurement of aptitudes, attitudes and intelligence.

(d) Measurement of learning.

(e) Measures of adjustment.

(f) Applications of the results of measurement and evaluation.

5. Techniques and Methods in Educational Psychology

(a) Scientific study of educational problems.

(b) Statistical techniques.

(c) Implications of research for the classroom teacher.

Classification II: In Terms of Learner and Learning

1. The learner (Pupil).
2. The learning experiences.
3. The learning environment or situation.
4. The learning process.
5. The teaching situation.
6. Evaluation of learning experience.

Classification III: The Educational Psychology Division of the American Psychological Association

1. Human growth and development.

2. Learning.
3. Personality and adjustment.
4. Measurement, evaluation and statistics.
5. Techniques and methods of educational psychologies.

The Learner through Out: This includes the study of growth and development of the individual and the concept of maturity in various aspects of personality-physical, mental, social and emotional. Study of learner deals with the influences of his family, social class and peer groups on his personality and behaviour. Social behaviour and social norms of his peer group; emotional health and problem behaviour of the learner are also studied in detail from the mental hygiene point of view. This also includes the study of the abilities, needs and motivational forces, like self-concept, life-goals, values, anxiety of the individual learner as well as the differences that exist among different individuals.

Learning Experiences: This includes providing activities and subjects according to the maturity level of the students.

The Learning Situation: In the learning situation, educational psychology studies such factors as class-room management and discipline, techniques and aids which facilitate learning, methods of teaching, evaluation techniques and practices, guidance and counselling.

The Learning Process: In the learning process, educational psychology deals with the nature of learning and how it takes place. It considers the various theoretical view points as well as experimental evidences to explain the role and nature of reinforcement, forgetting, problem solving, transfer of training and the learning of concepts, skills and attitudes.

The Teaching Situation: Effectiveness of educational psychology becomes relevant only when its methods and findings become a part of educational practices when the teachers apply psychological methods.

Evaluation of Learning Experiences: In recent years, evaluation of learning experiences has assumed great significance in the subject matter of psychology.

What, when and how to teach Questions of Educational Psychology ?

Educational psychologists are more concerned with the answer of these questions. The first question refers to the developmental processes that gradually mature as the child grows up. Similarly the problem of what to teach is important because of its close relationship with the process of maturation. Certain types of learning can be useful to the child only when he has matured sufficiently in certain faculties. We cannot think of teaching mathematics to a three year child, though he may be taught to count simple things. The problem of how to teach is equally important because there are ways and means of teaching which can make the education of a child more effective, meaningful and useful.

Different Facets

Educational psychology, being functional in its character is very helpful to all sections of society engaged in pursuing different dimensions of education at all levels of education i.e., formal, non-formal and informal.

Educational psychology is of great importance to parents, teachers, guidance workers, career masters, and psychoanalysts etc.

According to W.A. Kelly (1941), educational psychology is helpful in the following ways:

1. It provides a knowledge of the ature of the child.
2. It gives understanding of the nature, aims and purposes of education.
3. It gives understanding of the scientific methods and procedures which have been used in arriving at the facts and principles of educational psychology.
4. It presents the principles and techniques of learning and teaching.
5. It gives training in methods of measuring abilities and achievement in school subjects.

6. It provides a knowledge of the growth and development of children.
7. It assists in the better adjustment of children and helps to prevent maladjustment.
8. It helps to understand the significance and control of emotions.
9. It gives an understanding of the principles and techniques of correct training.

Psychology's Role in Education

An elementary knowledge of educational psychology would prove very useful to the parents who are undoubtedly the first teachers in the following manners:

1. The knowledge of educational psychology points out to the parents that they should show reasonable amount of love and affection to their children. They should bear in mind the maxim, "Love the child and the child will love you. Hate the child and he will hate you."
2. It helps the parents to understand the process of development and growth of their children.
3. Educational psychology acquaints the parents with the emotional, mental and physical needs of the children.
4. Educational psychology impresses upon the parents of the necessity of providing wholesome environment to the children so that they lead a happy life and are free from anxiety.
5. Educational psychology enables the parents to know that they should not take resource to repression and punishment which adversely affect the mental health of children.
6. Educational psychology enables the parents to observe keenly the behaviour of children. It enables them to control their habits.
7. It helps the parents to understand themselves, their roles and responsibilities towards their children.

The work of the teacher is like that of a gardener to a great extent. The gardener needs the knowledge of the plant life. The teacher also needs the knowledge of the learner. It is the duty of the gardener to ensure that all the plants grow and yield good flowers and fruits and he can do so when he is well-acquainted with all the details about them. The objective of the teacher is to ensure that all the learners under his care and charge develop into happy and healthy personalities and he can do so only when he knows how the learners develop and behave. This knowledge is provided to the teacher by educational psychology.

The work of the teacher may also be compared to that of an artist who must know his material thoroughly if he wants to produce a fine piece of art. What will happen to the artist if he starts his work without fully understanding the kind of material he has to work with. The teacher as an artist, is not only required to know the subject matter but also to know the child's nature and the techniques of moulding his behaviour in accordance with the objectives.

The work of the teacher assume all the more significance and needs more delicacy and expertness than that of the gardener and the artist as here, human beings are involved.

R. A. Davis in 'Applicability and Applications of Psychology with Particular Reference to Classroom Learning' (1943) has pointed out the significance of educational psychology as, "Psychology has made a distinct contribution to education through its analysis of pupil potentialities and differences as revealed by means of various types of psychological tests. It has also contributed directly to the knowledge of pupil growth and maturation during the school years."

G.M. Blair in 'The Psychological Interpretation of Teaching' (1947) has stated the importance of educational psychology to the teacher in these words," Modern teacher, if he is to succeed with his work should be a specialist who understands children, how they grow, develop, learn and adjust. He should be diagnostician, who can discover special difficulties of children and at the same time possesses the requisite skill for carrying forward the necessary remedial work. He should also be performing important educational and vocational guidance functions. No person untrained in the methods of psychology can possibly fulfil the obligations and tasks which are the responsibilities of the teacher."

Fundamental Issues

Principles and practices of educational psychology are needed by the teacher on account of the following considerations:

Knowledge of John and Latin: Sir John Adams has put it thus in his book 'New Teaching'. The verbs of teaching govern two accusatives, one of the person and another of the thing as, 'the master taught John Latin'." He says that there are two definite subjects-John, the student and Latin the subject which are governed by the verb taught". Now the teacher must understand both John as well as Latin if he wants to make 'teaching' effective. Educational psychology helps him in understanding 'John'. He may be a great scholar of Latin but he will not succeed in teaching Latin to John if he has no knowledge of the mental set up of John. Acquisition of knowledge is now no more the main object of education but it is still very significant in the process of education. Acquisition of knowledge is also a sort of modification in the behaviour of the child. For this purpose the educator will have to consider the mental processes of the child and not only the quality of knowledge which he is going to be put into the living mind. .

Knowledge of Individual Differences: No two persons are exactly alike. There is individual difference. Pupils always differ in their level of intelligence, aptitudes, likes and dislikes and in other propensities and potentialities. Different minds are to be trained by the teacher. There are gifted, backward, retarded, talented and handicapped children. All of them should not be treated in the same manner. Knowledge of educational psychology helps the teacher to cater to individual differences of children.

Educational Psychology and Process of Learning: Teaching and learning go side by side. All education depends upon the learning of new responses and the capacity of a human child to learn new responses. Educational psychology discusses the nature of learning theories and types of learning for different age levels and situations. Therefore, knowledge of educational psychology becomes essential to a teacher to study all these problems.

Knowledge of Educational Psychology Provides a Scientific Attitude to the Teachers: The knowledge of psychology can make the teacher more scientific in his educational practices and consequently he will be more objective and methodical in his work.

Psychology Proves Useful in the Methods of Teaching: Educational psychology has discovered many secrets about mental forces. Recent researches made in the field of educational psychology give us valuable suggestions for better methods of teaching and memorizing, for making desirable habits and eradicating anti-social tendencies. Educational psychology tells us how significant play and recreation are for the children and how play-way and project methods turn the work of learning into an interesting play.

Educational Psychology can Change the Outlook and Attitude of the Teacher Towards his Pupils: The knowledge of psychology can change the outlook and attitude of the teacher towards children by understanding them adequately.

Educational Psychology Helps the Teacher in his Own Mental Development: The study of educational psychology can help the teacher to understand himself. He will realise his own merits and weaknesses and make attempts to overcome his weaknesses.

Educational Psychology and Nervous System: The entire education depends on the function of the brain and nervous system. It becomes essential for a teacher to study the nervous system which controls human behaviour. He must have the knowledge of sensory organs which are the gate ways of knowledge.

Educational Psychology and Play: Play is a natural tendency having great educational potentials. Knowledge of educational psychology helps the teacher to provide for a varieties of activities for children.

Educational Psychological Measurements are Very Useful for the Teacher: Educational psychology has made many strides in this respect quite recently. It has produced many reliable tests and instruments of mental measurement. These are proving to be extremely useful in the field of education. We can quite easily measure mental capacities, basic intelligence, temperamental attitudes and special inclinations of children and base educational programmes on these findings. These measurements show that all the children differ in and that every child is a unique being. The teacher can know that children with I.Q. below 90 cannot do well in medical, engineering, administrative or other similar vocations. But he knows that such young ones are not doomed if they cannot do well in intellectual callings. He can easily explore some other fields where such children can also flourish.

Character Development: Educational psychology helps a lot to the formation and development of character. The teacher comes to know the methods he should adopt in inculcating suitable character traits, and moral principles among the children.

Educational Psychology and Productive Activities: A great stress is being laid these days on work experience and socially useful productive work. Educational psychology helps the teacher to know how various activities in these fields can be used for the fulfilment of the basic needs of children.

Educational Psychology Helps the Teacher in Guidance and Counselling: Students need various types of guidance and counselling. A teacher with the knowledge of educational psychology can render very useful service.

Educational Psychology Helps the Teacher in the Realization of the Aims of Education: The main aim of education is the harmonious and all-around development of the education. Development comes from within and the inner potentialities must be understood and approached for the desired modification in the development of the child. The knowledge of educational psychology helps the teacher to understand the inner potentialities which underlie the behaviour of the child.

2

The Fundamentals

Adolescents aged between 10-19 years account for more than one-fifth of the world's population. In India, this age group forms 21.4 percent of the total population. Characterised by distinct physical and social changes, the separate health, education, economic and employment needs of adolescents cannot be ignored. Adolescents are also entitled to enjoy all basic human rights—economic, social, political and cultural—but their inability to exercise these rights places the onus on policy makers and adults to implement separate measures to ensure their rights. Moreover, it is necessary to invest in adolescents as the future leaders and guardians of the nation's development.

The significant role of India's adolescence population in achieving its developmental goals must be recognised. It is, therefore, very necessary to cater to the needs, interests, goals and values of the adolescents.

As observed in Adolescence in India, "A prerequisite for policy planning and focus is a comprehensive situational analysis of adolescence." The lack of reliable data on the adolescent age group is a major impediment in discussing interests, goals and values of Indian adolescence.

Days of Youth

Three main stages of adolescence can be discerned:

Early Adolescence (9-13 years) : Characterised by a spurt of growth and the development of secondary sexual characteristics.

Mid Adolescence (14-15 years) : This stage is distinguished by the development of a separate identity from parents, of new relationships with peer groups and the opposite sex, and of experimentation.

Late Adolescence (16-19 years) : At this stage, adolescents have fully developed physical characteristics (similar to adults), and have formed a distinct identity and have well-formed opinions and ideas.

Groups of Adolescence : Adolescents are generally perceived as a homogenous group, yet they can be stratified on the basis of gender, caste, class geographical location (urban/rural) and religion. Adolescents also include a whole gamut of categories: School and non-school going, drop-outs, sexually exploited children, working adolescents-both paid and unpaid, unmarried adolescents as also married males and females with experience of fatherhood and motherhood.

Analytical Evaluation

An overview, based on the secondary data available, confirms the need for a separate focus on the health, education, employment and protection of human rights of adolescents. Reproductive health, in particular, represents the most critical area where an emphasis on the special needs and concerns of adolescents is required. In India, given its predominantly patriarchal set up, ideology of son preference, incidence of early marriage and high rates of maternal mortality, a strong focus on the needs of adolescent girls is warranted. However, both sexes are vulnerable to problems such as those of drug abuse, HIV/AIDS and other infections and sexual abuse.

Different Concerns

As already observed, there is a lack of reliable and scientific data on this issue. However, it must be accepted that on account of the influence of electronic media, Indian adolescent cannot remain unaffected by globalisation. Nevertheless, following interests, goals and values of Indian adolescent are discernible although it is very difficult to generalise as there are several subgroups on account of the vastness of the country and its plural culture.

Interests: 1. Recreational Interests: (i) Interest in folk dance (ii) Television watching (iii) Celebrating birthdays and attending parties. (iv) Folk dance and music (v) Pop dance and singing (vi) Watching movies (vii) Reading comics and sensational literature (viii) Travelling (ix) Interest in pen-friendship (x) Interest in television games (xi) Watching and Listening Cricket commentaries (xii) Playing cards (xiii) Trends towards for fun gambling (xiv) Interest in smoking as a fashion symbol (xv) Trends towards use of drug and pills. (xvi) Interest in fine arts (xvii) Exchanging jokes (xviii) Interest in drinking, it being status symbol

Religious Interests: (i) Usually sceptical of religious beliefs (ii) Disinterest in the observance of religious rites and ceremonies (iii) In difference to formal religion.

Social Interest: (i) Attending group parties, (ii) Mixing with the opposite sex, (iii) Interest in global matters, (iv) Demonstrating self identity in the group, (v) Group loyalty.

Vocational Interests: (a) Interest in professions related to Commerce, (b) Interest in information technology and especially computers.

Miscellaneous Interest: (i) Conversation in groups (ii) Interest in beautification of the body, (iii) Interest in new things, (iv) Trend towards foreign studies, (v) Trend towards settling in foreign lands, (vi) Heightened sex interest.

Goals: (i) Becoming rich over night. (ii) Getting power and exercising influence. (iii) Capturing political power (iv) Occupying higher posts. (iv) Becoming independent of joint family and having nuclear family.

Values: (1) Re-examination of traditional beliefs and customs and acquiring new ones, (2) Emancipation from home and becoming independent, (3) Knowing everything attitude, (4) Growing gulf between the values of parents and adults, (5) Critical attitude, (6) Indifference to respect for elders, (7) Declining faith in the leaders of all shades.

Related Steps

Serious problem of 10-14 Year Group: Since adolescents comprise a major part of the reproductive age group, addressing their needs will be critical in determining India's population. An analysis within the age group itself indicates that proportion of 10-14 year olds is greater than the 15-19 year group.

Problem of Gender Discrimination: Any programme for adolescents must recognise the problem of gender discrimination of the adolescents.

Problem of Under Nutrition: If India wishes to achieve the goals of 'Health for All' and adequate 'Nutrition for All', it must attend to the problem of under nutrition among adolescent girls. A sizeable number of adolescent girls are actually malnourished. This will increase the risk of difficulty to child birth.

Problem of Poor Understanding of Reproductive Health: A poor understanding of reproductive health and sexual issues creates several problems in this area.

Problems of High Level of Pre-marital Sexual Activity: In this regard, following trends are noticed:

(i) The magnitude of adolescent sexual activity is significant, and is higher in boys than girls. There is also under-reporting of non-marital relationships by adolescent girls due to fear of social disapproval.

(ii) Men are likely to be sexually active and at an earlier age than girls, and attitudes on premarital sexual activity remain conservative. Furthermore, the acceptance of premarital sexual activity is greater among boys than girls.

(iii) Parents and teachers play a minor role in giving information, and are usually reluctant to impart such information. The majority of information on sexual and reproductive issues is obtained from peers (which can sometimes be misleading and inaccurate).

(iv) Commercial sex workers usually serve as partners for first-time sexual encounters.

(v) Contraceptive use is low and rarely used in first-time sexual encounters, including with commercial sex workers. Contraceptive awareness is usually about sterilisation, which is unsuitable for most adolescents. Knowledge of HIV/AIDS, safe sex and preventive behaviour (like use of condoms) is low, across all ages and education levels.

(vi) Knowledge of sexual and reproductive issues is extremely poor. In some studies, 50 percent of female adolescents did not know about mensuration, and the limited knowledge was based on social factors (such as not being permitted to cook) than the actual physiological changes.

(vii) There is considerable interest among adolescent boys for information on reproductive health.

(viii) Education did not increase knowledge of sex and reproduction.

(ix) The educational system does not adequately meet the needs for imparting sex education.

(x) Sexual and reproductive decision-making by adolescents is constrained by age and gender factors. Adolescent women have little choice on whom and when to marry, and are usually not in a position to negotiate contraceptive use. This varies slightly with age, with an older wife more likely to make such decisions.

(xi) There is a huge unmet demand for adolescent health facilities, information and counselling services.

Unwanted Pregnancies and Abortions: There is a lack of knowledge of appropriate use of contraceptives. Son preference is another reason.

Maternal Mortality: This is on account of the fact that the body has not yet reached full maturity. Marriage age is very low.

Sexually Transmitted Deceases (STDs), including HIV/AIDS: Young people between the ages of 10 and 25 years make up 50 per cent of all new infections.

Drug Abuse: In India, it is estimated that a substantial number of drug users are in the age group of 12 to 18.

Violence against Women, Sexual Abuse and Trafficking of Girls: Available data indicate that a high incidence of rape occurs in the 10-16 year age group.

Gender Difference in Literacy and Education: The gross enrolment ratio (GER) for girls including adolescent girls lags behind boys. Likewise drop-out rates in the case of adolescent girls are higher than boys.

High Incidence of Unemployment Among Adolescents: Overall, the unemployment rates are almost three times as high for adolescents as that among aged 15 and above.

Depression Leading to Suicide: Every year, suicide is one of the most leading causes of death among them. Each year, 15 to 25 per cent of high school students seriously consider taking this course with depression being the prime motive.

Alcohol and Tobacco Abuse: Alcohol and tobacco abuse is very common among 2.5 to 3 per cent of children between 15 to 20 years of age.

Sex Encounter: In Delhi alone, 15 per cent of children in the age group 15 to 20 have already had their first sexual encounter.

HIV Infections: Sex encounter combined with the lack of awareness at this stage has also increased the possibility of HIV (Human immunodeficiency Virus) infections. India has currently an HIV infection rate of 1.7 per 1000 of which more than 40 per cent is concentrated around teenagers.

Emotional Stress: Family pressures to study and perform better indirectly result in emotional stress for a teenager.

Improper Company: Hanging around with improper friends may also lead to drug abuse, HIV and early pregnancy.

Miscellaneous Issues: Teenagers face numerous issues ranging from pubertal changes pimples, obesity, short height and changes in body structure, to medical problems like asthma, diabetes, thyroid disorders, eating disorders (anorexia) and bed welting.

Concerned Steps

Adolescent Clinic: Dr. Kumar suggests special adolescent clinics. 'Adolescent medicine' a new branch of medical science, might just be the sweet pill in teen's life.

National Policy: There should be a national policy that facilitates establishing adolescent care clinics in hospitals and health centers across the country.

3

Advanced Psychology

In modern times, during this age of science and technology, psychology has been considered as one of the youngest; yet one of the most influential sciences. It has influenced education in different ways and practically given a new turn, a psychological turn to the human mind. For a skilful teacher of the present-day society, knowledge of the child has been considered to be more important than the knowledge of the subject matter. Therefore, teachers in the modern society should be equipped with those psychological skills and competence, which are badly needed for the successful guidance of learning, adjustment and the growth of the child.

The subject 'Psychology' has two aspects-pure and applied. Pure psychology formulates broad principles brings out theories and suggests techniques for the study of human behaviour, which finds in its applied aspect, i.e. branches of Applied Psychology, Clinical Psychology, Crime Psychology, Industrial Psychology, Occupational Psychology and Educational Psychology. Therefore, Educational Psychology is nothing but one of the branches of Applied Psychology in the practical shape It is an attempt to apply the knowledge of Pure Psychology to the field of education.

It consists of application principles and techniques to human behaviour in educational situations. In other words. Educational Psychology is a study of the experiences and behaviour of the learner in relation to educational environment. In order to develop a clear understanding of the term 'Educational Psychology', it is necessary to understand the meaning of psychology and education separately.

Various Disciplines

Psychology as Science of Soul : About 2000 years ago, Psychology appeared as a separate branch of study. It was the genius of Aristotle that gave birth to this science. Yet, in its modern form, it is one of the latest of all disciplines. It has been changing its meaning from time to time. According to Rudolf Goeckel the term psychology has been derived from two words, "Psycho" and "Logos", Psycho means soul and Logos means "Science of" or "Talk about".

Thus psychology means "The science of soul". Goeckel named it as Psychologia. Soul is a being which dwells in the body and at the end of life it leaves the body. Since soul is a metaphysical entity, scientific investigation is not possible. Therefore psychology as the science of soul has been discarded by the modern psychologists. Therefore, the definition of psychology as the science of soul was discarded.

Psychology as Science of Mind : The philosophers again developed another definition of psychology as the "Science of Mind". After sometime controversy arose on the nature of mind. People began to feel that like soul, it is equally impossible to define mind scientifically. Ultimately this definition was discarded.

Psychology as Science of Consciousness : Psychology was again defined as the science of consciousness or immediate experiences. Ultimately, it was observed that consciousness forms only a very negligible part of the personality of an individual and the scope of psychology goes much beyond the study of consciousness. It also studies the sub-conscious and unconscious states of human mind. On this ground, the psychologists rejected this definition.

Psychology as Science of Behaviour : The above definitions given by philosopher-psychologists before the beginning of experimental psychology were considered to be very much inadequate and were rejected. Now it is defined as "the science of behaviour". To understand this definition, let us now discuss in brief the meaning of the science and behaviour.

Concept of Behaviour and Science : Science has been defined as "systematic study of knowledge" concerning the relationship between the cause and effect of a particular phenomenon. In order to collect the scientific data and systematised material, science employs various kinds of methods of enquiry such as observation, classification, formulation of hypothesis, analysis of evidence, etc. It also organises and develops our knowledge of the world, we live in. Psychology too aims at the same thing. It uses scientific methods to study human behaviour. It also helps us to understand, control and predict human behaviour.

Behaviour is a specific response which can be seen and observed in an active way. Psychology as the science of behaviour also aims at studying the behaviour of the individual and groups. We can study the behaviour of an individual in social mileu. As a social science it studies scientifically the socio-cultural problems of particular society. Hence it is the science of behaviour.

Educational Perception

"Education is an activity, which goes on in the society." It attempts to develop the personality of an individual and then prepares him for membership in a society. "Man without education would still be living just like an animal. It is education, which transforms man from a mere two legged animal into a human. It helps him to behave like a man and prevents him from behaving like an animal. Any modification brought about in the behaviour of an individual as result of his interaction with the environment constitutes learning." Thus modification of behaviour of an individual for healthy social adjustment in the society is education.

Psychology of Education : The term Educational Psychology is the combination of two words. Education and Psychology. So far, we have discussed the meaning of Psychology and Education separately. Let us now focus our attention to the meaning of Educational Psychology.

Psychology is the science of behaviour. It aims at studying the behaviour of individual and the group. Besides, this it also helps us to control the behaviour of the organism as a whole. Education on the other hand, implies the modification of the behaviour of an individual.

In order to modify the behaviour of an individual, the teacher must study the behaviour of the individual first. To study the behaviour of the child the teacher must take the help of true Psychology and to modify the behaviour of the child he must take the help of Education. Thus, Education and Psychology are interrelated. Pure Psychology helps to study behaviour and Educational Psychology as an applied branch of psychology applies psychological principles of Education to modify human behaviour.

Educational Psychology as outlined above is a branch of psychology concerned with human learning and development in educational settings. It involves scientific study of techniques that can be used to enhance learning. Studies conducted by the Educational Psychologists generally deal with the following three important areas.

Process of Teaching

It includes teaching methods, styles, management techniques etc.

Process of Learning

It includes application of principles of cognitive and developmental Psychology, taking into account individual differences and learning styles.

Surrounding Environment

It includes social context of the classroom or home environment.

Educational Psychology

Sl.	Education		Psychology
1.	Modern education is a group phenomenon. Hence some of the group psychological laws can be applied to the process of education viz. group dynamics.	1.	Psychology also deals with groups.
2.	Modern education is defined as for behaviour, of behaviour and by behaviour. Hence psychological laws, processes and findings can be applied to education.	2.	Psychology is surely a behavioural science.
3.	Educational goal today is all round psychology development of the individual. Hence psychology aids teachers in affording better educational development of children.	3.	Developmental psychology gives required insight into human develcpment in all of its aspects.
4.	Modern education caters to the needs, interests and abilities of children. Hence knowledge of psychology of needs and of interests enables teachers to plan educational programmes in a desirable manner.	4.	Psychology enables understanding of needs, interests and abilities of children.
5.	Education involves proper organisation learning of teaching learning situation. Hence it is a common meeting group of both the subjects.	5.	Psychology of learning gives insight into these areas.
6.	Education aims at the development of personality and character. Hence there are psychological aspects in this area also.	6.	Psychology analyses these aspects of development minutely.

According to Arthur Coladarci of Stanford University, Educational Psychology is the empirical foundation of education. It consists of those aspects of education which can be observed, tested and experimentally verified and as such Educational Psychology is the scientific foundation of Education. But effectiveness of Educational Psychology is proved only when its methods and findings become a part of educational practices, when the teachers apply psychological methods and when they develop and experiment attitudes towards their efforts.

Judd describes Educational Psychology "as a scientific study of the life stages in the development of an individual from the time he is born until he becomes an adult."

Charles E. Skinner states, "Educational Psychology is the branch of psychology which deals with teaching and learning."

According to Walter B. Kolesnik "Educational Psychology is knowledge of the study of those facts and principles of psychology which helps to explain and improve the process of education. Educational Psyhology thus is the body of scientific knowledge about two activities-Education and Psychology."

Inherent Nature

We often put a question-What is the Nature of Educational Psychology? The answer to this question becomes almost clear when we try to examine the meaning and definitions discussed earlier. Its nature is scientific as it has been accepted that it is a science of education. Its relation with education and educational psychology is also to throw light on its nature. We can summarise the nature of educational psychology in the following way.

(i) Educational Psychology is a positive and not a normative science: Usually normative sciences like Ethics and Philosophy decide the aims of education. It is not the function of Educational Psychology to decide the same. But once it is decided Educational Psychology will help us in telling whether aims are attainable or intangible. As a positive science, Educational Psychology will be concerned with the discovery of techniques, by which the educational goals can be attained out of scientific study. When psychology declares that a particular aim is unattainable, philosophers will then rethink and modify the goals of education.

(ii) Educational Psychology is a Behavioural Science: As noted earlier, the scientific study of how learning and other human behaviour have relevance to education is the principal concern of Educational Psychology. Thus Educational Psychology may be thought of as a behavioural science with two main referents-human behaviour and education. In the educative process human beings are the objects of investigation about whom generalisations are developed and knowledge is sought. The second important referent of education, Educational Psychology is concerned with behavioural questions that are related to the objectives and practices of education.

(iii) Educational Psychology is an Applied Science: The action of Educational Psychology is to be found not only in the nature of the subject itself but rather in its application in the classroom. Teachers primarily deal with groups of children not with psychological theory or experimental results, but their learning is constantly being applied to a unique set of circumstances. That is why teaching is a profession and not a trade.

Educational psychology is just an application of psychological principles in the field of education and also changing the behaviour of the individual. It is to predict behaviour, control and influence it. Thus it becomes an applied branch of Psychology.

(iv) Educational Psychology is a Social Science: Social psychologists study humans who interact frequently, if not continually, with each other and live in groups ranging from the family to the society. Social psychologists are not only concerned with the effect of the groups (whether family, peer, professional, cultural or social) upon the individual and vice versa, but are also interested in a wide variety of other personal interactions.

(v) Educational Psychology is a Counselling Psychology: We use the word counselling to refer to the functions of psychologists whose principal job is to deal with people who are in need of help or advice but not primarily who have emotional difficulties. A branch of psychology closely related to counselling is to be found in the work of the school psychologists—planning, teacher training, problem of parents, and the like. Educational Psychology thus encompasses counselling psychology.

(vi) Educational Psychology in an Educational Science: General psychology may be considered as the primary behavioural science. The domain of psychology is very broad, including the study of collective behavioural problems of individuals in educational situations. Educational Psychology collects necessary knowledge from general psychology to apply the same in educational setting. For example, to discover what makes teaching effective and what makes learning effective. We need the help of several special areas of general psychology. In Developmental Psychology the teacher learns about human growth from infancy (and even before) to maturity-how physical, intellectual, emotional, and social potentials mature and change as a child grows; what conditions foster healthy growth, and what conditions block it. Many changes in teaching methods and curriculum have come about as more has been learned about the ways in which children typically develop and how their needs change. Another focal point of attention has been the special problems of the child who is "different" in some way.

The Psychology of learning is concerned with acquisition and change of our patterns of behaviour, how those processes take place most efficiently, how learning of different kinds can be measured, what conditions help us retain what we learn and use it appropriately in new situations, and how learning varies with different levels of ability. Many kinds of learning "content" are involved in school work from simple muscular responses to highly complex intellectual process. A teacher's need for studying the psychology of learning is obvious.

It becomes evident that modern psychology offers a great deal of help to educational psychology to apply scientific principles to educational settings and thus educational psychology becomes an educational science.

(vii) Educational Psychology is concerned with Human Factor in Learning: *The Encyclopedia of Educational Research* (1960) defined the nature of Educational Psychology as follows:

Educational psychology is concerned with human factor in the learning. It is a field in which concepts derived from experimental work in psychological laboratories are applied to education, but is also a field in which experimentation is carried out to test the applicability of such concepts to education and to round out the study of topics of crucial interest to teachers. It is the study of the learning teaching process in its various ramifications.

(viii) Educational Psychology is a Growing Science: Historically, Educational Psychology began with William James and Edward Thorndike in the USA in 1808. Since then the field of educational psychology has been influenced by works in related fields such as developmental psychology, educational measurement, cognitive psychology, personality theory, counselling, individual differences, and most recently computer science researchers, who are involved in scientific study of techniques that can be used to enhance the teaching learning process are contributing many new ideas to be applied in the field of education:

(i) Not the Nature of Subject but its Application in the Classroom is its Real Nature: The nature of Educational Psychology is in no way concerned with the nature of the subject matter itself but with its application in the classroom situation. Knowledge of psychological theory alone cannot help the classroom teachers to deal with the students. Their knowledge in theory should be connected with classroom practice.

(ii) Psychological Foundations of Education cannot be Educational Psychology: Psychological foundation of education cannot be considered as deeper a science as Educational Psychology. It is to be considered as intermediary discipline that attempts to orient the students into the realms that are common between education and psychology. It is more concerned with the applicational aspect and not so much with the theoretical aspect of Educational Psychology. It aims at the application of the psychological knowledge to the field of education. It mainly emphasises on understanding the psychological aspects that serve as the educational foundation.

(iii) Educational Psychology is not Mysterious: Many people imagine that Educational Psychology is something magical or mysterious and that somehow educational psychologists have a superior or almost super human way of looking into the thoughts and feelings of the students. The notion is in other words, that there is a psychological method or approach, and that any one who knows how to use this and uses it successfully has an advantage over anyone who lacks it but in a true sense Educational Psychology is no more mysterious today. It is an ordinary applied science. It has no magic, no mysterious ways and no dark or hidden routes by which it gets its knowledge. Whatever educational psychologists have learned, they have learned through observation, and through careful observation in the classroom. Hence, Educational Psychology is neither magical nor mysterious.

(iv) Educational Psychology is not Common Sense: Some people go to the opposite extreme and assume that Educational Psychology is essentially nothing more than common sense. To them, Educational Psychology is nothing but what wise people have discovered from their experience, whether they have ever had formal training in the subject or not.

It would of course, be overstating the case to say that educational psychology has a monopoly of knowledge of human behaviour and its modification. The fact remains that application of scientific psychological principles in educational settings and the psychology of common sense in educational setting are different. For one thing there are statements that are accepted by common sense but not accepted by pyschology. One example of this is the common notion that those who are insane or seriously mentally ill have "lost their minds." In the other words, insane people are considered to be unable to reason adequately or accurately. This commonsense idea of insanity is far from the truth. Although intellectual abilities are sometimes disturbed in mental illness, a great, many individuals who are insane are not suffering for lack of ability to reason. If given an intelligence test, they do as well as others. In such cases, the difficulty is not in the intellectual realm at all but rather in the field of emotion. Thus, psychology must insist that insanity cannot be regarded as the "loss of mind".

On the other hand, a good many things that are accepted by psychology are not accepted by common sense. An example relates to the phenomenon of colour. The common sense view of colour is that the colour is in the object which we see. Thus, if we see yellow flowers and blue flowers in a vase on our desk, common sense says the yellowness and the blueness are actually in the flowers themselves. From the standpoint of modern science this view is entirely unacceptable. We have every reason at present to believe that the colour is not in the object but rather in the perceiver.

Area of Influence

Scope means, the limits of a particular subject in the field of its operation. What is to be included in its study or what subject-matter does it contain comes under its scope. Educational Psychology, as discussed so far, deals with the behaviour of the learner in educational settings and should limit itself within the four walls of the teaching-learning process and educational environment. It must try to solve the problem evolving in actual teaching-learning situations and help the individuals involved in this process.

The psychologists who deal with the problems of education are concerned with what to teach, when to teach and how to teach. A famous psychologist, Lindgren points out that Educational Psychology is concerned with understanding the learner, the learning process and the learning situation. The scope of Educational Psychology may be discussed under the following heads.

(i) The learner (student)
(ii) The learning process
(iii) The learning situation

(iv) The learning experience

(v) The teacher

(i) *The Learner:* The term 'learner' applies to students who individually or collectively participate in the educational programmes. These students taken collectively constitute the class. In fact, the behaviour of the class is none other than the behaviour of the students. There can be no teaching without there being a learner. Therefore, Sir John Adams once remarked "Teacher teaches John Latin. Teacher must have the knowledge of John's psychology; therefore, the teacher must study psychology."

The teaching of Latin without the knowledge of John will not be effective. John (the learner) thus becomes the center of the teaching-learning process.

From psychological point of view, John is a child and he should consider, not his needs, ambitions, fears and other emotions are not the same as those of an adult. Treat him, therefore, as a developing organism which is unique and not as a small model adult.

Two learners of the same age differ from one another in a number of ways. When one has a liking for music and dislike for mathematics and science another may have, dislike for music and for mathematics and science. Hence, while preparing the curriculum for the learners we must take into consideration the dual differences that exist among the learners.

However, intelligent a learner may be, he cannot become successful in life if he lacks motivation. Hence motivating the learner is very important. In the classroom, situation from the psychological view, not only motivation but also the developmental characteristics of personality, mental health, individual differences intelligence, etc., of the learner come under the scope of educational psychology.

(ii) *The Learning Process:* Learning is the process by which we acquire and retain attitudes, knowledge, understanding, skills and capabilities and these cannot be attributed to the inherited behaviour patterns or his physical growth.

Capacity for learning is related to innate physiological factors. Rate of learning depends on both inherited environmental factors.

Learning Levels

(a) Affective learning has to do with feelings and values and therefore influences our attitudes and personalities.

(b) Cognitive learning is achieved by mental processes such as reasoning, remembering and recall. It helps in the problem of remembering and recall. It helps in problem solving, developing new ideas and evaluation.

(c) Psychomotor learning has to do with the development of skills which require efficient coordination between our brains and muscles, as when we read or write or carry out physical skills such as balancing, skipping or jogging.

A number of other processes have been put forward to explain how we learn. All of them have conceived of learning as a process that progresses in stages.

(iii) *The Learning Situation:* It is difficult to imagine any period of our life situations, when we are not learning something, even though we are not always aware that we are learning. While walking down a street on any ordinary day, we continually modify our behaviour. Learning is commonly through experiences in response to environment. Thus learning situation covers all life experiences that modify our behaviour.

From academic point of view a learning situation refers to the classroom setting, which is composed of students, a teacher and a room. All have unique characteristics. In addition to these features we also have the behaviour of teacher and students. Behaviour includes not only overt physical activity such as talking, and doing, but also cognitive process like cognizing, thinking and evaluating. In the classroom and the school, the teacher is to help bring about desirable changes in student behaviour. Through the teacher's interaction with students and the students' interaction with one another, many desired interests, motives, social skills and several outcomes in the cognitive and psychomotor domains are acquired more efficiently than if there was no practical interaction.

(iv) *The Learning Experience:* Although Educational Psychology does not connect itself directly with the problem of what to teach or what learning experiences are to be provided for the learner, yet it has the full responsibility of suggesting techniques of acquiring the learning experiences. Once the task of deciding the aims and objectives of a piece of instruction at a particular stage is finished the need of Educational Psychology is felt. At this stage, Educational Psychology helps in deciding what learning experiences are desirable, at stage of growth and development of the learner so that these experiences can be acquired with a greater ease and satisfaction. In this area, Educational psychology has the subject matter which deals with the knowledge and principles of psychology which facilitates the selection of the desirable learning experiences for the learner.

(v) *The Teacher :* It is not enough for a carpenter to be good at sawing and polishing wood because every kind of wood has different characteristics and behaves in different ways under his tools. The skilled carpenter need to know about trees, their variety, their characteristics and how to make the best use of them, so it is with teaching. Teaching skills alone are not sufficient. He must understand the children as learners. He must try to recognize those characteristics that are significant in helping each child to learn more effectively.

Any teacher who knows anything about the learners is aware that growing up is more than growing bigger. Children are not little adults nor are adults big babies. It is essential, therefore, that teachers who are closely concerned with children during that period of life some of the most important developments take place should know as much as possible about the process of growing and developing.

One of the first things we notice when we try to understand the learners is how differently they are, how each develops at his pace and along his own path of progress. No child is typical. He is in his own way unique. Yet like the doctor who must recognise which symptoms are serious and which are trivial, the teacher must distinguish between those variations that are normal and those that may indicate a child's need for special attention.

Understanding the learner from psychological point of view is an attempt to find out as much as possible about a particular learner by spending some time with him and learning about his physical, mental and personality characteristics and relevant facts about the environment in which he is growing up. Recording of such child studies is important so that the information can be used in wider studies or, where necessary for helping a child with problems.

Infinite Avenues

In an important sense, it is not desirable to limit the scope of Educational Psychology to the above five areas only. Educational Psychology is a developing and a fast growing science. Like any other developing branch of science it multiplies itself every year. New ideas are coming into picture because of the results of new researches and experiments in the field. Society is dynamic in nature. So also is education. The new problems in the process of education and their solution are coming with a faster rate. Educational Psychology is trying harder and harder with the result of the development of new concepts, principles and techniques. For example, traditionally developmental psychologists were concerned with the study of the child development, but in recent years adolescence, adulthood and old age have drawn increasing interest. A major concern of developmental psychologists has been the process of socialization - how the immature, and relatively helpless infant is transformed into a functioning member of society. An important part of socialization is the process whereby language is acquired and this is an area of vigorous research activity. Although developmental psychology has been with us since the very beginning of psychological study, its current popularity is increasing. This example proves that it is unwise to fix the boundary of Educational Psychology by defining its scope. It will not only harm the progress of Educational Psychology but also prove as a great obstacle in the progresses of education.

The boundaries of Educational Psychology, therefore, must be left free for its future expansion so as to facilitate the inclusion of all that is created in this field. As a result of which we can solve most of the problems of education and help the teaching-learning process to meet the demands of exigencies.

Teacher's Role

The contemporary age has witnessed an ever-growing interest in the welfare and education of children. Because of the recognition of the significance of the period of childhood, the present age has been called "the children's century". Modern education is also described as child-centered. Besides this paedocentric knowledge and understanding of children, the teacher should have knowledge of Educational Psychology. It will give him larger awareness of the nature, abilities and needs of the students he teaches, of the processes involved in his work and his own capacities and limitations.

The Utility

Teachers in modern schools, whether primary or secondary, are often amazed at children's eagerness to learn, their creative problem solving, persistent efforts in self-development and their academic, athletic and artistic accomplishments. Trained teachers who are curious and scientifically oriented often wonder why and how children learn as much and even more effectively. The answers to these questions are relevant to the knowledge of psychological principles. The teachers can obtain positive results, if they can apply psychological principles in the classroom, laboratory, on the playground and in any learning situation.

Teachers and prospective teachers at the secondary stage of education, therefore should try to enhance their understanding of their students by studying Educational Psychology. Thus they can provide proper guidance for effective learning.

Education Psychologists have much to offer the secondary school teachers in understanding the learners, because they have extensive resources at their disposal. In their research, they have access to children of all ages and ability groups in ongoing complete learning situations. They also help the teachers in their understanding of the principles of teaching, especially in the field of learning, in understanding developmental tasks of adolescents, individual differences and mental health. In all these fields, the teachers and prospective teachers become successful in understanding the learner.

Student's Development

Modern education is concerned with the development of both the individual and society. It is the duty of the Teacher to develop the constructive potentialities of every learner as fully as possible. At the same time he should aim to preserve and enhance the conditions of constructive living in society. In addition to these, he should turn to the accumulated and continually expanding knowledge which makes up our cultural heritage and he should see that it is rich in curriculum resources. For the teacher should believe in a subject-child - community-centered education. When the teacher seeks the development of the learner, he should look to the following aspects.

(i) The teacher should enable the learners to achieve an inquiring mind, skills for effective communication, knowledge for maintaining, protecting and improving his health and for satisfying interests and skills and ethical character.

(ii) The teacher should enable the learners to achieve comfortable, useful and happy social relationships in their families, with friends and with other people at work and play. The learner should develop respect for humanity in general.

(iii) The teacher should enable the learners to attain economic efficiency by becoming an intelligent consumer and by preparing material suited to his talents and interests and to the needs of his society.

(iv) The teacher should enable the learners to develop civic responsibility, which involves a sense of social justice, an understanding of his society, participation as a citizen, tolerance, interest in conservation and devotion to the ideas of democracy.

In summarizing the role of the teacher in the development of knowledge of the learners, we can say that the teacher should look to the development of a community of individuals enjoying an increasingly satisfying constructive way of life. They involve the attainment of intellectual proficiency, occupational competence, effective group participation and leadership.

Besides the above areas, the teacher also gets help from Educational Psychology for the development of the learners in the following areas as well.

(i) Physical development, health and body care, including individual health, and elementary aspects of public health, grooming and understanding of growth.

(ii) Individual, social and emotional development, including mental health, emotional stability, growth of personality, and self-understanding and evaluation.

(iii) Ethical behaviour standards, and values, including observance of moral and civil laws, observance of the customs and mores of the culture, and the development of such characteristics as sportsmanship, kindness and helpfulness.

(iv) Social relations, a category which grows out of the preceding two and is devoted to the individual as a person in his personal, and social relations with others with whom he associates in home, community, and place of work.

(v) The social world, which considers the behaviour of the child in relation to the broader social setting of community, state and nation and includes geography, civics, economics, government, and the traditional Indian way of life.

(vi) The natural environment, as revealed by the physical and biological sciences, which emphasize learning to think scientifically and the use of scientific methods both as scientists and for solving problems in everyday living.

(vii) Aesthetic development, including both appreciation of

the arts and personal participation in art, music, crafts and other creative activities.

(viii) Communication, including an understanding of the language, effective use of language skills in reading, handwriting, composition, usage, spelling, punctuation, speaking and listening.

(ix) Quantitative relationships, consisting mainly of arithmetic, including understanding our number system, knowledge of how it is widely used in solving quantitative problems in society, and the development of problem-solving skills.

Report of Learnings : Within each of these nine broad and interrelation areas, objectives are further classified as indicative of four "types of behavioral change".

(1) Knowledge and understanding, which would include the objective of learning " how to use table of contents of a book".

(2) Skills and Competence, under which we would place such objectives as " skill in untangling unfamiliar words."

(3) Attitudes and Interests, under which we would include "enjoyment of a wide variety of reading materials," and

(4) Action Patterns, which "refer to broad generalized ways of behaving" such as ways of responding to problem situations through the union of intelligence with good working habits and scientific methods of thinking. According to Campbell-Stewart, Educational Psychology helps the teachers in the following ways:

(i) To outline aspects of the learning process: Teaching methods rest fundamentally upon the psychology of learning. A teacher aims at modifying the experience and responses of his students in many ways. He should, therefore, know the conditions of the learning process thoroughly. Psychology helps him by rendering a most systematic and exhaustive analysis of the learning process.

(ii) To outline the main phases in psychological growth from infancy to maturity: The infant, the boy, the adolescent and the young man have different outlooks and attitudes. A systematic study of the characteristics of each one of these developmental phases will not only be interesting but also rewarding for a teacher who desires to be successful and effective in the classroom. Detailed information regarding these stages of growth is furnished by psychology.

(iii) To match subject matter and processes to be learned to labels of development and psychological principles: A practical outcome of the study of development stages is the equipping of the teacher with the skill to match the class instruction with the mental levels of the learners. Educational Psychology also helps in the formation of the guiding principles which are the bases of this correlation of the curriculum and teaching to the psychological growth level of the learner.

(iv) To give some training in assessing and making allowance for the social matrix beyond the school in which the child and the teacher live: As the child leaves the school he is exposed to many social influences, a large number of which are only too often adverse, nullifying the healthy socio-cultural effect of the education received at the school. Streets, cinemas, cafes, etc., are few instances of the sources of these undesirable influences in the beyond-the -school social matrix. In order to assess their pernicious or non-pernicious effect and in order to counteract their undesirable influence on the child. Educational Psychology aims at training the teacher in adopting suitable remedial measures. Some of these measures are: organization of sports and games, conducting of psychological test, guidance of the students and their parents, etc.

(v) To give the teacher insight into his own psychological process and his own role as teacher: A teacher should learn to control his own conflicts before he starts

> teaching. If he does not do so the students merely serve as more or less suitable materials on which "to react his unconscious and unsolved difficulties," Knowledge of Educational Psychology helps the teacher to know himself.

Some of our teachers develop an undesirable attitude towards their students due to poverty, ill-health, insecurity of service, incompetence to do the allotted work, emotional tensions, inability to get on amicably with colleagues, etc. These and host of other unfortunate factors affect the teaching-learning situation adversely.

Our society, on the other hand is unfavourable towards the teaching profession. Teaching has been accepted as a 'failure belt'. It is the refuge of the "unproductive men and unmarriageable women". Because of such an attitude of the society towards teaching profession, our teachers do not feel for their profession. If this is reinforced by an already existing painful tension in the mind, of the teacher, his plight becomes all the more miserable because of this additional inner enemy.

Educational Psychology which helps a teacher to know his own inner nature. He also understands the mechanism of the factor leading to his failure as a teacher. The knowledge of his own self and his profession helps him to improve both as a person as well as a teacher.

Educational Psychology also helps the teacher in proper management of the classroom to promote learning and minimize disruption. It teaches him how to present his lessons to both large and small groups-and when to do which. It also teaches him how to predict certain learning patterns of students of different ages and from different backgrounds to comprehend the importance and limitations of the theories employed in teaching strategies, and to utilize the many tools and techniques that are available to him. Besides, studying. Educational Psychology will remind a teacher how challenging teaching can be, and how gratifying it is when a teacher devotees his time and energy to this work.

Function of Educational Psychologists

Educational psychologists incorporate knowledge of the teaching process, the learning of the teaching process, and the learning environment in strategies that are designed to enhance learning. They study topics such as cognitive and developmental psychology, principles of measurement and classroom management. Educational psychologists also conduct experiments, some in the classroom and some in laboratories to find their own answers to unresolved questions and so on.

4

Main Factors

Different Standpoints

H.C. Mckown has given a very vivid description of individual differences, "In the whole world there are probably no two things alike-no two trees, not two leaves, flowers, blades of grass, rocks, drops, clouds, animals, houses, pianos, books, baseballs or photographs, even though at first glance they appear to be identical. Similarly no two human beings are alike, they differ physically in size, weight, height, colour of eyes and hair texture of skin-and in a thousand other details as well as in thousands of details of mental, social and spiritual life" Not only this, an individual reacts to the same situation in different manners at different times. Mass procedures, no matter, how well-intentioned, fail to accomplish the desired results in educational programmes, unless they are supplemented by adequate attention to the individual needs of the learner. In the words of Charles E. Skinner, "Today we think of individual differences as including any measurable aspect of the total personality." Differences in children may be slight, moderate or extreme.

Types of Individual Differences: Following are the important types of individual differences:

1. *Differences in Physique:* This means tall or short, thin or fat, fair or black, etc.
2. *Differences in Health:* It means healthy or ill, weak or strong.
3. *Differences in Intelligence:* Here the range is very wide-from almost nil intelligence to 140 or above. On the basis of one's I.Q., one can be classified to fall in any of the idiot through genius categories.
4. *Differences with Reference to Achievements:* Pupils differ in achievements in school subjects and their efficiency in vocation.
5. *Differences in Affective Factors:* There are differences in attitude towards ideas, subjects, things and people etc. Likewise differences in interests.
6. *Differences in Motor Ability:* This means control over muscles. The performance of some in some mechanical task is superior and the performance of others is inferior.
7. *Sex Differences:* Sex differences operate in different ways.
8. *Differences with Reference to Learning Ability and Speed of Learning:* This is evident from daily example. Take a class-room. Some boys learn things quickly-other take days to learn it and some do not learn at all.
9. *Differences with Reference to Race and Nationality:* Many studies lead us to conclude that people belonging to different races and nationalities differ in respect of nature, physical and mental traits, interests and personality etc. It can be intelligence also.
10. *Personality Differences:* Many classifications of personality differences are made. According to Hipprocrates, people are of four types:

    (a) sanguine,

    (b) choleric,

    (c) melancholic,

    (d) phlegmatic

    According to Jung, people can be classified into three types:

    (a) Introverts,

(b) Extroverts,

(c) Ambiverts.

Terman has classified people on the basis of intelligence into nine categories-from genius to idiot.

11. *Differences with Respect to Development:* It includes social development, emotional development which includes emotional maturity, emotional stability, etc.

Threefold Broad Classification of Individual Differences

(1)	(2)	(3)
Physical Characteristics Like appearance, colour, height, size, sex etc.	Demographic Characteristics Like age, caste, socio-economic status etc.	Cognitive Behaviour Like thinking, remembering, creating and problem-solving etc.

Vital Facets

Teaching-learning process can be efficient and effective only when individual differences of students are recognised and suitable steps are taken to meet them so that individuals are in a position to develop according to their optimum capacity.

Some students go faster than others and such students may be given double promotion or separate streams formed or some additional work given to them so that their progress is not retarded due to slow learners. Similarly, steps will have to be taken to ensure that the slow learners also make satisfactory progress commensurate with their capacity and ability to work.

A deaf, dumb, blind, undersized, oversized, too fat or too lean learner needs guidance in the selection of such a vocation where his physical defect may not be a handicap and he may be able to earn his living in an honourable manner. Such students need special educational courses. Ordinary schools fail to do justice to them.

There are some students whose parents are very dominating with the result that their children develop inferiority complex. Too lenient parents allow their children to be freelancers and such children suffer from other complexes and develop bad habits.

Children of the rich and the poor have altogether different situations to be faced with. The problems are as numerous as the learners.

The programme of guidance is not confined to the selection of subjects, schools, vocations etc. All children need guidance in every aspect of their harmonious development. They need guidance in fields such as recreation, moral and religious, social adjustments, cultural pursuits, physical development, etc.

Democratically, all individuals are equal but physically and psychologically all individuals are unequal and in other words each individual is different from the other. All the same, all are agreed that equal opportunity or equality of opportunity must be provided to every individual for drawing out the best that an individual has so that an individual achieves optimum development. It has been aptly stated by Benjamin S. Bloom, an American educator, "A society which places such great value on education and schooling that it requires the individual to attend school for a long period of time must find the means to make education attractive and meaningful to the individual learner." This implies that education should be individual-centred. But in spite of the loud talk on child-centred or individual-centred education, it is observed that there is very little practical action in this regard.

Undoubtedly, all the students need guidance in one or the other aspect, some need more guidance and others less. Without proper guidance the superior child may go astray, the average one may become backward and the backward may be lost to the society altogether.

Techniques of Teaching

In view of the individual differences, it is quite clear that the same curriculum, same methods of teaching and same discipline and in some cases even the same educational institution will not serve the individual needs of children. Ideally speaking each student needs a particular setting and individual instruction with a lot of group interaction. This, however, is not feasible in normal life. At the same time individual differences of children must be catered to. There are seven broad areas, in which a lot of work could be done to take into consideration individual differences. These are:

1. Streaming of students, i.e., making ability groups.
2. Curriculum planning, i.e., providing advanced and ordinary curriculum in different disciplines.
3. Disciplinary treatment.
4. Guidance and counselling.
5. Special schools for the handicapped children.
6. Combining individualised, group and class instruction.
7. Using maxims of teaching and mnemonics.

Following are the general guidelines for meeting individual differences:

1. Courses should be selective to meet the needs of individual students.
2. Opportunities for acquiring manual and mechanical skills should be provided.
3. A wide range of pupil experiences may be provided in the school.
4. Remedial instruction should be made available to such students who need it.
5. Courses should be organised in such a way as bright pupils can learn at their own speed and slow pupils follow their own speed.
6. Guidance regarding co-curricular activities should be provided.
7. Counselling should be provided to students.
8. Assignments should be adapted to the needs of students.
9. Special care should be taken to accept the under-achieving child as a unique individual. His particular needs should be immediately attended to.
10. Efforts may be made to re-establish child's confidence in himself.
11. The teacher should seek the cooperation of other teachers and the parents of the under-achievers.

12. In case of deep-rooted emotional problems which lie at the root of under-achievement, referral may be made to a child guidance clinic after taking the parents into confidence.
13. Students should be taught to recognise their handicaps, and counselled in methods to overcome or compensate for them.
14. Some programme of parents education may be taken up as many problems of the students result from unsatisfactory home conditions.
15. School programme should take into account the needs of those students who are not likely to go to college and those who would join college.
16. The school programme, administration and management should be made flexible enough to allow for adjustment to individual differences.

Inceptional Methods

On account of differences in ability and in previous experiences all children are not at the same readiness (preparation for action) for learning when they enter school or when they learn a new topic or unit in the same subject or when they are promoted to the next class. This makes difference in the new situation because of differences in basic concept formation and the level of knowledge required as foundation on which to build a new lesson.

Thorndike has propounded the Law of Readiness. The law states, "When any conduction unit is not in readiness to conduct, for it to conduct is annoying. When any conduction unit is in readiness to conduct, for it not to do so is annoying."

The law is indicative of learner's state to participate in the learning process. According to Thorndike, readiness is preparation for action. Readiness does not come automatically with maturation. It is a law of preparatory adjustment, not a low about growth. Thorndike termed the neurons and synapses involved in the establishment of a specific bond or connection, a conduction unit. According to this law, for a conduction unit ready to conduct, to do, is satisfying and for it not to do so is annoying.

Educational Implications: Teacher should prepare the minds of the students to be ready to accept the knowledge, skills and aptitudes. For this, he should provide opportunities for those experiences in which students can spontaneously participate. In other words, he should arouse their capacity to link the experiences with their everyday life. 'Simple to complex' is the important maxim. Aptitude tests may be given to the students to find out their readiness to learn.

Dimensions of Individual Differences in the Cognitive Domain: Various dimensions of the cognitive behaviour of the students are as under:

1. Thinking
2. Remembering
3. Analysing
4. Interpreting
5. Reasoning
6. Problem Solving

Identification of Cognitive Differences: Following are the important methods adopted for identifying cognitive differences of students:

1. Intelligence Tests
2. Aptitude Tests
3. Creativity Tests
4. Academic Achievement Tests

Educational Impact

1. Small classes may be organised.
2. Much responsibility may be given to the students for organising their programmes.
3. School marks should not be accepted as the sole evidence of successful student development.
4. Undue reliance should not be placed on tests and measurements.
5. Case histories of each child from kindergarten through higher secondary school must be made available to concerned persons and kept up-to-date.

6. A good system of accessible cumulative records must be developed.
7. Time table should be arranged in a way that the teachers may compile cumulative records and use them.
8. Opportunity to secure advice from specialists in diagnosis of difficulties should be provided.
9. Time for home visits or conferences with parents should be provided.
10. School personnel and parents should accept the statement that honest labour performed to the best of one's ability is worthy of commendation, whether the work be in the shops or offices, factories or farms.
11. Professional service to aid teachers in developing the attitudes, skills and techniques necessary for successful counselling should be provided.
12. Necessary material for testing and recording data needed to understand the individual child's needs, aptitudes and interests be provided.

Using Existing Cognitive Level as Base: Here several maxims of reaching like linking present knowledge with the past and future, direct to indirect or whole to parts may be adopted.

Use of Mnemonics (Aiding the Memory) for Strengthening Memory: For instance for remembering reading, writing, arithmetic, rights, responsibilities and relationships, the term 7 R's may be used. Likewise 4 H's for head, hand, health and heart may be used.

Meaning of Affective Domain of Learning: Affective domain as already mentioned includes interests, attitudes and values. In this domain also, there are wide differences among learners.

Personal Ends

Meaning of the Term Interest: The word interest owes its origin to the Latin word 'intersec' meaning making a difference or its matters. We may, therefore, say that whatever matters to us is of interest to us. Following are some of the definitions of interests:

Crow and Crow state, "Interest may refer to the motivating force that impels us to attend to a person, a thing or an activity."

"An interest is a disposition in its dynamic aspect" according to James Drever.

James M. Sawhrey and Charles W. Telford define interest as, "Favourable attitude towards an object."

McDougall is of the view, "Interest is latent attention and attention is interest in action."

Factors Affecting the Development of Interests: How Interests Emerge? According to "Encyclopedia of Educational Research by Harris, interests of the learners are influenced by the following factors:

(i) Socio-economic status of the family.

(ii) Aptitudes of the learners.

(iii) Personality patterns of the learners.

(iv) Individual differences in general.

The Interest

1. There is an intimate link between interests, wants, drives, motives and basic needs.
2. Interest is a great motivating force and it persuades us to take up various types of activities.
3. There is a close relationship between interest and attention.
4. Some interests are inborn and some are acquired.
5. Our interests dominate us and we interpret everything in the light of our interests.
6. Our interests lead to action and generally yield satisfying results.
7. Strong interests resist fatigue and avoid failure.
8. Interests are superior to our attitudes of mind. An attitude is simply a bent of mind but does not ensure action.
9. Our interests are always shifting.

Broad Types of Interests of Learners: Broad categories are:

(i) Academic interests

(ii) Interests in hobbies etc.

(iii) Play Interests

(iv) Vocational Interests

(v) Sex Interests.

Significant of Interests and Class-room Implications: School work becomes interesting to the student when he finds that it is related to him as an individual and it meets his needs to a considerable extent. He is interested when he realizes that learning is a means to his goals and that the learning experiments will make difference to him personally and when he appreciates that he has a great stake in the results.

Identification of Students Interests: A teacher should identify the interests of the students by using the following measures:

1. Observing their activities.
2. Noting the questions they ask.
3. Keeping in view the topics of their conversation.
4. Take into consideration the books they read.
5. Observing their spontaneous drawings.
6. Noting their wishes.
7. Studying their self-reports of what is of interest to them.
8. Administering interest tests to them.

In order to interest a child in a subject, a teacher must know a lot about the student and about the subject. He must understand the pupils' wants, problems, tendencies, goals and interests at their current stage of development. He should share responsibility with them. Participation of a teacher in a foot-ball game has a great value than being a mere spectator.

One of the ways of arousing interest in class-room activities is to make students participants rather than spectators or members of an audience. A variety of co-curricular activities should be organised so that students can choose activities in which they are interested.

Interest inventories may be used to find out the interests of the students and accordingly steps taken to develop these.

Failure to understand students' interests tends to reduce effectiveness of teaching. The kind of person a student would become is determined to a large extent by the interest developed during the childhood years.

Different Views

Meaning and Nature of an Attitude: Anastari has given the meaning of an attitude in these words, "An attitude is often defined as a tendency to react favourably or unfavourably toward a designed class of stimuli, such as a national or a racial group, a custom or an institution."

According to Frank Freeman, "An attitude is a dispositional readiness to respond to certain institutions, persons or objects in a consistent manner which has been learned and has become one's typical mode of response. An attitude has a well-defined object of reference. For example, one's views regarding class of food or drink (such as fish and liquors), sports, maths or democrats are attitudes."

Thurstone states, "Attitude denotes the sum total of a man's inclinations and feelings, prejudice or bias, pre-conceived notions, ideas, fears, threats as conceived about any specific topic. Thus a man's attitude about pacifism means here all that he feels and thinks about peace and war. It is admittedly a subjective and personal affair."

According to the definition given by G. W. Allport, "Attitude is a mental and neutral state of readiness, organised through experience, exerting a directive and dynamic influence upon an individual's response to the objects and situations with which it is related."

1. It is a point of view, or a frame of reference, substantiated or otherwise, true or false which one holds towards an idea, object or person.
2. It includes certain aspects of personality as interests, appreciations and social conduct.
3. An attitude is learnt.
4. An attitude is adopted.
5. An attitude has several aspects such as direction, intensity, generality or specificity.
6. The attitudes of a student are formed as a result of his experience and interaction with real situations.

Components of an Attitude: According to Harrison, an attitude has three components:

1. Beliefs
2. Emotions
3. Behaviour

Types of Attitudes

Positive Characteristics	*Negative Characteristics*
(i) Assisting others	(i) Prejudice
(ii) To be caring	(ii) Entering into arguments and conflicts
(iii) To be unselfish	
(iv) To be at peace with the world	(iii) Tension

Factors Leading to Individual Differences among Learners: These are:

1. Cultural background.
2. Home environment
3. Maturity level of the learners.
4. Neighbourhood environment.
5. Physical surroundings
6. Political environment
7. Religious environment
8. School environment
9. Social environment

Role of the Teacher in Developing Positive Attitudes: Following factors are very helpful in developing positive attitudes in the students

1. Personal example of positive attitude.
2. Friendly, sympathetic but attitude of firmness on the part of the teacher.
3. Understanding the background and needs of the students.
4. Appreciation of individual differences and accordingly adopting disciplinary measures.
5. Making teaching-learning affective.

Measurement of Attitude: The two most frequently used methods for the measurement of social attitude are: "The Methods of Equal Appearing Intervals" developed by Thurstone and "The Method of Summated Ratings" developed by Likert.

Learning Standards

Meaning of Value: Educators and thinkers differ regarding the precise meaning of the term 'value'. Nevertheless, there is no doubt that values guide our behaviour and conduct, set goals and determine actions towards different events, objects and situations. They are the moving spirit in our lives. The following are some of the important definitions of a value.

A. K.C. Ottaway observes, "Values stand for ideas men live for."

D. H. Parker thinks, "Values belong wholly to the inner world of the mind. The satisfaction of desire is the real value, the thing that serves is only an instrument. A value is always an experience, never a thing or an object."

Kane says, "Values are the ideals, beliefs or norms which a society or the large majority of a society's members hold."

M.T. Ramji writes, "A value is what is desired or what is sought."

T. Parson points out, "Value is an element of a shared symbolic system which serves a criterion or standard for selection among the alternatives of orientation which are intrinsically open in a situation."

Classification of Values: Strictly speaking there are no hard and fast rules to classify values as they are closely interlinked and interrelated.

Values are individual as well as social. Individual values refer to the good of oneself and social values refer to the good of others.

Values may be classified into three categories: biological values, intrinsic values and instrumental values or as instrumental values and terminal values. Plato classified values into three categories- Truth, Goodness and Beauty.

Classification of Values

1.	Aesthetic	–	appreciation of beauty and joy
2.	Emotional	–	courage, endurance, friendliness, harmony and heroism
3.	Material	–	love of money, pleasures of life
4.	Mental	–	impartiality and perseverance
5.	Moral	–	benevolence, gratitude, honesty
6.	Physical	–	beauty, truth, grace, health and strength
7.	Social	–	civic sense, cooperation, courtesy, devotion to duty
8.	Spiritual	–	meditation, pursuit of ultimate reality.

The Values

1. Values can be developed.
2. Environment plays an important role in the development of values.
3. Values held by adults may not necessarily be handed down to the younger generation.
4. Educational experiences, undoubtedly promote certain values and cast others aside.
5. Quality of peer action plays an important role in value development.

Role of the Educational Institutions: Since students spend a good deal of their time in educational institutions, these play an important role in the development of their values.

Following factors should be carefully attended to :

Activity Programme for Developing Values: Following are the important activities to be undertaken by the school in this regard:

1. Community prayer in the school.
2. Cleanliness programme in the school.
3. Community service programmes.
4. Social service programmes in fairs and festivals.
5. First-aid programmes.

6. Celebration of national days and festivals.
7. Dramas, etc. depicting values.

Talks: Emphasis should be laid on the unity of all religions, harmony among communities and national integration.

Personal Examples: The most important aspect of the programme is that the teachers should set examples of good conduct and behaviour which the students may imbibe in themselves.

Concluding Observations: It may be observed that a special responsibility for creating a value-oriented environment lies on the V.I.P.'s, leaders of all shades and all those persons who matter in different walks of life. In fact, by and large, people tend to think that these are the persons responsible for the erosion of values. They must set the highest standards of ethical morality.

New Findings

Meaning of Creativity: Following definitions point out the meaning, nature and various dimensions of creativity:

Zbigniew Pietrasinski defines creativity as "an activity resulting in new products of a definite social value"

According to Wilson, R.C., Guilford J.P. and Christensen P.R., "The creative process is any process by which something new is produced an idea or an object including a new form of arrangements of old elements. The new creations must contribute to the solution of some problem."

Components of Creativity

Ability	*Fluency*	*Flexibility*	*Originality*	*Elaboration*
It is the ability of the individual to see the problem.	It is the ability of the individual to give a number of Successful responses to a given stimulus.	It is the ability of the individual to use different approaches in responding to a stimulus.	It is the capacity of the individual to give original response to a stimulus.	It implies generating new ideas.

In the words of Torrence, creativity is a "process of becoming sensitive to problems, deficiencies, gaps of knowledge, missing elements, disharmonies and so on; identifying the difficulties, searching for solutions, testing and retesting hypotheses and possibly modifying and retesting them and finally communicating results."

According to Drevdhai, J. E., "Creativity is the capacity of a person to produce compositions, products or ideas which are essentially new or novel and previously unknown to the producer."

Various Mechanisms

1. Creativity is a gift of God.
2. Creativity is based on intelligence.
3. Creativity is intuition.
4. Creativity is the process of novelty cell in the brain.
5. Creativity is the presence of 20-22 mental abilities.
6. Creativity lies in the personality of an individual .
7. Creativity is like madness.
8. Creativity is based on heredity.

Why special Stress on the Education of the Creative? Torrance says, "Society is downright savage toward creative thinkers especially when they are young." Suppression of the creativity of the child means learning disabilities, behaviour problems, drop-outs and mental conflicts and above all, a loss to mankind.

Identification of Creativity: We may use both test and non-test techniques for the identification of the gifted.

Guilford and Merrifield have developed test techniques that measure fluency, flexibility, originality, redefinition and sensitivity to problems.

Getzels and Jackson have used five different measures of creativity in their research.

(a) *Word-Association Test:* Students are required to give as many definitions and number of different categories into which they could be placed.

(b) *Uses of Objects Tests:* The student is asked to give as many uses as he can for a common object.

(c) *Hidden Shapes Tests:* A student is required to find more complex form of figure on card in a simple form.

(d) *Three Different Endings:* Here a student is required to suggest three different endings to incomplete short fables.

(e) *Make-up Problems:* A student is required to make-up as many mathematical problems he can on the basis of information given in a complex paragraph.

There are the Minnesota tests of creative thinking, comprising non-verbal tasks like picture construction, creative design, circles and squares etc.

Tornat's check list comprising eighty-four characteristics for identifying the creative children is also very helpful.

Characteristics of a Creative Child: A creative child is :

1. Adventurous.
2. Bold.
3. Complex.
4. Dominant, self assertive.
5. Dreamer. But not a day-dreamer.
6. Emotionally sensitive.
7. Independent of judgment.
8. Introvert-Deals with things and not with people.
9. Non-conformist.
10. Psychologically healthy.
11. Resourceful, radical.
12. Risk-taker.
13. Self-accepting
14. Self-assertive
15. Self-controlled.
16. Self-sufficient.
17. Sensitive to environmental stimuli-which means sensitive to loopholes and gaps in the environment.

According to Getzel and Jackson, the characteristics of a creative child are four:

(a) Less popular with teachers.

(b) Independent of judgment.

(c) Unconventional.

(d) Humorous and playful.

A creative child is constantly probing, discovering, imagining, fantasying, asking questions, guessing and wondering.

Real Problems

School is, in fact the proper place where an organised effort should be made to develop in children the basic foundations of creativity. Deliberate attempts need to be made to develop an environment of creativity.

The teacher can provide certain conditions which will increase the fluency, flexibility, originality and exploration of the students' thinking/ behaviour. The following are the important conditions which can foster students creativity.

1. Create a supportive environment.
2. Adopt a multidisciplinary approach to teaching.
3. Allow the students ask unusual questions.
4. Ask challenging and provocative questions.
5. Assign/suggest activities of an interdisciplinary nature.
6. Develop a spirit of inquiry and to speculate, cultivate a deliberate pace of thinking, etc.
7. Encourage debates, discussions, quizzes etc.
8. Encourage children to experiment, innovate, discover, hypothesise or imagine possible solutions to any pressing issue.
9. Depend upon creative discipline. Do not depend on excessive discipline. It reduce students' creative potential.
10. Love them and let them know it.
11. Provide activities like drama, dance, music etc.
12. Provide materials which develop imagination of the students.
13. Provide opportunities to students for self-initiated learning.
14. Pose open-ended, divergent questions with the focus on alternative responses and novelty, and not on right or wrong.

15. Show consideration to imaginative and unusual ideas of the students.
16. Enthuse pupils that their ideas have values.
17. Use teaching aids that stimulate imagination.

Meaning of Self-concept: Self-concept implies a person's perception or view of himself. Self-concept is what the individual thinks of his actual self. Some psychologists refer to as personal field, behavioural field, life, space, or psychological field. Self-concept plays an important role in the development of personality of an individual. The positive self-concept is likely to enable an individual to lead a happy, contended and well-managed life. His development is optimum. It is, therefore, important that children are trained to learn from the very beginning to develop a positive self-concept which is socially desirable. The idea of self starts growing from the period of infancy and grows during childhood, adolescence and maturity. As the child grows up, he starts feeling that he is separate from others. He slowly begins to learn that certain things belong to him. The part of the environment in which he lives is known as his phenomenal self and the rest of the environment of which he is aware or to which he responds is called phenomenal environment or perceived environment and not self. Following figure adapted from A. Ward Combs and D. Snygg's book, *Individual Behaviour: A Perception Approach to Behaviour* explains these concepts.

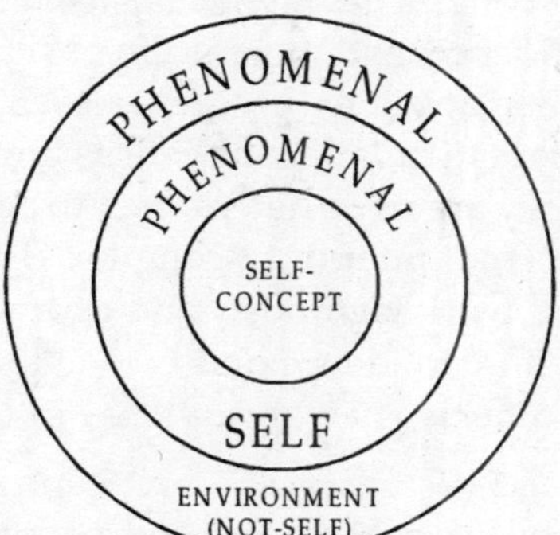

Diagramatic Representation of the Concept of Self-concept : As the child starts advancing he starts feeling that he has a personality and an identity of his own which is different from others. He may be a part of the total environment but it is not his own. Hence there is a line of demarcation between phenomenal self and phenomenal environment as indicated in Figure. It indicates what the individual thinks about himself. Self-concept is the 'me' part of the individual.

The phenomenal self includes all the aspects of the environment with which the individual identifies himself, i.e., the family, the school etc.

Components of Self-concept: Components of self-concept are—beliefs, ideas or perception an individual has about oneself-one's physical, emotional, psychological and social achievements and characteristics.

Self-concept

1. Self-concept is organised. An individual organises a lot of information about himself.
2. Self-concept has several dimensions.
3. Self-concept is hierarchical.
4. Self-concept becomes increasingly differentiated with the increase in age.
5. Self-concept is stable.
6. Self-concept is negative as well as positive.

Self-concept and Student's Performance: A student with a positive or high self-concept has high self-esteem. High self-concept develops self-confidence and poor self-concept hinders initial school adjustment and academic progress also. Students with high concept tend to accept their failure as well as limitations. They are better achievers. They are more determined to achieve their goals. They do not suffer from inferiority complex. They are free from mental sickness and work vigorously and express their ideas and beliefs to others with confidence and conviction. They have the ability to impress others. They are rational in their approach.

Development of Self-concept: Self-concept is based on what children believe their teachers, peers and parents think of them. Positive self-concept is developed through love, encouragement, positive comments and understanding attitude of the teachers and parents. Teachers should adopt suitable strategies and provide opportunities to children to develop their self-concept.

5

Gradual Growth

Evolution is a continual process. The study of growth and development helps people to understand what life means. That is, one must study the changes that normally occur in body, thought and behaviour over the course of a life span. Right from the time of conception to death at a ripe age, the human organism runs through various stages of growth; each stage being a ladder-step taking to the final goal of life. An infant and an adult are paradoxically "like and unlike" each other in very many ways: one is erratic, impulsive and playful and the other seasoned, reasoning and thinking and artful; one is waxing and the other waning, one is like a rising star and the other a setting star. Biologically, it takes a long span of time for a neonate to become an adult, to become big, to grow in height and acquire weight although all the physical organs are already present at birth. Growth is a natural tendency with all organisms.

Concept of Growth and Development

Growth and development are generally used interchangeably though the scientists consider growth to be one aspect of development. Ordinarily the term growth refers to the 'increase' caused by the biological process in which the organism becomes bigger in size, and heavier in weight. Starting his life almost from an invisible dot, the human organism grows to be more than five feet in height and more than 150 pounds in weight. Growth indicates the enlargement of cells, fibres and muscles, elongation of the skeleton and increase in the general volume of the body-parts and organ-systems. Growth brings about perceptible changes in one's structure and form: it is quantitative in the sense that can be measured in inches, points and dynes. Marked structural changes are noticed as the organism advances in age. Day after day and year after year, as the child looks different in appearance, we conclude that the child is growing.

'Development' is a wider term indicating advancement, more unfoldment, a progressive change - a sort of growing forward to a greater maturity; it is a process of qualitative transformation which brings about maturity and functional improvement.

Gessel stresses "Development is more than a concept. It can be observed, appraised and to some extent even 'measured' in three major manifestations: (a) anatomic (b) physiologic and (c) behavioural...... Behavioural signs, however, constitute a most comprehensive index of development states and development potential"

Development is growing up characteristically. It is related to growth in as much as that it denotes more specifically the changes in the character and efficiency of the organs, organ-systems. For example, the bones as they grow, they become larger but changes also take place in their ossification, hardness and the ability to bear weight and shocks; elasticity gives way to solidity which gives strength. Similarly the heart grows, becomes bigger and it also undergoes qualitative transformation when it becomes capable of pumping out more blood and thus stand the rigorous of vigorous exercises. Filling up the soft-parts of the brain, elongation of the exons and dendrites of the nerve cells are instances of development in which the internal physiological processes stimulated by them are integrated (or responded to) in a way which enables the individual to master further anew environmental stimulations. The better the child develops, the stronger he becomes to fight knowledge of the environment and the environmental hazards like diseases. Development is an interactive process causing the organism to acquire physiological capacities and psychological capabilities.

Growth **:** "Many people use the terms "growth" and "development" interchangeably. In reality they are different, though they are inseparable. Neither takes place alone.

(i) The term "growth" is used in purely physical sense. It generally refers to an increase in size, length, height and weight. Changes in the quantitative aspects come into the domain of growth.

(ii) Growth is one of the parts of the developmental process. In strict sense development in its quantitative aspect is termed as growth.

(iii) Growth may be referred to describe the changes which takes place in particular aspects of the body and behaviour of an organism.

(iv) Growth does not continue throughout life. It stops when maturity has been attained.

(v) The changes produced by growth are the subject of measurement. They may be quantified and observable in nature.

(vi) Growth may or may not bring development. A child may grow (in terms of weight) by becoming fat but growth may not bring any functional improvement (qualitative change) or development.

Development **:** Development, by contrast; refers to qualitative and quantitative changes. It may be defined as a progressive series of orderly, coherent changes. *The Webster's Dictionary* defines 'development' as "the series of changes which an organism undergoes in passing from an embryonic state to maturity". These changes refer to physical, emotional, intellectual changes which we shall discuss under the following points:

(i) Development implies overall changes in shape, form or structure resulting in improved working or functioning. It indicates the charges in the quality or character rather than in quantitative aspects.

(ii) Development is a wider and comprehensive term. It refers to overall changes in the individual. Growth is one of its parts.

(iii) Development describes the changes in the organism as a whole and does not list the changes in parts.

(iv) Development is a continuous process. It goes from womb to tomb. It does not end with the attainment of maturity. The changes, however small they may be, continue through the life span of an individual.

(v) Development, as said earlier, implies improvement in functioning and behaviour and hence brings qualitative changes which are difficult to measure directly. They are assessed through keen observation in behavioural situations.

(vi) Development is also possible without growth as we see in the cases of some children where they do not gain in terms of height, weight or size but they do experience functional improvement or development in physical, social, emotional or intellectual aspects.

Hence when observed in minute details, both growth and development show differentiation. But in a wider and practical sense both terms are used to denote any changes in the organism's physical as well as functional behaviour. These changes which cover physical, emotional, intellectual and social aspects of human life are roughly divided into four major classes by Mrs. Hurlock:

(i) Changes in size,

(ii) Changes in proportion,

(iii) Disappearance of old features,

(iv) Acquisition of new features.

All the types of changes have qualitative as well as quantitative aspects and hence generally growth and development go hand in hand. And it is in this sense, that the two terms are to be used collectively. Both, taken together explain the total changes-functional as well as constitutional changes in the body and behaviour of the individual with the lapse of time after the conception.

Difference between the Two : However, growth and development are so closely linked that at times it is hardly possible to clearly distinguish between the two. Nature has set limits to the extent of growth of every animal and hence no animal would grow beyond those limits. Macy and Kelly declare that "physical development does not necessarily mean increase in size. There are modifications of the body composition taking place constantly. In the body, for example, gain in weight comes partly from increase in neural, glandular, and muscle tissue; in childhood the gain comes principally from bone and muscle tissue; while in adult years, the gain is from an accumulation of fat tissue".

No boundaries are set for development. Normally the growth may stop by the time a boy or a girl crosses further, depending upon one's professional work and labor. Not only does one develop physically but also socially and intellectually. Acquisition of new skills and assimilation of more knowledge constitute those qualitative changes which characterise 'development'. Quantitative measurement of the structure may reveal the pattern of growth a child is following and it is nowadays very easy to find out from the school health records whether the child is growing or not. Similarly tests have been devised to objectively measure strength, an indirect-index of the qualitative change in muscles and bones- and determine the extent of the development. In the same way, intellectual capacity and ability which are the indices of mental development, can be noticeable in the players and athletes who day after day give better performance in activities involving strength, speed, cardiovascular endurance, etc. Ordinarily when children reveal their motor skills, intellectual ability. etc., differences in their growth and development can be spotted without much difficulty.

Physical development is prominent in athletes who regularly take exercise while people with sedentary habits lag behind in this sphere. Similarly voracious readers show signs of mental development. When athletes behave wonderfully well during play and do not lose mental equilibrium when defeated, we normally say that they have developed emotionally too. Social development is purely qualitative in nature because it reflects one's adjustment in the environment.

Development and Growth's Study : Regardless of individual background and concerns, it is desirable to examine our purposes in studying growth and development. We want to acquire the following abilities:

1. The ability to recognize individuality. This implies the ability to recognize the uniqueness of each child's traits and view of life.
2. An understanding of the theories and principles of growth and development so that one can understand development in terms of the varied hereditary, environment and self influences usually involved.
3. An increased effectiveness in observing and interpreting the pattern of individual behaviour.
4. The ability to differentiate and evaluate the effectiveness of varying points of view in child study.
5. The development of a point of view and set of principles basic to guiding children more effectively in the learning and adjustment processes.

Thus, the student of child development should be involved not merely with learning a number of facts, but also with developing skills which can help him both personally and professionally throughout his life. This necessitates the continuing and purposeful observation of children in action, to supplement regular class study. As time goes on, he will be able to apply his knowledge and experience to interact more effectively with children.

The Tenets

Development psychologists believe that an accurate picture of the principles of growth and development is essential for the teacher. They are as follows:

(1) *Growth in Some Direction is Inevitable:* All living organisms have to grow come what may. Propensity to grow is inherent in the organism. Because of malnutrition or some other environmental factors, the functional capacity of the child may not improve. Yet he has to grow and become

bigger to the extent to which his heredity has set limits. It has been found that mental development is not much affected by malnutrition in childhood, provided the child received normal diet later on and that unfavorable conditions are not allowed to continue. All persons gain normal height even if they are not subjected to any special diet and physical exercises. Only those who exercise shall have better physical functional ability. There is, in each individual, an urge to grow and become bigger. Some individuals strive to grow into athletes, others into Mathematicians. The inner urge for growth will certainly take some form or direction.

(2) *Mental Growth is Dependent upon the Changed Structure:* Along with increase in child's physical proportions, his ability to experience things enhances because physical growth and mental activity go hand in hand. When a child is found to be poor at perception and comprehension, it is because various organs of perception are not fully developed to receive cues from the environment and he is not in a position to sift the wrong from the right. Gradually the brain also becomes capable of accumulating experiences. A child and an adult differ from each other in physical as well as mental growth. Perception and execution of complex motor skills involving a very high degree of neuromuscular coordination is beyond the mental limits of the child while an adult having richer experience of years, takes little time in picking up hints and behaving accordingly. Qualitative mental activity is not possible without proper growth of the nervous system.

(3) *Characteristically, Children are Egocentric and Adults Socio-centric:* A child's behaviour is motivated by the intra-organismic drives which lead to the achievement of biological ends. When the needs connected with this process are not satisfied, the child revolts. As the child matures, he also learns to consider "other things" before his self. Much of his instinctive behaviour gets modified because the society demands certain norms, standards, customs and traditions as well as etiquettes to be observed

and followed in the manner of walking, talking, dressing up, eating and the like. The adult behaviour is guided more by social norms and standards. Childhood, in fact, is a state of animal-hood. The child does what pleases him and what strengthens his ego. In infancy, for example, all activities of the child, including play, are individualistic in nature. Childhood is not bound by the shackles of social norms and standards.

(4) *Growth is a Creative Process:* Right from the time of conception to adulthood marked differences in structure and form appear-thus resulting in behavioural variability. Transforming a infinitesimal zygote into a child, is the nature's highest form of creativity. As a child advances in age, year by year marked changes become visible in his behaviour. Instinctive behaviour which hitherto was more or less fixed, starts giving way to variability. Behaviourally what a child is at the age of one year, he would not be so at the age of five and the child at the age of fourteen is entirely different from the one at five. The process of growth creates novel, cognitive, conceptual and motor forms of behaviour as the child marches ahead in time.

(5) *Heredity sets Limits for Development in terms of Potential:* Even if environmental factors such as food, air, exercise, etc., are abundantly available, the organism would never grow beyond the limits nature has already set on various animals and their respective species. Even twins may differ on anatomical characteristics. Certain races are tall while others are short statured.

Similarly short children born of short parents would not gain height despite the best nutritional facilities and physical exercise. No teacher of physical education and sports should hope to increase the height/size of the individual which is already determined and demarcated by his hereditary forces. Many parents and teachers still erroneously believe that certain physical exercises can help children gain height. The teacher of physical education has to take special note of this fact. The activity programme has to be framed keeping in view these facts concerning the anatomical structure and its developments. Similarly many other hereditary traits cannot be developed beyond a certain limit. A born imbecile will never become a genius despite all efforts. Effects of certain congenital defects and deformities might be attenuated. Yet the total cure is impossible.

(6) *Different Aspects of Growth, Develop at Different Rates Some children start toddling earlier than they start babbling;* some start articulating sounds before they step into the phase of upright locomotion. Parents often worry when there is some delay in the appearance of a particular trait or characteristic at a particular period of time. Children characteristically speak three to five words at twelve months of age but in the next three or four months they seldom use words and often even forget the ones they knew. Language growth slows down for the time being because the child's physical energy and enthusiasm for learning are thoroughly occupied with the thrills of upright locomotion. Physical growth proceeds rapidly during puberty. Children probably learn more new things in the first five years of life than at any comparable period during the rest of their lives. In most of the children there is no synchronization between the physical and the mental growth. Some children become psychologically mature earlier while some excel mentally earlier than others. Ultimately all aspects of growth catch up by the time maturity is reached.

(7) *Various Organs of the Body grow at Different Rates:* Each organ reaches its maximum extent or dimension at different times. But within this chaos, a definite order has been found by the researchers. They speed up first reaching their peak growth rate only after about three months after the adolescence spurt has begun. In other six months, it is the turn of the calf muscles. Four months later, the hips and chest begin to broaden at an accelerated rate followed by the shoulders. In both sexes, the length of the trunk and the depth of the chest reach peak growth last of all.

(8) *Growth is Characterised by Fluctuation:* Many factors may

be held responsible for fluctuation in growth. Generally infancy or pre-school years are periods of accelerated growth while later childhood and late adolescence are periods of slackness. They are, in fact, periods of consolidation. After adolescence, the growth tapers off. Some psychologists have found certain individuals still growing-though imperceptibly-even at forty. Nutrition, physical and mental stresses and strains and other environmental factors influence the rate of growth. Some time, with all other factors there is still fluctuation in growth with certain children. For this, some internal and external factors may be responsible. Fluctuation in growth is not a drawback but an internal law and can easily be spotted if periodic check-up is made and proper records are kept. A month-to-month and year-to-year study, through psychomedical and ability tests, can reveal fluctuation.

(9) *Any Breaks in the Continuity of Development will generally be due to Environmental Factors:* Given an adequate environment, development will ordinarily take place in a relatively predictable way. Infants will grow physically as do most other children in the culture. They will learn to crawl before they walk. By the age of two they will have a rough working knowledge of the language that surrounds them; and toward the end of childhood they will experience rapid physical changes culminating in sexual maturity and adulthood. Motor, or intellectual development may be impeded in cases of severe childhood diseases or as a result of certain maternal diseases while the child is still in embryo. In much the same way, diet, drugs, and illness can affect children directly at various stages of their development and stunt both physical and intellectual growth. And, according to a principle already stated, the effects of these conditions will be most pronounced during the period of most rapid growth.

(10) *Correlation and not Compensation is the Rule in Development:* It has often been assumed by grandmothers that nature makes up for deficiencies in some areas by compensating

for them in others. Thus, children who develop with frail and uncoordinated bodies, will most likely be given exceptional minds to make up for it. Only rarely will mother nature give the same individual both a superior body and a superior mind.

In reality, mother nature is probably not responsible for such events. Striking incidents of compensation that can be gleaned from personal experience or anecdotal evidence are probably most often the result of considerable direct effect on the part of the individuals concerned. Because all individuals have a need for acceptance by others. Children who are unsuited for the competitive aggressive sports of their peers because they are significantly smaller, may naturally become more interested in intellectual or other matters. The point is that the compensation is not a natural phenomenon, but results instead from the individual's activities motivated by whatever needs are predominant at that time. That correlation rather than compensation is the rule is supported by evidence from a number of studies of gifted children.

(11) *Development usually Proceeds at the Rate at which it Started:* Children who learn to walk and talk at an early age are likely to be advanced in all areas of development throughout their childhood. This does not mean, of course, that they are more intelligent and better developed physically than children who mature more slowly. Although their biological clocks may be faster, they are not necessarily programmed for more superior development.

(12) *Development is a Life long Process:* Generally growth and development go hand in hand. When the boy or an individual child grows in structure it also develops in function. But it is not the universal truth. A time may come when he may grow but does not develop or he may develop but does, not grow. Again growth may stop at a particular period, but development continues after growth has ceased. Development thus, is a continuous process. An individual changes both physically and psychologically and encounters new adjustment problems throughout his life.

(13) *Development Involves Changes:* The life of an individual is dynamic in nature. It is never static. From the moment of conception to the time of death, it undergoes changes. At each stage of human development, changes take place, whether for good or bad, as a result of accumulation of experience. The aim of such developmental changes are achievement of genetic potentials or self-actualization.

(14) *Early Development is more Critical than Later Development:* Milton, the world famous poet once said, "The childhood shows the man, as morning shows the day." Right from the beginning of the early childhood, one can predict the future of an individual. Freud, in his study about personality maladjustment emphasises on the significance of early years of life. Erikson also opines that "childhood is the science of man's beginning as man". Thus, most educationists and the psychologists feel that the early development of the child is very critical. Early pattern of life is relatively unchanged as time goes on. The early impression of the child remains for all times to come. Therefore, the first five years of the child have been called "The critical period". From this age onwards the foundations are laid for future life. The environment in which the child lives during this period has strong impact on his hereditary patterns. Hence guidance is most needed in the early stage of life.

(15) *From Infancy to Childhood each Individual has his own Rate of Growth:* The rate of development varies from individual to individual. While some develop rapidly others develop slowly. Dull children continue to be dull and the bright children maintain their brightness. Children having mental defects stop growing at an early age in comparison to the normal children From physical point of view, a child who is tall and heavy for his age, will continue to be tall and heavy to his age, and a child who is weak for his age, will continue to be so. Such rate of growth is a tendency and it may be influenced by environment.

(16) *The Pattern of Growth is Continuous and Gradual:* Behaviour of an individual does not become mature and perfect soon after birth. It is a slow continuous and gradual process. To enter into a stage or level, it takes time. Early childhood lays the foundation for later childhood and later childhood for adolescence. Therefore, it is not possible to demarcate sharply the different stages of development. It is a continuous process. Physical growth and mental and social development is also a continuous process. The process of continuity is maintained even in the development of traits.

(17) *Growth is a Process of both Differentiation and Integration:* People vary in their behaviour because of differences in their genetic constitutions. From birth till the end of life man's behaviour changes at each progressive stage. This change in behaviour pattern occurs due to new discrimination and generalisation of different factors. Now we shall discuss how the child discriminates and generalizes mental processes.

The complex mental processes are the combinations of simple processes like sensations, feelings and images. Behaviourist also build complex behaviour patterns from simple reflexes. At the first stage of life the child is in a state of confusion but gradually according to his age and mental ability he is able to discriminate things properly. For example, when the child utters the words mummy, daddy, etc., he may use the same word 'mummy' for every woman. But when his intellect develops properly he uses the same word for one person only. At first the child does not know the actual relationship with different people. But gradually he learns to distinguish between them. Again another example may be stated that in early infancy emotions begin as undifferentiated generalized excitement. But day by day anger, fear, love, and delight begin to be distinguished from each other. In the social development the child also selects his friends, peer groups, and companions through the process of discrimination.

In growth and development integration and coordination of different physical parts, mental activities are more important as differentiation because the growth and development of every individual is a process of integration. Staging a drama, appearing at a competitive examination, playing cricket, giving a lecture, writing an essay, organising a social function are seen as simple unitary responses but all the activities require some mental and physical capacities in an integrated way. For example, we expect more achievement from a three or four year old child when he starts his first alphabet learning. But until the proper movement of his hand, and proper mental development he cannot write a single letter. Therefore without proper integration and coordination among different organs, no success is possible.

From the above discussion it has been found out that growth is both differentiation and integration. These two processes happen together. Both are important and fundamental aspects of growth and learning. Thus, we must keep these two in mind while framing the curriculum and selecting methods of teaching.

(18) *The Effect of Training Varies with the Stage of Maturation:* In the process of growth and development the role of maturation is more important. But what do we mean by maturation? It is appropriate inner growth which develops readiness for learning. Without proper development of inner organs of the body, the child is unable to acquire new skill by guidance or training or education. Therefore training and teaching will not be fruitful unless actual maturation has taken place. But from our day to day experience we have seen that many parents don't have any knowledge about this inner growth. They lay much emphasis on education and training and expect notable results. Now psychologists have conducted many investigations upon this factor of growth and development. The outcomes of their studies indicate that the teacher or the parent cannot put new things into the child until he is mature for that. Real matured child can learn easily.

Therefore proper training or instruction should be given at the right level of maturation and that may produce right results. In the process of teaching the subject matter for curriculum, and evaluation procedure, the level of maturation of the child must be taken into consideration.

(19) *There are Wide Individual Differences in Growth Pattern:* Individuals differ in respect of their physical appearance, mental ability, school achievement, height, and weight, habit and skills, temperament etc. This individual difference occurs due to genetic factors, environmental influence and many other reasons. But in the process of growth and development children vary in their rate of growth. It implies wide individual variations both in their rates and pattern of growth. From our modern research it has been found that growth is a creative force which results in new experience and ability. According to one's own intelligence and ability, and influence of his own environment he is capable of making a unique pattern of growth. Thus, this variation occurs spontaneously in growth pattern.

(20) *Both Rate and Pattern of Growth can be Modified:* Both rate and pattern of growth can be modified by the conditions within and without the body. Although the patterns of growth are family definite for all children yet 'some' modifications can be envisaged. When environment does not offer equal opportunity to all, the natural flow of growth is modified. Amount of activity, psychological challenges, learning facilities, security, affection, discipline, etc., are a few factors which determine how fast and to what extent the potentialities of the child will have opportunity to develop.

Children living under abject poverty and constant mental strains when freed, will show positively modified growth patterns. Growth brings differentiation as well as integration in behaviour. The processes are closely knit. It is impossible to understand the 'physical' child without understanding, at the same time, the 'thinking', the feeling and the 'impulsive' child. Likewise it is impossible to understand a mentally 'matured' child without evaluating his social development. There is a close relationship, for example between his total adjustment at school and his emotional growth, his physical health and his intellectual adequacy; his intellect is related to his physical health and his intellectual adequacy; his intellect is related to his physical well being: his physical growth and health are deeply affected by his emotional development; his emotions are influenced by the school success or failure, by his physical health and by his intellectual growth. His growth—physical, intellectual and social - is a product of his family history, his personal history and his current satisfactions and strains. Differentiation is a marked sign of growth; each organ, each aspect of the child's personality reaches its fullness by the process of differentiation; integration aims at synthesising all aspects to give the individual a sort of uniqueness and "wholeness".

(21) *Developmental Process and Education:* Opportunity for good education and learning help developmental processes—being an inextricable aspect of an individual's personality. Acquisition of knowledge, experience and motor skills clearly point out the direction and the pattern of an individuals growth. Gesell claims that innate capacity for growth "is a gist of nature. It can be guided, but it cannot be transcended by an educational agency". The patterns of behaviour which develop through learning, clearly indicate the cultural influences. Generally, children studying in public and convent schools seem to be maturer than children studying in ordinary schools. Urban children seem to behave in a more mature manner in the field of sports than do the children from rural areas.

The above generalizations about growth and development serve as a sort of directive principles of programme-planning in educational setting. Generality may solve a great number of problems of education and yet 'individuality' may always pose itself as the biggest problem to the educationist and the psychologist alike.

Change based on Development

Developmental changes are continuous and gradual. The importance of these continuous changes among children has been highlighted by research in the field of child psychology and child education. Because of these developmental changes certain characteristics emerge in the life of an individual, which put a permanent stamp on his whole life. Besides these, the ultimate success or failure of his life are determined largely by the way he happened to have spent his early infancy and childhood period. It is the real period of learning. During this period, the most significant patterns of thought and behaviour are formed. Therefore, the study of early infancy and childhood in human development is the most significant.

Different Stages

Life begins at the moment of conception, when the ovum (the female reproductive cell) is fertilized by the sperm (the male reproductive cell). Not only before birth, but also after birth for many years the child is a helpless organism until and unless he is helped by the continuous process of growth and development and attains maturity. When one attains maturity he ceases to be an adolescent and labelled as an adult member of the society. He is supposed to play a responsible role in the society.

Before being called as adolescent, he is named as child or infant, etc. All of these names—infant, child, adolescent and adult, etc., are linked with various stages of growth and development through which the child passes from birth to death.

There are certain common developmental or practical characteristics belonging to each stage. The human organism shows peculiar quantitative and qualitative changes in his body and behaviour with the help of which we can say at what particular age an individual belongs to which definite stage of his life.

The life span of an individual can be divided into the following stages.

Name of the stage	Period and approximate age
1. Pre-natal (pre-birth) stage	From conception to birth,
2. Stage of infancy	From birth to five years.
3. Childhood stage	From 6th to 12 years or in strict sense up to the onset of puberty.
4. Adolescent	From the onset of puberty to the age of maturity (generally from 13 to 19 years)
5. Adulthood.	From 20 years and beyond or from the age of attaining maturity till death.

Psychologists studying child behaviour tend to discern distinctive phases in the development of the child, and they conceptualize the whole development process as consisting of certain identifiable stages. Though logical objections against stage concepts are strong, the concepts may be useful for practical purposes.

There is no single scheme of stages of development. Depending upon the aspects of behaviour studies, and the investigators frame of reference, there are different schemes of developmental stages. It is not possible to discuss here all the schemes of development stages.

Dr. Earnest Jones has divided human development into four phases.

1. Infancy (1 to 5 years)
2. Late childhood (6 to 12 years)
3. Adolescence (12 to 18 years)
4. Maturity (18 years onward)

James Ross deviated a bit from the above divisions. Instead of four, he says, the stages of development are five in number.

1. Infancy (Birth to 3 years)
2. Early childhood (3 to 6 years)

3. Later childhood (6 to 12 years)
4. Adolescence (12 to 18 years)
5. Adulthood (18 years onward)

Dr. Earnest Jones tells us that 'we grow up twice achieving a pseudo-maturity before puberty. At this age "nature seems to undo most of her pioneer work and begin again the process of building up and consolidating." In his opinion adolescence and adulthood arc recapitulations of infancy and late childhood respectively. Before adolescence, each year of growth brings rapid changes and each year itself is a separate stage of development. Reckoning the span of each developmental stage is more a matter of convenience than a rule.

Tradition and Environment

Since we all have similar beginnings, it is interesting to ask what makes us all so different as we grow older. One answer is that, except in the case of identical twins, we have different heredity. Another answer is that we have different environments. There is further more a constant interplay between heredity and environmental influences and our physical and mental characteristics are the complex results of both factors.

Inception of Life

Each of us begin life at the moment of conception. Conception is the moment when the ovum (the female reproductive cell) is fertilized by spermatozoan (the male reproductive cell). Thus a single cell smaller than the head of a pin, later multiplies and become many cells. This cell results from the fertilization of a female's ovum by a male's sperm. Heredity is determined by complex organizations of chemical materials within the nucleus of the fertilized cell. These chemical materials are contained in nuclear structures which are known as chromosomes or coloured bodies.

Microscopic studies have shown that there are forty six chromosomes in every body cell. Within each sex cell whether male or female, there are 23 pairs of chromosomes before the maturational process takes place. Within each chromosome there are strings of microscopically small particles, the genes. The genes are the physical substances passed on from parent to offspring. Those are the carriers of hereditary traits.

The moment of conception is regarded as one of the most important moments in the life of an individual for the following reasons.

(i) The first important reason is that at the moment of conception, when the ovum is fertilized by the sperm, is the determination of the newly born child's hereditary endowment.
(ii) Whether the child will be male or female is determined once and for all at the moment of conception only. Nothing after this moment can change the sex of the child.
(iii) The third important condition determined at the time of conception is whether the child will be single or multiple. Thus number of offsprings is also determined at this moment.
(iv) The fourth condition determined at this moment is the ordinal position in the family; whether the child will be first born, second born in the family has a lifelong influence on the behaviour pattern of the child and his personality development.

Resembling Heredity

Since the combination of genes an individual receives from his two parents is a matter of chance, only in rare situations will two children get identical combinations and hence identical heredity. This is only possible in case of identical twins (or identical triplets, identical quadruplets, and so on).

Identical twins develop from the same, zygote. If a zygote divides into two cells, each separately goes to form a new individual.... Since each cell has the same genes as the zygote, the heredity of the two individuals will be identical. These are known as identical twins; they are always of the same sex and are identical in many other respects.

Not all twins, however are identical. Host twins are fraternal twins; they develop from two separate eggs of the mother and hence begin as two zygotes formed independent by the union of two different sperms with two different ova. Fraternal twins are no more alike genetically than ordinary brothers and sisters (siblings) born at different times. Fraternal twins may or may not be of the same sex.

From the foregoing, we come to know that we have different heredity. Therefore, we differ from each other. The diagram on the previous page will give us a clear picture about the influences of heredity upon the life of an individual.

Surrounding Environment

Like heredity, environments also plays an important role in growth and development of an individual. It is everything, other than heredity, that influences an individual's growth and development. It starts from the period of gestation in the mother's womb. Of course, it must be pointed out at this juncture that it is a mere superstition that everything the mother does affects the unborn foetus. Some ladies spend the months of pregnancy visiting art galleries in the belief that they are improving the child's mind. While malnutrition of the mother or disease or any such factor can affect the uterine environment of the foetus, external factors like visit to beautiful places or listening to music cannot have any direct effect.

The environment influences an individual all through his life from "womb to tomb". Environment refers not only to the physical surroundings but even to the thoughts and attitudes of others which exert an influence on the individual. It is very difficult to study the environment because it is also unique to each individual. Let us take the case of two brothers playing in a room. Though the physical environment is the same for both, the psychological environment is not the same. One boy is older and is playing with a younger brother while the latter is playing with an older brother. Their past experiences too cannot be identical and therefore their reactions to the situation are also different. Hence psychologists are faced with many problems when studying the effect of the environment because it is impossible to keep it constant and introduce a few variables.

Heredity and environment influence human development. For example, differences in eye color are hereditary, differences in social attitudes are largely environmental, and differences in intelligence have both hereditary and environmental origins except in the case of identical twins, where they are purely environmental.

Hereditary and environment in interaction with one another, produce the wide range of individual differences observed among people. Heredity gives a predisposition for high intelligence of activity level, but the extent to which the potential becomes a reality is determined by the interaction of genetic endorsement.

Inherent Nature

Nature and nurture are jointly responsible for the development of personality characteristics, abilities and skills of an individual. In this connection we shouldn't treat Nature and Nurture separately in determining their contribution to particular type of behaviour. Therefore the issue in Nature versus. Nurture should not be raised. Nurture, or the environment, seems to determine whether the potentialities will be realised. For instance, a person has the genetic potentiality to be educated, but his potentiality may fail to be expressed because of poverty or illness which comprise the environment. The potentiality always acts through the environment and the result of the joint of Nature and Nurture is the behaviour of the persons as seen by others. The greater the potentiality and the more favourable the environment, greater will be the result of the joint action. Thus an individual is the product of an interaction between nature and nurture.

Complex Issue

There is always a controversy between the psychologists, biologists and educationists whether heredity or environment is a more important factor for growth and development of an individual. This controversial issue is very significant for the teachers. If we say that heredity is responsible for the growth and development of an individual, then the teacher has nothing to do. He has simply to watch how the innate potentiality of the child gets unfolded. If, on the other hand, we consider environment to be responsible, for the growth and development of the child, then the role of teacher becomes very important. When he becomes the sole moulder of the students according to his own ideals, he can shape or pattern the life of the students in the way he likes. Thus, he occupies a pivotal place in the process of growth and development. Role of heredity and environment in the process of growth and development from the external point of view is not at all desirable. Those who support heredity to be the only factor responsible for growth and development argue that nothing can be done to improve the individual beyond the limits laid down by heredity. On the other hand, those who support the role of environment to be the most important factor are guilty of exaggerated optimism that there are no limits to the growth and development of an individual.

But it is not possible to have a watertight compartment between the two factors of heredity and development to work for the growth and development of the child. It is not possible to point out the traits which are exclusive hereditary or environmental. Besides this, most of the modern psychologists are of the opinion that because of the interaction between the energies inherited by an organism and development of an individual, it is impossible to estimate the amount of contribution made by heredity and environment for the growth and development of an individual. Nor is it possible to have watertight compartments between the two factors. From the moment the child is conceived in its mother's womb, the two factors work hand in hand and continue to play their roles throughout his life. A study of both the points of view brings us to the conclusion that heredity or environment alone cannot be the sole determinants of the status of an individual. The combination of the two factors in obvious and implicit ways makes the individual what he is.

A child is purely a product of heredity at the time of conception. He receives this heredity from his father and mother, who are having different traits, qualities and characteristics. Each of them contributes to the heredity of the child through genes. A child becomes a distinct individual with distinct characteristics of his own because of the interaction of genes. Hence the teacher cannot change the influence of heredity on the child. A child who has inherited poor intelligence cannot replace it with superior intelligence by the help of a teacher. A teacher can only help in the development of his intelligence within the given limits.

The influence of heredity of the child begins from the very beginning of life. Soon after conception, the organism comes in contact with the environment. The effect of this contact becomes apparent only after the birth of a child.

It becomes very easy to understand the influence of environmental factors because of the marks left by the forces operating in the environment in which the children live. Being influenced by environment they learn different attitudes, values, etc. Malnutrition for a long period and poor hygienic conditions develop certain functional deformities and diseases which leave a permanent mark in the life of an individual. The teacher plays an important role in moulding the environment of the child. In order to become a successful teacher, he needs to understand the concepts and role of heredity and environment in the life of a child.

Learning after Getting Matured : Maturation is considered as the chief competitor of learning as a modifier of behaviour. Maturation is regarded as those stages of growth and development which takes place from within the subject without the help of any special training, practice, experience or stimulation. For example, at a particular stage, a child starts crawling or sitting or standing or walking. At a particular stage of its development, a tadpole starts swimming and a bird starts flying. All these changes in behaviour are the result of maturation. But the ability to talk by a parrot, the ability to drive a motor cycle or to swim in a river, etc., are the products of learning.

Learning sometimes depends upon maturation. A child can learn a thing better, only when he reaches a particular maturational level. For example, during the age from 1 to 5 a child can learn the language better, a stimulus response function. All our sense organs are bombarded by the stimuli of the environment and we respond to them. The sense organs help us to understand and to interpret the environment, to discriminate between good and bad stimulus, to decide to welcome which stimulus and to avoid which one. All these are stages or processes of learning activity.

Different senses contribute differently to the learning process. This is illustrated by an interesting experiment by C.H. Hongik. A number of white races were divided into 5 groups to learn a maze. Some learnt it with all senses intact. Others learnt after being blinded by operation, some others after being blinded and deafened. Another group after being blinded and rendered anosmic (made intensive to adore). The last group was deprived of all these senses.

Learning Process

Learning to an extent is also a function of maturation. One cannot teach a new born baby to walk or to pick up tiny objects with his four fingers, however much one may try Before anything is learnt by a person, his sensory-motor and also the nervous system including brain must reach a certain level of maturity. The predetermined sequential stages of maturity of the sensory-motor and nervous system of an individual comprise the "critical time" for that learning.

Similarly there is critical time for other important tasks like toilet training, reading, learning socially approved behaviour, etc. If a child is taught a behaviour before the critical time i.e. before he attains the maturational level for the task, he fails to do so. If he is taught that task after the critical time, he also fails to master it effectively as is proved from the language problems of the wolf-children.

Academic Relevance

To be successful in the teaching-crafts, a teacher, therefore, must have a thorough knowledge of the process of child development. A mere bookish knowledge of child life, however, will not be of much help to a school teacher. Descriptions and researches contained in the literature on child development are, of course, very enlightening for a teacher. But unless supplemented by concrete observations of and experimentation with children, a mere bookish reading will be of little value in actual school or home situations.

A sound knowledge of various characteristic features of child development through infancy, childhood and adolescence is indispensable for the teacher owing mainly to the following reasons.

1. It gives him the most authentic knowledge regarding the human staff that he deals with the children.

   It enables him to understand the root causes of their good and bad behaviour.
2. It helps him to match his teaching techniques and standards with the developmental level that a child has actually attained. He is thus enabled to avoid being too difficult, too easy or too common place in the classroom.
3. By enabling him to understand his own infancy and childhood periods it facilitates him to understand his own self This self-understanding proves immensely helpful for him in becoming a better teacher and a better person.

6

The Cultivation

Human being is the best creation of God, but he does not receive the best education by the study of science or religion, philosophy or political science, education or Psychology, Art or literature or by earning a Ph. D. or a D. Litt degree from a recognized university, but by the study of truth about how to live and how to be socialized. Sociability not only establishes his superiority over other animals but also provides him with capability of making sound adjustment and maintaining effective and influential social relations. Traits, habits and instincts come into being during childhood. Then they provide the criterion for the characteristic reaction of man to his environment. The child's respect for his elders, love for the youngsters, cooperation with peers and hospitality towards strangers, etc., depend on the process of the development of his personality in the environment of school and family. The more he learns sociability in this stage, the more he becomes sociable in his later life and the less he faces problems. So both the school and the home play an important role in the social development of the child.

Man is a social being. He comes in contact with the society and starts his interaction with it from the moment of his birth.

The span of social relations gradually increases and continues till death. So it is a process from womb to tomb. Considering from social point of view, the childhood is the most valuable phase in human life. Real socialisation starts from childhood. The social habits along with the social instincts that he gains and his interaction with different persons and environment shapes his personality for the whole of his life. Hence it is a prime necessity on the part of a teacher to have the knowledge of how the social personality of a child develops and what are its main constituents.

At the time of birth, the child is neither social, anti-social nor unsocial. It depends upon the environment and experience of his life. His personality is shaped accordingly. At the time of entering the school, the child does not have egocentrism. Rather he expresses interests in the persons, objects and events of his surroundings. He takes part in group-activities. Qualities like distributing things among friends, cooperation, friendship, social interaction and leadership are the main characteristics of his behaviour at that time. With the increase of his experience with other elements of the world, these qualities become the traits of his personality.

Social Growth

Social development is a multi-faceted process in which children acquire talents and behaviour that allow them to function, within a social environment, in a manner that is mutually beneficial to their well-being and that of others. Through social development, children and youth establish inter-personal relationships, acquire a sense of sex-role identity, and develop social standards and a sense of conscience.

Social development is influenced by many different socialisation forces. These affect children's acquisition of the habits, values, and knowledge that facilitate their attainment of goals and enable them to function satisfactorily as members of society. In other words, children learn a complex network of clues that indicates the appropriateness of their actions for specific situations. For example, students' behaviour in one teacher's classroom may be very different from their behaviour in another classroom or on the playground.

A variety of social agents, or determinants, influence the socialization process needed for effective social interaction. These social determinants may include biological factors, social structure and cultural-group membership, the unique social interactions that children and adolescents have with parents and other, cognitive and situational determinants.

Children are not just passive recipients in their acquisition of social behaviour; rather they are active participants in their environments through their social interactions. Students actively incorporate the standards of external social agents and they process those mental structures that enable them to construct schemes or programmes that facilitate appropriate behaviour in other social situations.

System of Culture and Society

Social development varies with children's social and cultural system. Children are cultured differently based on their cultural backgrounds and on parental beliefs related to the nature of children and how they should behave as adults. For example, American-Indian, Oriental, and Anglo-American children are cultured to have different values and behaviour. However, it appears that children's acquisition of social traits and skills is independent of culture and that the process of social development is similar across cultures and social systems.

Importance of the School

School or any educational institution occupies a special position among the various factors that influence the social development of a child. School is basically a social institution. It can be called a society in miniature. So it can serve as a model of society with all the social characteristics. The amount of influence that school can have on the child depends on the caliber and will of the teacher.

Along with the discussion of child's physical, perceptual and cognitive development, psychologists are highly interested in infant's social and moral attachments. The reasons are many.

Firstly, the human beings are highly social and a child's birth is a social event in itself. Then as he grows he is influenced and shaped by the social and moral behaviour of people surrounding him. He also influences others. So it is a two way relationship and needs a good understanding among those involved.

Secondly, during early years an infant's behaviour is not clear but confusing as it does not have any uniqueness. Without a proper examination, we can't find out the possible psychological roots as causes of such behaviour.

Thirdly, there is the question of nature and nurture of the child. Different aspects of child's personality should be known to us. We must know about the inherent aspects and the factors that change due to influences of circumstances. Here social experiences take an important place in the child's life.

Finally, the effect of early deprivation trauma should be studied. The factors that produce a well-adjusted and balanced child and the cause that produce a permanent scar in an individual's psychology, must be properly studied.

Different methods and ways are open for the experimenter to study early sociability of human beings. Simple cases can be studied by mere observation. Then there longitudinal studies continuing for many years and experimental studies. We may conduct cross-cultural studies to know the difference in sociability of human beings caused by different social backgrounds. Then there are the studies of child's social behaviour in different socio-economic set-ups. Sociability of upper class, middle class and lower class children tend to be different and its cause and effect is to be properly studied.

Societal Development

Various thinkers have defined social development in the following way:

1. *Garrett:* "Socialisation or social development is a process whereby the biological individual is converted into a human person.

   This definition is based upon the distinction between the term individual and person. We cannot name each and everybody as person. The person always possesses some personality. The personality is the product of social interaction between him and his social environment. Socialisation and social development-the process of social interaction-helps the individuals to attain personality characteristics.

2. *Sorenson:* "By social growth and development we mean increasing ability to get along well with oneself and others".

   In this way Sorenson explains that during the process of social development there is a progress in the social abilities or skills of an individual. With these increasing abilities he tries to bring improvement in the maintenance of social relationships. He tries to mould his behaviour and seek adjustment and harmony with others.

3. *Freeman and Showel:* "Social development is the process of learning to conform to group standard mores and traditions and becoming imbued with a sense of oneness, inter-communication and cooperation."

This definition lays stress on the following:

(i) Social development refers to the process by which a person acquires the necessary knowledge, skills and dispositions that make him an acceptable member of his own group.

(ii) It develops group loyalty and encourages mutual dependence, cooperation and cohesiveness.

(iii) It is the process which helps an individual to behave in accordance with social traditions and mores and thus makes him able to adjust to his social environment.

In the light of all these views we can come to the conclusion that social development or socialisation is a process

(i) which begins with the infant's first contact with other people and continues throughout life.

(ii) it is the net result of his constant interaction with his social environment.

(iii) it helps in learning and acquiring various social qualities and characteristics, and

(iv) with the result of such learning the individual becomes adjusted to his social environment and can maintain proper social relationships.

Growth during Infancy

The child's attitude, social relationships and pattern of behaviour are to a great extent determined by his early social experience. In the beginning all these are "home-grown" and the foundation of sociability is laid in the homes.

Sociability is not innate and it must be learnt. Every social behaviour is an acquired trait. The period between six weeks to six months, is said to be a 'critical time' in the development of attitudes. For a sound and organised social development both "the types of opportunity" and "number of contacts" are important. Mothers, in upper and middle socio-economic families can give favourable opportunities to their children for contact with the members of their families while those who belong to the lower groups lack such opportunities. So their social immaturity is shown in a quiet, retiring and disinterested attitude towards people and social activities.

At birth the infant's perception is non-distinctive. He wants his physiological needs fulfilled. It does not matter who fulfils them. She may be his mother or a caretaker, it may be a soft pillow or a hot water bottle. When the child is six weeks old, the first social smile appears and between second and third months of life, the baby's ability to distinguish people from inanimate objects develops. He then becomes more attached to people and shows different types of emotional behaviour when detached from them. But still he is unable to distinguish people. Some psychologists call this stage as "discriminating responsiveness to people". It is the beginning of true social behaviour.

The baby, between the second and third months becomes interested in people. He tries to attract his attention towards him or watch his facial expression. He shows special relationship with his mother.

When the baby is four or five months old, he wants to be picked up and to be given a soothing and warm touch. He smiles, in response to the person who speaks to him. After one month he can distinguish between scolding and smiling, friendly and unfriendly voices. At the age of six or seven months he differentiates between familiar and strange persons. He smiles at friends and shows anxiety towards unfamiliar persons.

During this period "attachment behaviour" shown towards the mother is intensified. He smiles at her and tries to vocalise a word to her.

The age of eight or nine month is a period of imitation for the child. He imitates the speech, simple motor activities and gestures of others. When he is one year old, elders can refrain him from doing a thing by uttering the word 'No'.

When the child is one and a half years old he shows "Negativism". It means stubborn resistance to requests and demands of adults. The resistance may be physical or the child may remain silent or even tense.

At the end of second year a state of equilibrium is seen in a child. He cooperates with adults in many simple daily activities and follows their directions. Now he becomes more social in his behaviour. He plays with others and especially with the children of his own age. He even shares his playing materials with them.

Most babies become interested in viewing coloured pictures, television and listening to radio. Though they cannot understand the meaning of the subject matter, still they observe and become fascinated by the constant change in light, colour and pictures on the screen of the television or on the pages of the comic books.

Growth during Childhood

Childhood consists of two phases known as early childhood and late childhood. Pattern of socialisation changes from one phase to another. Early childhood has been characterised as the "first stage" of socialization. At this stage he gathers training and experience to be a member of gang in late childhood. Area of relationship of the child increases every year and his talking, playing, etc., increases accordingly. The importance of social development during early childhood lies in its qualitative aspect rather than quantitative aspect. That means, it is not important to count the number of social relationships the child has, rather it is important how he develops intimacy with his environment. His future socialization depends upon the pleasurable social contact at this stage.

Early childhood is a crucial time, so far as social development is concerned, because the child during this time, learns the basic social attitudes and the pattern of social behaviour. From two to three years of age, the child's level of social relation is generally low. After three years of age his socialization shows the prominent symptoms of conversational interactions, dominance, leadership, dependent submissiveness, conformity or compliance with the wishes of others, etc. He also shows some unsocial or antisocial behaviour, but they are also important to the socialization of the child. Some prominent social traits develop during early childhood, which are discussed below.

Firstly the child shows negativism or resistance to adult authority which reaches its peak between the age of three and four years. After that it declines. According to Macfarlane, "Negativism is an interesting combination of self-assertion, self-protection and of resistance to excessive pressures. Children learn that resistance is their best defence in the face of erratic training or when quick tempered persons push slow tempered persons too fast. The child's negativism takes the form of verbal responses and silence. They sometimes do not hear or understand an order or request or they try to neglect them".

Another trait of socialisation of the child is imitation, which implies that the child becomes interested in other children in and around him and tries to imitate their speech, action and emotions. By doing this he tries to prove himself a member of the group. The child does not imitate at all. He chooses the person or persons from whom he gets warmth and affection and imitates their behaviour. At times the child develops a desire to excel or outdo others. This results in rivalry and he tries to brag about his possessions. This is common in case of siblings in a home. When the child is frustrated he expresses aggression. By showing aggressive behaviour he tries to establish his dominance over others. From rivalry and aggression quarreling starts and the child takes away the toys of another child, distracts his work, screams, cries, kicks, hits and bites. These outbursts are short in duration and easily forgotten. At the age of three years such quarreling is frequent and after that improved social adjustments bring about a decrease in the frequency and intensity of quarrels. Children of the lower socio-economic levels quarrel more than those of the higher. Boys are more quarrelsome than girls.

Upto the age of four years, the boys and girls play together, without any specific preference for a particular sex. After four the discriminating attitude begins and it becomes prominent after five years. Then they play different games. In the opinion of Marshall it is a kind of aggressiveness shown by the boys towards the girls. The girls are also antagonised by this.

Between the age of two and three years the child plays alone without any interest in other children. Then comes "Associative play" and "Cooperative play" in which he is a part of a group. At the age of four years he starts team play. He becomes conscious of other's acceptance or rejection of his play activities. He starts playing 'neighbourhood-games' such as tag, hide-and-seek, cat and mouse, cops-and-robbers, etc. Games at this age are simple, involving few rules and lack any type of competition.

Late childhood has been named as "gang age" in view of an increasingly strong desire of the child to be a member of the gang. During this stage, social-development is rapid and the child is no longer a selfish, self-centered individual. He is a well-adjusted, cooperative member of his peer-group. Child's behaviour shows more maturity than before. When the child reaches the age of six, his negativism decreases, though again at the age of ten and eleven they show a type of rebelling attitude against adult authority by which they try to establish their self appropriateness.

The circle of friends of the child widens as he does not want to be confined to his home and family members. When the child enters the middle school, his puberty begins and boys as well as girls spend more time outside the home. Generally a gang consists of children of same sex. They form teams not only to play but also for other activities like stealing fruits, smoking and some other socially unacceptable behaviour.

By forming gangs they raise money for charity, make things

or act out plays depending upon the nature of the community they belong to.

The child learns to compete with others, to cooperate and work as a member of a team, to accept responsibilities and to see them through, to take the part of others when mistreated or neglected and to be a good sport in adversity as well as in success. During the childhood, boys and girls prefer the companionship of the individuals of their own sex. The girls think themselves more matured than the boys of their age but at the same time they see them enjoying more social independence. So they develop antagonistic and unfavourable attitude towards the boys. Boys and girls of this age develop an attitude of hero worship towards someone who possesses qualities they admire. The children select a member of their gang as leader, who must be superior in most respects to the rest of the group especially in intelligence, dependability, diplomacy, self-confidence, emotional stability, athletic ability and awareness of the wishes of the others. Again the leader must be an extrovert.

Influence of Group

Late childhood is also called 'play age' because during this period overlapping of play activities is the characteristic of the younger years and those of adolescence of different social class backgrounds differ, qualitatively and quantitatively. Bright children are generally more solitary and take part in fewer activities. Within the play activities of boys construction of tools, drawing, painting and clay modelling are marked, while girls prefer sewing, drawing, painting and singing. The child who fails to establish good social relations spends more time in day dreaming than the socially well-adjusted child.

During late childhood the child develops interest in understanding people and things which formerly hold little or no meaning for him. After the child enters the school he becomes aware of his racial group and religious-group membership and tries to follow the attitude of elders. He develops a self-concept and understands his social class. He defines his social class status in terms of the occupation of his parents. The self-concept of boys and girls is different. The boys think that they should be able to run fast, play rough games, need to be smart, climb, swim carry things and above all they must have more ability than girls. On the other hand, the girls think that they must stay close to the houses play quietly and gentler than boys; sitting and talking about dresses; they need to know how to cook, sew and take care of children.

Teacher's Role

For the development of social traits in the child and to build him as a good citizen, the school, family and society are to play a very crucial role. In all these environments social development of the child is well-directed and well-shaped by teaching learning process. Education in very valuable for the child. Parents and elders should teach their children how to cooperate and keep good relation with all family members. Direction, advice and above all encouragement are basic for the development of the child. They should not be neglected but be given love and affection. Otherwise his social growth is retarded. He becomes autocratic and selfish. Selflessness, tolerance and cooperativeness are the qualities which should be inculcated in the child. Hard and rigid behaviour, sometimes causes mental instability. Many parents out of fear of danger, do not give their children independence to do any work and they themselves do that work for the child. By this, the quality of self-independence is hampered.

In case of schools or other educational institutions proper environment should be created to facilitate social growth of the children. School can arouse in the children qualities like friendship leadership, cooperation, responsibility, pity, unity, etc. This cannot be achieved only by advice. For this co-curricular activities should be encouraged. Sports and games, staging of drama, discussion, excursion, scouting, Red Cross, etc., are helpful for the child in the development of social traits. Human relationship is the foundation of sociability. So it is the first and foremost duty of the teacher and school to see how best students can keep direct relation among themselves and engage in constructive work.

Qualities based on Society

1. *Sympathy:* It is a social quality. One should not only express explicitly sympathy in the sorrow of others, rather he

should cooperate in order to do away with the misery of others. This is true sympathy. Sympathy should be active but not passive. It starts from home. Its learning cannot be rendered simply by means of advice. If the child receives sympathy from his family members and gets required help in the time of need, he develops exactly the same quality for others. These qualities may not be explicit in the child, for the child's power of observation, imagination, thinking and gathering experience may not be enriched. So he fails to express sympathy for others. For this reason the elders, by means of concrete examples should eradicate qualities like hate and jealousy from the child's mind. The child first applies these qualities to his own people. This is extended to others at a later stage.

2. *Friendliness:* Sympathy and sentiment for one and all creates friendship. A child of two or three years can make contact with other children of his own age if they are left together at a particular place. This contact develops into friendship. Generally similarity in interest, age, height, social and economic status serves as foundation of friendship, selflessness, cooperation, etc. It has been observed by examining the students of a class that many students are interested to create new friends and some others lead isolated life. This happens due to individual differences in the personality. The child with whom others become interested to mix and make friendship with are called 'stars' and friendless students are called 'isolates'. Apart from this, there are some students who become intimate with only one friend and there are others who have many intimate friends. The former is called 'paid' and the later is called 'friendship gang'. This difference should be marked by the teacher and he should steer them in the right way. He should take steps to facilitate the isolate child to enlarge his circle of friends and become sociable.

The followings are some reasons for the isolation of the student.

(a) *Anti-Social:* Some children show rough behaviour. They show anti-social behaviour like disturbing others at the time of study, quarreling frequently, beating others, stealing books and money, tearing up of the books and notes, etc. For such reasons other children are not interested to keep relation with him and finally he is isolated.

(b) *Socially Indifferent:* Some children are always thoughtful, inattentive and shy. They are introverts. Thought, imagination and attention of such students are always self-directed. They are not hopeful in creating friendship and lead a busy life. Their mental health needs to be restored. For, the teacher should apply principles of love, sympathy and consolation and engage them in responsible work by which they can be brought back to social mainstream. Sometimes the suggestion of psychologists proves useful in such cases.

(c) *Underdeveloped:* The students whose social and moral maturity does not keep tune with their growth in chronological age lie behind other general students and feel isolated.

The students who are friendly with all and with whom others want to make friendship show some distinct qualities. The qualities that make a student popular and friendly to all are his patience, good health, efficiency, responsibility, dependability, cooperation, service and help to others, and love for all, etc. Again good adaptability and emotional balance make him popular among friends.

Competition based Cooperation

Cooperation is one of the finest social traits. When the child, for the first time leaves his family and enters into the other environment his span of social relations widens. He develops group behaviour. After becoming the member of a group, he tries to be cooperative. Group cooperation gives birth to group competition. One group of children compete with another group for which all members of a group are to be united. It is difficult to say which of the two qualities—cooperation and competition starts first in human life, because during infancy and early childhood brothers and sisters in a family compete among themselves to be nearer and dearer to their elders. This type of competition is also possible in a classroom.

It should not be misunderstood that family only serves as a ground for competition. It also facilitates cooperation. Experience and moral educations makes competition change into cooperation. Competition cannot be blamed, since without competitive attitude, the child cannot continue his endeavour for development and perfection. But both cooperation and competition have their own limits. They should respond to the needs of the society. Though competition is helpful for the child, it has some drawbacks, because at times such a competitive mentality makes the child jealous and he undergoes tension. So proper balance should be maintained between these two qualities and that is the duty of the teacher. Apart from these if the competition is fair and constructive, social health is restored.

For the all-round development of the child, good social moral upliftment should be given proper attention in the school curriculum. The behaviour of the child should be closely and intensely observed by the teacher which will guarantee the healthy development of the child social and moral.

The whole series of anatomic and physiological changes taking place between the beginning of pre-natal life and the close of senility may be considered as the physical growth. The study of physical growth of both children and the adolescents is very interesting and helpful also. Ordinarily, people make an estimate of the age of the children from their size and treat them accordingly. They also expect them to behave in a manner appropriate to the level of their physical growth. But the basic growth of the child is determined by two factors: heredity and environment. The hereditary factor refers to the characteristics of their family and race and environmental factors refer to healthy or unhealthy surroundings in which the children live, their nutritional and climatic factors, etc.

The behaviour of the child gets influenced by physical development in two ways: direct and indirect. Directly, it determines what children can do. For example, a child, who is developed according to his chronological age, can compete with his peers in games and sports on equal terms. If not, he fails to compete with them and gets himself isolated from the peer group.

Indirectly, physical development influences the attitude of

the child towards self and others. In other words, it is his adjustment to the human environment. For example, children who are overweight cannot adjust with their thinner mates. As a result of which they develop a feeling of personal inadequacy. If, on the other hand, their friends refuse to play with them because they are too slow, they develop a feeling of "martyrdom" in addition to the feeling of inadequacy. Such a feeling creates a havoc in the personality development of the children and the adolescents.

Physical Development

Physical growth brings bodily and physiological changes (internal as well as external) in an organism from the conception till death. These changes take place in the following dimensions.

(i) *Changes in Physical Structure:* Changes in terms of height, weight, body proportions and general physical appearance are considered as changes in the gross physical structure of an individual.

(ii) *Change in Internal Organs:* Changes in the functioning of glands, nervous system and other body systems like circulatory, respiratory, digestive, muscular, lymphatic and reproductive are known as changes in internal organs.

Physical growth does not occur at a regular rate. It occurs in periods, phases or waves. Sometimes it appears slowly and sometimes rapidly.

Researchers are recognizing more and more that a child's physical development has a strong influence on his personality. Researcher Tanner, put it this way:

> "All the skills, aptitudes, and emotions of the growing child are rooted in or conditioned by his bodily structure. Behind each stage of learning lies the development of essential cell assemblies in the brain; behind each social interaction lies a body image conditioned by the facts of size and other features....... How fast a child grows and what type of body structure he has can exert a crucial influence on the development of his personality. The child's sense of identity is strongly linked to his physical appearance and ability."

Early Childhood Growth

The period of infancy covers knowledge of the entire pre-school age, from birth to about 5 to 6 years. In the first few weeks the human embryo and foetus grow at an extremely rapid pace both in size and structure through the multiplication of cells. Within a period of nine months, from the time of conception, the human organism grows from an almost weightless cell to about seven to eight pounds. By the time the human infant is born the rate of growth shows an enormous decrease as compared with that of the foetus. Even then the most rapid physical changes and the most striking growth of the whole post-natal life takes place during the first year. This early period of rapid growth is uniquely significant for education.

Important Significance

(i) *Rapid Growth and Development:* Infancy is the period of growth and development. Inner as well as outer organs, develop rapidly at this stage. There is rapid growth in terms of height, weight and size. There is rapid development of emotions and almost all the emotions are developed in the child during this stage. This stage is marked by intensive motor activity and restlessness.

(ii) *Dependence:* An infant depends upon his mother, father and other family members for the satisfaction of his basic needs. He is a helpless creature and can move and function only with the help of others. Even for the emotional satisfaction, he depends upon others. He expects that everybody around him should love him and give him his entire affection and attention. He wants to love and to be loved and in this exchange he totally depends on the mercy of others. In this way the child at this stage is dependent but as he moves into the later years of his infantile behaviour he slowly proceeds towards independence.

(iii) *Self-Assertion:* Although the child is a helpless one and depends upon others for the satisfaction of his needs, he is quite self-assertive. He tries to dominate his superiors and elders. His wishes must be fulfilled. He thinks he is always right and those all around him should obey him. He is the prince without a crown.

(iv) *Period of Make-believe and Fantasy:* Infants live in the world of their own creation. This is a period of rich but baseless imagination. As at this stage the infant has limited potentialities and aspires more than what he can actually get in actual life. He compensates himself in fantasy and make-believe.

(v) *Selfish and Unsocial:* In infancy the child is almost completely geocentric and selfish. He does not want to share his toys or give any of his possessions to anyone else. He wants to have all the things, even love, admiration and affection reserved for him. He does not care for the social and moral codes and principles and places his self-interest at the premium.

(vi) *Emotionally Unstable:* Infancy is the period of violent emotional experiences. The emotions at this stage are marked by intensity, frequency and instability. They are spontaneous and the infant is hardly able to exercise control over them. He is not able to hide his feelings and in this way, the emotional expression of the infant is generally in the overt form.

(vii) *Sexual Development:* Although the sex organs at this stage are not developed, yet the sex tendency is in a continuous stage of development. The findings of psychoanalysts like Freud and others have clearly shown that the sexual life of the infant is as rich as that of an adolescent. The infant passes through the three stages, sexual development stages of self-love, homosexual and heterosexual. At the initial stage, the child-derives pleasure from his own body by sucking his thumb or touching the sex organs. Later on he seeks the satisfaction of his sex impulse outside and develops sentiments of love for the mother or father depending upon his sex. Finally the child develops heterosexual tendency and in this respect the male child gets attached to the mother and the female child to the father.

(viii) *Respiration and Circulation:* During infancy, the lungs develop rapidly and breathing capacity is increased. The heart also grows in size and its action becomes stronger but slower than at the embryo stage. The pulse rate which was one hundred and thirty for boys and one hundred forty for girls at birth drops gradually so that it is ninety-five for boys and ninety for girls. Parents and teachers must realise that the developmental rate of the heart varies with children. Recognition of this fact can help us to prevent tragedies resulting from too great a strain laid on this organ.

(ix) *Muscular Development:* The very slow development during infancy shows a slight acceleration at age three. Development proceeds from the bigger to the smaller muscles. Thus, an infant thrusts out his arms in play, but immaturity of the smaller muscles of his wrists and fingers prevent their manipulation.

This is determined by maturation of necessary muscles. A child will sit up, stand or walk only when the necessary muscles have matured. But this process of muscle maturation is very slow during infancy and these motor skills are acquired very slowly. Prior to this maturation, actions are awkward and they involve many unnecessary movements. In trying to grasp an object, an infant will exhibit several unnecessary movements of the shoulders, upper arms and elbows. The use of the thumb occurs only after the ninth month. As the infant advances in age, greater maturity of the muscles results in the unnecessary movements being dropped and action being refined. There is also greater strength and speed in the movements.

When the human infant is born, he weighs about 7 to 8 pounds. In length, he is about 20 inches. In the very first year the weight triples and the length increases by about 40%. The rate of growth slows down considerably during the next three years and after that it becomes steady.

Growth in weight is influenced to a great extent by nutrition. Infants from poorer families are weightless and are shorter in stature as compared with infants from rich families. There is also variation in growth rate due to sex-difference. The male infants are larger than female infants of the equal age.

Period of Childhood

Childhood begins with the school going age round of about 5 or 6 years and ends with the beginning of adolescence, i.e. about 12 years in case of the girls and 14 years in case of the boys.

During childhood period, height and weight progress at a fairly uniform rate. But, motor development including posture, motor skills, coordination, locomotion, etc., which begin from infancy, go on unchecked.

Physical Growth

The rate of physical growth continues to be slow. Between the ages of six and nine years, children grow about three to four pounds annually. This slow trend continues during the next phase also. Between the ages of nine and twelve years, increase in height is only an inch per year. Weight increases by about two or three pounds per year but this increment varies from month to month. This slow period of growth is called the pre-puberty lag. The growth is slowest for girls between the ages of nine and ten years, while boys grow slowest between ten and eleven years.

An average six year old is about three feet tall and thirty-five to forty pounds in weight. As the growth rate is slow at age nine, the child is about three and half feet tall and nearly fifty-five to sixty pounds in weight. Girls are generally shorter and lighter than boys. The most significant physical change occurring during this period is the lengthening of the limbs. The legs especially grow vary fast and children appear long-legged. Though children are generally healthy, postural defects are likely to appear now. In our efforts to correct this, we must try to find out the causes which may be infection, malnutrition, fatigue or even emotional disturbance.

The lungs continue to grow and the breathing capacity increases. The heart has not yet attained its full growth. Between the ages of nine and twelve these organs are almost, but not fully developed. Hence we must prevent children from exerting themselves too much.

Muscular Growth

The slight acceleration in muscular development that had set in after age three, still continues. Muscle tissue increases and coordination improves. By age six, a child has reasonable mastery over the basic skills. Hence the child is very active, and enjoys games that involve much physical activity. But his imperfect muscle-coordination makes him prone to falls. Since the muscles of the orbit are not developed fully, long reading sessions are prohibited for the six year olds. Between the ages of nine and twelve, muscle growth increases and coordination also improves. The child's actions are more refined and skillful. Reading sessions can also become longer now.

Children between the ages of six and nine have a reasonably good mastery over the basic motor skills of sitting, standing, walking and simple finger manipulation. Improving muscle coordination helps the child to acquire new skills and improves the already acquired ones. Thus, the six and seven year olds may be seen trying to climb a stairway by taking two steps at a time. They also try climbing and jumping down from high places. By age twelve, muscle coordination is almost perfect. At this stage improved coordination of hand and finger muscles helps the child to produce good handwriting.

Varied Activities

A child at this stage is full of energy and action. The school authorities, therefore, should take care that the early education of the child takes cognizance of this significant physical factor. Consequently, primary education should be predominantly informal. It should have ample provision for interesting and diversified activities.

Most of children grow according to the average pattern of development characteristic of their age level. Some children however, differ markedly from the average in many respects. Some of them go through the whole developmental process more rapidly. Others more slowly, than the average growth rate typical of their age. Some children show striking individual peculiarities in the trend and speed of growth at various levels of development.

They may thus be advanced at one stage of their development and retarded at another. Throughout these developmental variations however, every child keeps on undergoing almost ceaseless growth in various parts of its body

Sex's Role

During the first ten years, the boys are slightly superior to girls in most of physical growth. The tempo of physical development, however, is faster on the whole in girls than in boys.

On the average, the period of rapid growth, following the onset of puberty, starts two years earlier in girls than boys. The significant year in which most rapid growth usually occurs is the 12th in the case of girls (about one year before the first menstruation) and the 14th or 15th for boys. Between the age of 11 and 15 years the girls usually excel the boys in weight and height. Growth in girls, however, stops abruptly after the menarche. The average girl reaches her mature stature by 16 1/2 (sixteen and half) years. The average boy, on the contrary, continues to grow until he is almost 19.

The body proportions of young boys and girls are very similar in general. Boy's skeletal frames become broad at the shoulders. Their general growth is characterized by heavy muscles and greater strength. In girls the pelvis widens and the hips broaden. Pads of thicker fat in certain areas of the body result in the typical softness of the female figure.

These developmental proportions are typical for the two sexes. Nevertheless, there are a great many children whose course of growth does not fit in with the average pattern of physical development described above.

Different Sorts

Many attempts have so far been made to classify individual children into physical types. The most commonly recognized racial and familiar traits usually forming the basis of such classification are variations in skin colour, form and colour of hair, shape of head, ear and nose, colour and shape of eyes, general structure, span and weight. It may be pointed out that these variations are more or less permanent. They persist in the individuals from family to family and from generation to generation. In changed environments, these physical traits may undergo some modifications but their general nature remains fundamentally unchanged on the whole.

Classification by Scammon

One classification of physical types is presented by Scammon. His four types of children based on their physical growth are as follows:

1. The Lympoid: This is a physical type in which the rate of growth of the child increases rapidly until 11 to 12 years and then decreases almost as rapidly to the adult level.
2. The Neural: It is the type of rapid early growth at 3 or 4 years gradually slowing down and reaching almost adult level by 12 to 14 years.
3. The General Type: It is characterized by a rapid rise in growth in early infancy followed by another rise around puberty.
4. The Genital Type: It is marked by a slow growth in the early years which becomes very rapid at puberty.

Views of Kretschmer : Another interesting classification based on physical peculiarities, is presented by Kretschmer. His physical types are also four in number. Their salient features are:

1. *Pyknic Type:* This is characterized by round trunk and short extremities.
2. *Asthenic Type:* Small trunk and long extremities are the distinctive features of this type.
3. *Athletic Type:* This type shows a moderately proportional development of the body.
4. *Dyspalastic:* This is a mixed type of physical growth.

   A thorough knowledge of physical typologies might not be very helpful for a teacher in his actual school work though it proves very insightful for the school medical officer. Some general information regarding the salient characteristics of physical growth among children, however, is almost indispensable for any successful teacher because obviously proper guidance in the field of physical health is as essential for a child as any other help and guidance.

Significance of Education

It is not possible to have watertight compartments between physical, cognitive, emotional, social and moral development. They are closely interlinked. The growth and development of any one of these aspects affects the growth and development of the other. Therefore, physical growth is not an exception to it. It influences the other aspects of growth and development in other directions also. For example, growth and development of the nervous system influences the growth and development of intellectual powers.

Emotional and social adjustment is also linked with physical growth and development. While the children having normal physical growth and development are accepted by their age group, the physical deviates, who are very small, very large, too fat, etc., remain isolated. They are often nicknamed, ridiculed and denied participation in the play and recreational activities enjoyed by children of the same age. It brings serious maladjustment and personality problem. The young child, if intelligent enough, becomes aware of the fact that he differs in appearance and physical abilities from other children. His attitude towards self is injured and self-confidence is shaken. In this case either he becomes shy and timid or becomes aggressive in order to compensate for his inferiority feeling. Besides this, the balanced growth and development of the internal as well as external organs depends on the balanced functioning of the body systems. The functioning of the body systems decides the interest, attitude and the total behaviour of an individual. For example, glands and their functioning affect his emotional behaviour to a great extent. Similarly his anatomical development, the development of circulatory, respiratory system, etc., give the persons the required abilities for participating in various motor activities.

Thus physical development has a great impact on the total make-up of an individual. Therefore, it needs a very careful attention. It can help the teachers to achieve one of the most important aims of the educational process to bring an all round balanced development.

Implication of Education

Children between the ages of three and five years are too young to cope with the work of the primary school. But they are mature enough to start preparing for it. Kindergarten training is therefore, very important. It is here that the child gets the first experiences of school life. He memorises short nursery rhymes, sings with others, learns to obey simple commands and follows directions. He gets accustomed to being separated from his mother and learns to adjust to a fixed schedule. He is also taught to work and play with other children of his age. Hence, the song-dance-and-play atmosphere of the nursery school is just a happy place where learning is a joy.

Activity must form an integral part of nursery training. As the children acquire new motor skills, they have an innate urge to practice them. Action songs, games that involve varied activities like running, skipping and jumping are enjoyed by them. As repetition and drill are also enjoyed, the same action or drill can be repeated profitably.

Children between ages six and nine years have a keen desire to read and write. But their muscle coordination is still imperfect. Hence the teacher must not over-emphasise reading and writing. Handwriting also cannot be expected to be very good at this stage. Between age nine and twelve, reading can be encouraged. The teacher can also help the child to improve his handwriting.

7

Adjustment Problems

Many a significant change have taken place in the school during the last decades, but probably none is of greater significance than the increased concern over the personal and social adjustment of the child. From a rigid emphasis on academic learning very often at considerable cost in terms of his adjustment, schools have come to recognise not only the importance programmes designed to promote the more personal and social aspects of his growth, but also of making the regular classroom programme much more guidance and adjustment-oriented. The primary responsibility for the child's adjustment lies with his parents who set the basic pattern of adjustment through the security they provide him, particularly in his early years. The teacher's influence is only slightly less important, for it is he who, in the main, holds the key to whether the experiences the child undergoes in school throughout his formative period will lead to satisfaction and self-fulfillment—or to frustration and self-defeat.

Ways of Adjustment

Throughout life, the individual has to adjust to the demands of his external environment as well as to those of his physiological and psychological make-up. Thus, the individual is continually eating, drinking, seeking affection or approval, trying to gain status. The adjustments he makes in response to these demands are not always the most desirable or wise from the standpoint of his long-term welfare but they are, nevertheless, adjustments in the sense that they are attempts to satisfy some of his needs. Only in death does the individual cease to adjust.

Adjustments may be defined as the process by means of which the individual attempts to maintain a level of physiological and psychological equilibrium; or more simply, adjustment refers to behaviour directed toward tension reduction. Implied in this definition is a state of harmonious relationship existing between the individual and his environment so that adjustment is a matter of the interaction between the capacities of the individual and the demands of his environment. Thus, adjustment is specific to a given individual under specific conditions and the term adjusted is meaningful only in terms of 'adjusted to what?' It follows that adjustment is related to such factors as the particular culture in which one lives, the sex of the individual, his socioeconomic status, and other factors peculiar to him and to the environment to which he must adjust. Thus, a boy from a lower socioeconomic group who refuses to fight may be considered maladjusted by the standards of his social milieu whereas the boy of a higher socioeconomic group who does fight may also be considered maladjusted by the standards of his social group.

Adjustment is only relative and temporary. It is impossible for the individual to become adjusted for no matter how contented he may be over the fine meal he has just had, he can be out of harmony with his environment in a matter of hours if his next meal is not forthcoming. Furthermore, he almost invariably has problems in connection with his personal life or his business that disturb his adjustment. Thus, when we say we are trying to promote adjustment on the part of the child, we really mean that we are trying to develop his capacity for adjusting on the assumption that, if he can learn to face in an adequate fashion the problems with which he is confronted today, he may be expected to be adequate in meeting the problems of tomorrow.

The question may be raised as to the desirability of promoting adjustment on the part of the individual. Since adjustment implies the question 'adjusted to what?', one might wonder if it is in their and society's best interest to have people adjust to conditions of poverty, slums, and other negative features of their environment. A different aspect of the same question concerns the extent to which progress on both the social and the personal level is being brought about by persons who are maladjusted. Generally, the producer, the achiever, the reformer are maladjusted in the sense that they are not in harmony with the conditions they find. The drifter and the loafer, on the other hand, tend to be perfectly contented with conditions as they are—no matter how bad. We do not want the child in school to be too content with his present state of ignorance: we want him to be under a certain amount of tension so that he will be jarred out of his complacency and made sufficiently anxious so that he will learn. As we have seen, motivation with regard to any form of learning—whether academic or in the area of personal and social adjustment—is simply a matter of raising the anxiety level of the individual as a means of spurring him to learn more appropriate behaviour. Thus, the child who boasts must be made sufficiently anxious by the inadequacy of his present behaviour that he will seek a more adequate adjustment.

Adjustment is, of course, directly connected with the concept of needs—or more specifically, adjustment refers to the adequacy of the behaviour patterns by means of which the individual habitually satisfies his needs. Thus, in as much as everyone has, at all times, multiple needs to satisfy, everyone is perpetually faced with adjustment problems and everyone is, therefore, potentially capable of being adjusted or maladjusted depending on the adequacy of his need-satisfying behaviour. A person is considered maladjusted, for instance, if he consistently satisfies his needs of the present while increasing the severity of the problems of satisfying his future or his more basic needs, e.g., the child who satisfies his needs through daydreaming rather than developing the skills which would permit him to convert his fantasies into actualities. Likewise, adjustment implies that the individual must satisfy his needs within the framework of the rules, regulations, and mores of the social group in which he finds himself. For, unless he can satisfy his needs in ways consistent with the standards of society, he is likely to find that his behaviour involves him in conflict with the social order and leads to further problems of adjustment.

The adequacy of the adjustment which the individual makes depends in considerable measure upon the severity of the adjustment problems with which he is faced. If the situations to which he must adjust (in relation to his potentialities) are such that he can satisfy his needs without undue difficulty, he is less likely to resort to asocial or a typical behaviour and he is, therefore, more likely to be adjusted. Severe and continued frustration of his needs, on the other hand, is likely to lead to maladjustment as the individual in desperation grasps at any straw that will cause even a momentary reduction in the tension associated with the frustration of his needs.

The severity of the adjustment problem with which the individual has to cope would depend on such factors as (a) the nature of the need being denied; (b) the extent to which it is being denied; (c) the extent to which other needs are also being denied; (d) the possibility of substitute goals and partial satisfactions; and (e) his basic security and the degree of his awareness of the frustration of his needs. As long as his frustration concerns only a few of his needs, or even a larger number but to a minor degree, the individual can generally get along much just as a car can run even though not all cylinders are supplying maximum power. However, when the problem becomes unusually severe, he is likely to become desperate and deviant behaviour is likely to result.

How to Adjust in Learning ?

All the laws and principles of learning apply to the concept of adjustment—whether the behaviour involved is desirable or undesirable—in exactly the same way as they do to the learning of academic material. Thus, not only does the individual learn his adjustments but his learning follows the same sequence of steps as we discussed in the chapter on learning, namely:

(a) The individual is motivated by virtue of a need being temporarily unsatisfied.

(b) He looks to some goal as a potential satisfier.

(c) Progress toward this goal is blocked by a barrier. (Note: This barrier may be physical, personal, social, societal, or cultural, or it may involve a conflict between incompatible goals.)

(d) Emotional tension develops and varied response ensues as the individual attempts to reach the goal and reduce the tension.

(e) The goal—original or substitute—is usually reached and equilibrium is restored.

(f) Those reactions which are instrumental in reaching the goal and reducing the tension are learned whereas those not effective in this connection are dropped.

The very fact that learning takes place only when the individual's present pattern of response is no longer adequate in meeting the demands of the situation implies that a certain degree of inadequacy and incompetence is characteristic of any learning situation. However, since an adjustment problem relates to the individual in a much more personal way than does the learning of, say academic material, it is more likely to involve feelings of inferiority and insecurity and these are quite obvious in the insecure person's tendency to derogate others, his poor reaction to competition, his oversensitivity to criticism, and his over response to flattery. Thus, if the individual's present behaviour patterns are adequate for him to cope with the situation readily, he has no adjustment problem. If, however, the situation in which he finds himself is one in which he lacks the ability to attain his goals, he is faced with an adjustment problem, and the more severe the problem, the greater his insecurity and the more likely is the development of a typical and ineffective behaviour.

Aspects—Negative and Positive

Behaviour patterns are learned as a result of the individual's attempt to reduce tension associated with the frustration of his needs. Once learned, they maintain themselves by providing some satisfaction and they develop into habit motives which give stability and permanence to his behaviour, hence, Shaffer and Shoben's definition of personality as the individual's persistent tendencies to make certain kinds and qualities of adjustment. The fact that behaviour is learned in the process of satisfying one's needs may seem hard to believe in view of the short-sightedness of many individual's behaviour on certain occasions and that of a few individuals on most occasions. Yet this is the case and, even though the learning of undesirable behaviour generally tends to be less conscious and less deliberate than the learning of desirable behaviour, it is nevertheless learning in the accepted sense of the term; it is the modification of behaviour as a result of experience and is explained on the basis of the same principles as any other form of learning. All behaviour—however stupid or shortsighted—has a purpose as the individual interprets the situation: very often his overconcern with the immediate situation causes him to select immediate goals that are not in line with his long-range welfare. The unlearning of undesirable behaviour, on the other hand, calls for considerable effort since, once established, any form of behaviour becomes such an integral part of the total personality that it is quite resistant to change. It is especially resistant to change in the case of the insecure person who cannot afford to take a chance experimenting with other modes of adjustment.

Generally, if he keeps trying long enough, the motivated individual is able to overcome or circumvent the obstacle to his goal or reach a substitute goal which is reasonably satisfying. If his behaviour is completely ineffective with respect to the attainment of his goal, he will, of course, be forced to continue trying other modes of reaction until some degree of satisfaction is achieved through substitute behaviour. There are times, however, when the individual's behaviour is only partially ineffective, leading to goals which are partially satisfying. Unfortunately, since it provides some satisfaction, such behaviour will tend to be learned in accordance with the laws of learning even though it is not in the individual's best interest from the standpoint of his long-term adjustment. It is also characteristic of this type of behaviour that it has to be repeated continually in a desperate attempt on the part of the individual to drain off the tension as fast as it accumulates. This is rather evident in the case of people who boast or show off despite the poor reception their behaviour gets from others.

It may also be that the individual reaches a goal which,

though satisfying in terms of his motivation, may involve him in difficulty with the rules of society. If he is not sold on the rules involved, his only concern is in not getting caught and, if he is able to avoid detection, he is 'ahead of the game.' On the other hand, society makes a deliberate attempt to have its rules and regulations internalised by the individual and, to the extent that it is successful in so doing, the individual will not be able to violate the constraints of society without automatically upsetting some other need or destroying some value of importance to his continued adjustment. Thus, sexual immorality may or may not result in guilt feelings depending on the extent to which it has become accepted as wrong by the particular individual. Likewise, the delinquent may not see where he is wrong and may feel discriminated against when society punishes him. In other words, social problems are not necessarily personal or clinical problems. When a problem is both social and personal, adjustment is more difficult since the person must first resolve the personal before he can deal effectively with the social aspects.

There may also be times when the individual cannot attain his goal without some form of outside help. This may entail nothing more than a need for coaching in a special skill such as dancing, or it may call for psychological counseling which, when provided, will allow the individual to achieve reasonably complete adjustment. On the other hand, the obstacle may be of such magnitude and resistance, by reference to the individual's potentialities, that he may never attain his goals. In such cases, he is likely to become desperate and to aggravate rather than solve his problem. His only salvation may lie in his being removed from the situation or in his being provided with considerable support. If this is not possible, his only escape may be in breakdown, with possible eventual recovery with psychiatric help and improvement in the conditions that caused the difficulty.

Thus, maladjustment arises out of attempted solutions at tension reduction which give only partial or temporary relief, or out of attempts which, although acceptable at one time, become so entrenched as habits that the individual is not able to outgrow them. It generally occurs in situations which are so resistant that the individual exhausts all the more desirable alternatives, or in situations which are so complicated that he cannot get insight into the relative dangers of the attempted solutions.

Adjustment differs from maladjustment in degree rather than in kind. Normal adjustment simply entails behaviour that is within the range of tolerated differences, where the limits of such a range are uncertain and highly flexible. More specifically, the adjusted person shows a relatively high degree of integration and consistency in his behaviour, displays behaviour that is essentially effective in attaining his goals, faces problems realistically, and devotes his energies to the realisation of his purposes. In addition, he has found satisfactory solutions for the major problems which he faces and has effective ways of releasing tensions so that he is relatively free from conflict and tension. On the other hand, when the individual is caught between a resistant obstacle and a persistent motivation, frustration and tension will mount to the point of causing excessive interference, and even disorganisation of behaviour. It may be, for instance, that internal conflicts will cause the person to be at cross purposes with himself with resulting indecision and inability to coordinate his efforts in the attainment of his goals. If this pattern tends to be typical of his behaviour, he may be said to be maladjusted, although there is no dividing line at which a person ceases to be adjusted and becomes maladjusted.

Maladjustment may be revealed through any number of symptoms, many of which—at least in their milder forms—are also characteristic of normal adjustment. Among the more common, we might mention the following: explosive behaviour, general restlessness (including nail biting and other nervous habits), preoccupation (daydreaming, absent-mindedness, worry), withdrawal (excessive reading for vicarious excitements, shyness and general avoidance of social situations), and minor physical dysfunctions. Another set of symptoms such as crying, temper tantrums, fixations or delays in normal growth, dependence on others, lack of motivation, inability to make decisions or to assume responsibility, attempts to win sympathy, and selfishness are often signs of immaturity rather than maladjustment, i.e., reflect failure to learn more mature ways of behaving rather than the learning of undesirable behaviour patterns. On the other hand, they can also be indicative of maladjustment, at least in the sense of a lack of harmony existing between the individual and his environment. Furthermore, regardless of differences in the background of immaturity and maladjustment, both are difficult to deal with: to the extent to which they have resulted in some satisfaction to the individual and are incorporated into his self-image and changing calls for major reorganisation of the total personality. Furthermore, an improvement in behaviour cannot take place in a vacuum and immature or maladjusted persons are likely to encounter difficulty in finding people endowed with sufficient patience to put up with them, let alone provide them with the permissive and supportive environment they need in order to improve.

Different Methods

As we have seen in the earlier part of the chapter, the individual learns certain behaviour patterns by means of which he attempts to satisfy his needs. Thus, the boy who is frustrated as a result of inability to find satisfaction for needs of social recognition or self-esteem by being on the honour roll, compensates by making the football team or rationalises that only sissies are interested in academic work, or even perhaps develops neurotic symptoms such as headaches that prevent him from studying so that his inability to make the honour roll is quite understandable. These habits, known as adjustment mechanisms are neither disorders nor symptoms of maladjustment: they are simply the adjustment the individual makes when confronted with certain needs, on one hand, and certain situational realities, on the other.

Adjustment mechanisms can be arranged according to any number of systems depending on the basis of classification used. None of them is too satisfactory; behaviour is the resultant of multiple causations and is invariably so complicated that it tends not to fall into neat categories. Thus, a given mechanism may resemble the other mechanisms in its category from one standpoint but also resemble mechanisms in adjacent categories in other respects. Furthermore, a certain adjustment situation may give rise to any number of different adjustment mechanisms so that being able to identify the mechanism displayed by a given individual at a given time, either by itself or in terms of the category to which it belongs, is of limited value in dealing with the underlying problem. Yet despite these arguments and the obvious necessity of considering any classification as merely suggestive, classifying adjustment mechanisms is probably justified on the grounds that it brings out the common features among them and tends to make for a greater understanding of their nature.

Probably the simplest classification system is one in which adjustments are divided into those that are direct, i.e., reactions by means of which the individual attempts to overcome the obstacle and reach the original or a substitute goal, and those that are indirect, i.e., reactions in which the individual withdraws, rationalises, or generally gives up trying to reach the goal he has set. A more comprehensive classification system is that of Shaffer and Shoben in which adjustment mechanisms are divided into five categories:

(a) adjustment by defense;
(b) adjustment by withdrawal;
(c) adjustments involving fears and repression;
(d) adjustment by ailment; and
(e) various non-adjustive reactions. In general, the discussion in this chapter will follow this outline in a somewhat abbreviated form and the reader is referred to their excellent text and other sources for additional information.

The mechanisms to be discussed in this section are those in which the individual is still attempting, by minimising his failure or attaining success by other means, to defend himself against feelings of inferiority occasioned by his failure to attain his goal. As we have seen, all adjustment mechanisms relate to feelings of inferiority but, whereas these feelings may lead to withdrawal or even ailment, the mechanisms in this category represent attempts on the part of the individual to maintain self respect through a defense against such feelings. Included in this category are a variety of reactions ranging all the way from attention-getting devices to the more serious attempts to project the blame onto others, with compensation and rationalisation being the most common.

Compensation represents an attempt on the part of the individual to overcome feelings of inferiority arising out of personal limitations in a given area by striving for success in the same or a different area. Thus, Demosthenes is said to have overcome a speech impediment by practicing speaking with pebbles in his mouth. Likewise, a boy may compensate for relative weakness in academic work by becoming an athlete or he may compensate in a peculiar area, e.g., collecting snakes or college banners, where, because the competition is less keen, he is more likely to attain relative success.

A common form of compensation concerns compensation through others. Parents, for instance, who perhaps feel inadequate as a result of their lack of education will go out of their way to have their son or daughter go to college and even to graduate studies. This type of compensation implies identification of the person with the individual through whom he compensates in order to get vicarious satisfaction of his needs through the achievement of the latter. Thus, a father will identify himself with his son with the result that the son's academic achievement becomes that of the father. Compensation through others is involved in the popularity of sports and of movies in which the spectator identifies himself with the players and obtains vicarious satisfaction through their achievement. Two observations in connection with such compensation are in order:

(a) With the present emphasis on professional-type sports, high schools and colleges are reducing drastically the number of their students who can derive satisfaction for their needs through actual participation rather than through identification with the team;

(b) Parents who compensate through their children can occasionally make it rough on the children: the parent who harbors a deep sense of inadequacy and frustration as a result of his inability to get past the fourth grade may do his son considerable damage by insisting upon unrealistic standards of academic achievement. In the same

> way, the alumnus who could not toss the pigskin ten yards when he was in college may well demand the head of the coach whose won-lost record is somewhat short of perfection.

Compensation is also involved in such common attention-getting devices as boasting, lying, and exhibitionism as well as in more complicated reactions such as compensation against evil in the abstract in which the individual crusades with unusual zeal against such 'evils' as tobacco, alcohol, or sex as a means of defending himself against feelings of undesirable compensation, particularly when it applies to the area of sex. Thus, teaching and nursing might be considered forms of sublimation of the sex drive.

Rationalisation consists of giving plausible but untrue reasons for one's behaviour as a defense against having to admit that, by objective standards, the behaviour is silly, irresponsible, or otherwise unacceptable. Rationalisation is an unconscious mechanism: when false reasons are given knowingly, they are lies, not rationalisations. Rationalisation is a face-saving device which goes back to Adam's "The woman whom thou gavest to be with me, she gave me of the tree, and I did eat." It may take on any number of forms, including 'sour grapes' or 'sweet lemons', or the blaming of incidental causes, e.g., kicking the stool for its having been in the way.

A more serious form of rationalisation is involved in the mechanism of projection, wherein the individual perceives in others the traits or motives in which he feels his own inferiority. Thus, the child accuses the teacher of having hostile feelings toward him while, in reality, it is he who is hostile toward the teacher. Prejudices and logic-tight compartments, in which obviously false beliefs are held despite logical evidence to the contrary, also have elements of rationalisation and projection along with various degrees of delusion.

In mechanisms involving withdrawal, the individual is no longer seeking to achieve satisfaction for his needs through the attainment of his goal but rather runs away from the frustrating situation. Those mechanisms are generally undesirable since they do not solve the problem and yet remove the individual from the pressure that would force him to do something more constructive than simply withdraw. Teachers should be particularly aware of the relationship between simple withdrawal and more serious forms of maladjustment such as schizophrenia and should be alert to danger signs. They should be aware of the fact that the child who never misbehaves, who is often the model child may be in grave danger of later difficulty and is, therefore, a more serious case of maladjustment than is the troublemaker who is fighting to satisfy his needs.

Probably the simplest and the most common forms of withdrawal concern bashfulness, timidity, negativism, and general seclusiveness in which the individual, perhaps as a result of having been the victim of frustration and failure along with repressive discipline refuses to take part in situations which may mean further failure. Another well-known form of withdrawal is fantasy, or daydreaming, in which the individual becomes the conquering hero for whom success and revenge are unlimited or the suffering hero whose misfortunes cause even his enemies great sorrow. Fantasy is not harmful in itself; it may even give the individual ideas that he can then proceed to put into practice. However, it possesses the danger of being used in lieu of more constructive behaviour, for as long as the individual finds no satisfaction for his needs, he will be forced to continue seeking some adjustment but, when he gets partial satisfaction from his fantasies, he is more likely to rely on them more and more and, as a result, become progressively less capable of doing something more constructive about his problems. On the other hand, not all retiring children are in immediate need of a psychiatrist: some people enjoy peace and quiet and teachers should refrain from using social participation as the sole criterion of adjustment.

A less obvious form of withdrawal consists of plunging into a number of occupational or social activities or becoming drowsy, or turning to alcohol, narcotics, or even sweets as a way of running away from one's problems. Occasionally, a person with severe problems which he can neither resolve nor escape from will turn with a vengeance to his work or will get ; involved in numerous activities in an attempt to forget. Sometimes, such a person will have a nervous breakdown and people are likely to pity him and commend him for having worked so hard that he became ill when, in reality, the hard work was the result of the same difficulty that eventuated in the breakdown but not its cause.

Procrastination is another common variety of running away from difficult situations which is indulged in by very normal people. Also common is retrogression in which the individual goes back to a more immature mode of behaviour, e.g., adults resort to crying as a way of solving problems and the preschool child who has become quite grown-up may revert to infantile behaviour when a new baby is born in the family.

Apprehension and Suppression

Everyone has at least minor fears. In fact, fear (insecurity) is a basic component of all adjustment mechanisms: in compensation, fear is dispelled by overassertion of adjustment, while in withdrawal, the individual avoids fear-producing situations. On the other hand, persistent and excessive fears, particularly of an abnormal nature, i.e., phobias, are indicative of maladjustment. A person might have an intense fear of dogs as a result of having been bitten by a dog but it is something else for an individual to have frantic fears of high places, of low places, of crowded places, of wide open places—none of which is a normal stimulus for fear.

Generally, such abnormal fear can best be explained in terms of the individual's having had an unpleasant experience in connection with which he or she feels some degree of guilt. Because of these guilt feelings, there is a tendency for the individual not to face the situation but rather to repress the incident into the unconscious as a means of avoiding anxiety. But a repressed incident is not a dead incident and it comes up to consciousness again in a disguised form. So the girl who has been sexually assaulted in a situation in which she feels she was not completely blameless finds her fear of the original situation transfer from one object or situation to another till, for no apparent reason, she now fears being in a large room or has an intense fear of being left alone even for a few minutes— stimuli which are symbolic of being without protection. Repression serves the purpose of protecting the self but it is one of the most dangerous mechanisms because the underlying dynamics cause unexplained behaviour. As long as problems are kept in the open, they can be understood and dealt with but, once repression has taken place, the individual can be helped only by a competent clinician.

Also involving the repression of guilt feelings is the mechanism known as reaction formation, in which a person goes out of his way to be nice and considerate of another person as a way of reacting against the opposite feelings which the individual harbors with some guilt. Thus, the mother whose career ended with the birth of her child may react to a desire that the child be dead by granting his every wish and working well beyond the call of duty in seeing that no harm befalls him. Such behaviour may become quite compulsive for, as in the case of the obsession-compulsion of Lady Macbeth, the behaviour is related only indirectly to the goal and the compulsive reaction has to be repeated in a desperate effort to relieve the tension which seems to accumulate as fast as it can be dissipated by such relatively ineffective means.

Additional Devices

When the individual is caught in a conflict, he may unconsciously resort to ailment as a way out of his predicament. These ailments do not have an organic basis—at least they do not have an organic basis that we know of—but rather are of psychogenic origin. They are generally known as psychoneuroses (or simply neuroses) under which can be grouped two broad areas of physical dysfunction: (a) various forms of hysteria such as localised pains, paralyses, and anesthesias; and (b) motor psychoneuroses (or functional hysteria) such as occupational cramps, stammering, and stuttering. A number of servicemen, for instance, suffered from shell-shock during the First World War and war fatigue during World War II, both terms referring generally to some form of hysteria. Thus, to use a fictitious example, a soldier is in the front lines. He is very scared and wishes he could be somewhere else, but among the values he has incorporated into his self-concept are bravery and loyalty which prevent him from leaving and 'letting his buddies down.' If he is wounded, perhaps in a minor way—immediately he is taken away from the danger zone and his conflict is resolved: he is no longer afraid nor does he have to feel guilty about not being in the front lines since it is accepted that wounded men should be out of combat. In due time the wound heals but a certain pain or stiffness remains in the wounded area so that he cannot rejoin his unit in the battle lines. He has—unconsciously—made an adjustment of a neurotic nature as a means of avoiding conflict.

Many psychologists feel that the majority of speech disorders such as stuttering and stammering are cases of functional hysteria. Likewise, a good fraction of the cases of arthritis, hay fever, asthma, migraine, headaches, backaches, and other ills affecting the average person are considered to be of psychogenic origin, and medical doctors estimate that over half of their clientele is made up of people whose ailments are psychogenically induced.

The cure in cases of hysteria is generally slow. First, the person must be motivated toward a cure: the soldier will not improve as long as he knows that the day he is discharged from the hospital he will be back in the firing zone. Then he must be given the means of saving face, for he cannot get out of the hospital cured the day armistice is signed. Since it is relatively difficult to change the basic personality of the individual which led to the hysteria, it is quite a problem to change the basic motivation and it is typical of patients suffering from hysteria to be indifferent to their troubles. In fact, since the hysterical symptoms serve to reduce the conflict, it is quite likely that, unconsciously, they actually enjoy their ailments and have no inclination to get rid of them.

It is generally agreed that persons with hysterical symptoms tend to be socially immature and highly suggestive so that when they are ready to be cured they may respond to treatment by a specialist who can convince them that a cure is possible. An interesting case of such a cure is that known as stocking anesthesia in which a patient whose leg is completely insensitive to any feeling will, at the suggestion of the therapist, recover feeling in the leg as a stocking (which has been put on the leg for suggestion value) is gradually rolled down an inch or two each day. Also, generally useful in the treatment of neurotic patients, is the common practice among medical doctors of giving them painful injections and foul-tasting medicine as a means of making their symptoms unsatisfying, but such treatment may serve to convince the patient of the reality and severity of his illness. Furthermore, cures of this type merely remove the symptoms and, unless something is done about the underlying conflict, curing one symptom will only lead to the occurrence of other symptoms and even of more serious difficulties.

The Retaliation

As stated before, when behaviour is only indirectly related to the goal and, therefore, yields only partial satisfaction, the individual finds it necessary to repeat it in a desperate attempt to drain off tension as it accumulates. In such cases the individual is likely to be in a constant state of tension as evidenced by digestive upsets, insomnia, diffuse motor activity, and anxiety. To the extent that the person fears taking the risk involved in attempting to reach the goal, he is incapable of taking positive action: the worrier, for instance, does not take positive steps to solve his problem; he simply continues to worry—often not even knowing what he is worried about.

Among the more common forms of non-adjustive reactions might be mentioned: (a) neurasthenia, which is a form of persistent anxiety state characterised by nervous exhaustion as in the case of the chronic invalid, and (b) hypochondria, a general preoccupation about health and an exaggeration of minor disorders. In these cases, as in the case of hysteria, there is generally to be found in the background of the individual a favourable experience with illness. Thus, the woman who feels lonely and neglected, as a result of her children and husband having developed interests outside the home, may find that illness on her part keeps everybody home in the evening for a change. She may unconsciously feel that being sick is an effective way of satisfying her needs. As with hysteria, the cure is difficult to achieve: the person must first become convinced that giving up the partial satisfactions connected with being sick will be more than compensated for by the satisfaction of being well. It is, of course, much better to avoid the development of such symptoms. A good rule to follow with regard to hysteria and neurasthenia, for instance, is never to make illness a pleasant experience. Thus, the child who has a headache at nine-o'clock should be put to bed for the rest of the day—minus comics and TV. If he is realty sick, the rest will do him good, while if the headache is of a psychogenic origin, putting him to bed will discourage the formation of hysterical symptoms. It is, of course, necessary to deal with causal factors. Perhaps some of the pressure at school should be lightened or the child should be made to realise that it is not necessary for him to be sick for people to take notice of the fact that he exists.

Mechanism of Adjustment

All people have needs: therefore, all have to make use of adjustment mechanisms. In fact, adjusted as well as maladjusted persons make some use of most of these mechanisms. Adjustment and maladjustment are a matter of degree and, even adjusted people daydream, rationalise and develop forms of hysteria such as migraine headaches. On the other hand, many of these mechanisms can be considered potentially dangerous—although each would have to be evaluated in terms of the particular individual involved and the particular situation in which he finds himself. Speaking in general terms, adjustment mechanisms are considered undesirable in the following cases:

(a) when they displace some more constructive mode of adjustment;

(b) when they are relatively ineffective in satisfying needs;

(c) when they introduce greater problems than the need they satisfy; and

(d) when they create adjustment problems in other people as in the case of fighting. Perhaps a more adequate—although less explicit—guide for the evaluation of adjustment mechanisms can be found in Shaffer's statement that only those adjustments that fail to satisfy individual and social needs are maladjustments.

Understanding Child's Nature

Every experience which the child undergoes affects his adjustment one way or another. It is, therefore, essential that the teacher understand each child as an individual if he is to provide educative experiences that will be conducive to his maximum growth. Actually, the average teacher can be only partially effective in this respect: not only does he not have the time and opportunity to make a through study of each child while at the same time attempting to have the class as a whole attain certain academic standards, but he is also relatively untrained in the area of the psychodynamics of behaviour. To make matters worse, behaviour, being the product of multiple causation over a period of years, is relatively complicated. In the field of medicine, the trouble can be identified by the symptoms and, once this is done, a rather complete understanding of the disease including its etiology and its treatment is attained. In the area of maladjustment, on the other hand, symptoms rather rarely identify the trouble since learning plays an important part in determining the behaviour by means of which the individual attempts to satisfy his needs. Hence, each case tends to be unique so that labeling a child an extrovert really does not tell us how his behaviour can be improved or how he can be handled best. Likewise, let us hope that the adjectives good and bad will soon drop out of the vocabulary used by teachers to label children and that they will be replaced by the concept of understanding and helping them.

Nevertheless, in the final analysis, it will be the teacher, not the psychiatrist or the clinician, who will do most for the vast majority of children in the development of effective behaviour. Qualified or not, the teacher must make understanding of children and their behaviour one of his primary responsibilities—for understanding children is an integral aspect of teaching them, not something one undertakes when things get out of hand. And whereas love is not enough, it is essential, and, when coupled with sensitivity and a good grasp of the basic principles of psychology, it will go a long way. In fact, it will go the whole way with most of the children in the classroom, for children don't have personalities made of glass: they have a wonderful resiliency to stress and strain and all they want—and all they need—is perhaps a little help here and there, but mostly, just a chance to grow.

Unfortunately, the easy way (the lazy way) is not to bother, simply to present academic material, make assignments, and ignore the fact that children are people with individual characteristics and problems. To understand children calls for time and effort, and the more understanding a teacher is, the more they will come to him rather than to other teachers who won't help them. But it is time and effort well spent for it pays dividends in pupil adjustment and in teacher satisfaction. A little help given at the right time will often put the child back on his feet and it is surprising to see the number of children, perhaps drifting in the wrong direction, who have found themselves as a result of a little understanding on the part of a sympathetic teacher. In fact, it is debatable whether any saving is effected by ignoring students except in the case where, in final desperation, they drop out of school. When they remain in school, whatever saving is involved, if any, is very shortsighted even from a purely selfish point of view, for neglected students soon fall behind, become discipline problems, and generally multiply a hundred-fold the teacher's problems. It just makes good sense to set up a definite appraisal programme designed for such purposes as knowing the child as an individual, providing the faculty and the guidance staff with information upon which to base counseling, increasing the child's self-understanding, and providing the basis for effective parent-teacher cooperation.

If we are to understand the child, we must know something of the experiences to which he has been subjected to and the forces which have played upon him. Thus, the child who has been mishandled throughout his childhood may well have deep-seated problems that will defy superficial treatment. This would often be true of delinquent children, for instance, who rarely get the understanding and the help they need in order to be able to change their pattern of behaviour. Of course, each child is unique and no group diagnosis can be made as to the causes or the treatment of delinquency. Many delinquents, for instance, simply have not internalised the constraints of society, a situation likely to occur when adults make unreasonable or inconsistent demands on the child or when they allow him to grow like Topsy without any demands being made upon him. He needs discipline but only when it is consistent and based on love and security does it lead to character formation, i.e., only then can he grow in self-direction. Thus, the delinquent is often confused by the conflicting demands made upon him by the different cultural groups to which he belongs, e.g., to fight in his neighbourhood but not at school.

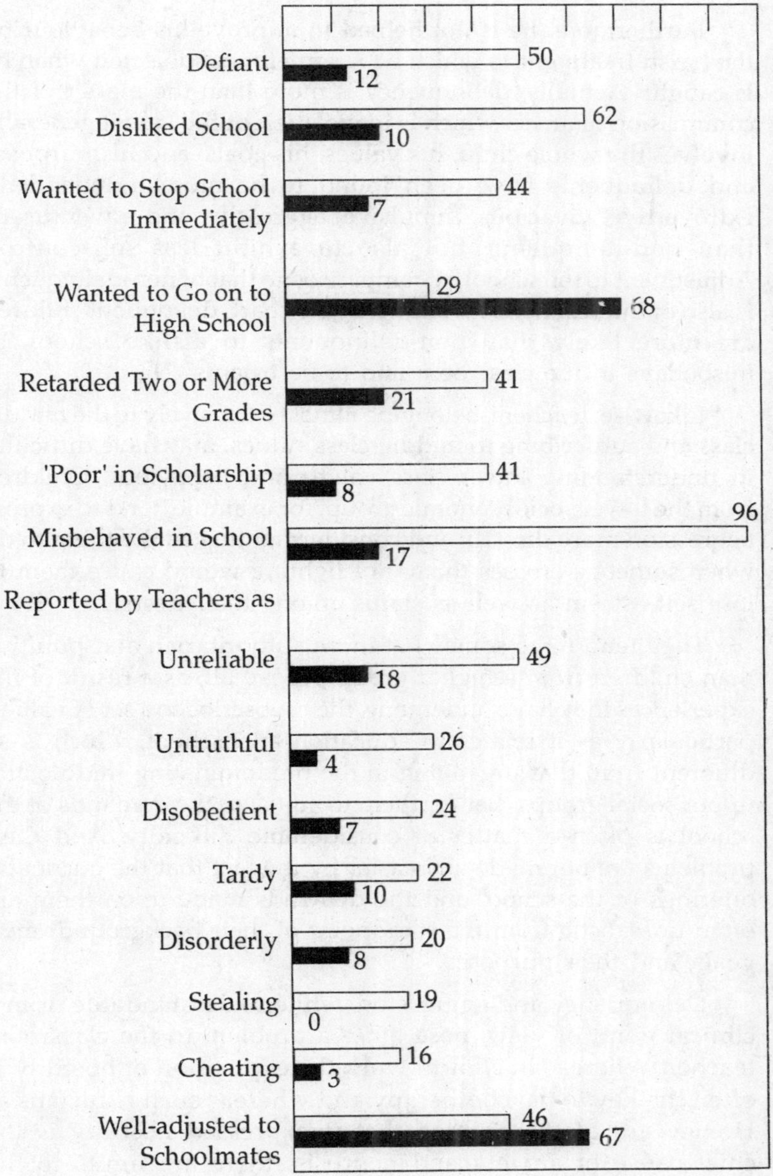

Fig. *Reactions of delinquents and non-delinquents toward the school situation*

Furthermore, he is not helped to improve his behaviour by the harsh treatment to which he is sometimes subjected when he is caught. Actually, delinquency is more than the matter of the commission of an act which is in violation of the law: it generally involves the whole child, his values, his goals, and his purposes and delinquents have been found to be more independent, extrovertive, vivacious, impulsive, aggressive and adventurous than non-deliquents, but also to exhibit less self-control. Adjustment to the school by comparison to that of non-delinquents is also of interest here. As shown in the chart, delinquent children are more likely than non-delinquents to dislike school, to misbehave in the classroom and to be truants.

Likewise, teachers, belonging almost exclusively to the middle class and subscribing to middle-class values, may have difficulty in understanding lower class values and behaviour. Children from the lower socioeconomic group, for example, tend to express aggression more directly and consider fighting as the thing to do when someone crosses them: not fighting would cause them to lose self-esteem as well as status among their peers.

They tend to be somewhat more authoritarian and punitive than children from a higher group. Above all, as a result of the experiences they have undergone, they subscribe to a set of values, particularly as it relates to education and school, which is so different from that prevailing in the predominating middle and upper social groups that for them to adjust to the demands of the school is often a matter of considerable difficulty. And their problems are not made any easier by the fact that the curricular offerings of the school and the demands made upon them are often unrealistic from the standpoint of their background, their goals, and their purposes.

Delinquency and aggression, while understandable from a clinical point of view, pose quite a problem to the classroom teacher. Whereas in clinical work the expression of hostility is often the key to psychotherapy and whereas such clinicians as Homey are of the opinion that unexpressed hostility is the chief cause of anxiety and neurosis, there are limits to the extent to which the teacher can allow feelings of aggression and hostility to be expressed in the classroom so that, no matter how desirable such expression may be from a mental health and personality development standpoint, it has to be curbed. To the extent that a permissive atmosphere exists in the school, the child can express hostility without guilt feelings but, in view of the social situation involved, care must be taken to channel hostility into constructive ends rather than let it interfere with the growth of other children or with the morale of the group. In the meantime, when delinquency or aggression does occur, the teacher needs to remember that it is a symptom of something relatively basic rather than merely an undesirable act. Perhaps the child is acting in accordance with his system of values as derived from his socio-economic and cultural group and may need re-education and a redetermination of his goals and values. He may not even know his behaviour is unacceptable. Perhaps he is trying to tell all concerned that the demands and the standards imposed upon him are unrealistic and that the curriculum is unsuited to his needs. In the same way, the child who is absent frequently because of headaches and other minor ills resulting from his unconscious attempt to avoid a difficult situation, may need understanding and a lightening of the demands made upon him so that he can learn to see the school as a pleasant place in which to be.

Pupil's Appreciation

In order to be effective, a pupil appraisal programme must be systematic and based on sound theoretical considerations. The problem involved is that of accumulating whatever data are pertinent to the uniqueness of the individual, including his own reactions to these data and to himself as a person. It is necessary to consider all the children—not only the troublemakers as is so often done now—and to make as complete an appraisal of each individual child as possible. Since behaviour involves the whole child, problems in one area are likely to lead to problems in other areas so that an understanding of the child calls for seeing the total child in his total environment. It is also necessary to see him in perspective by considering his present status in terms of his previous experiences, his unresolved difficulties, his present values as well as his present and future goals.

This calls for taking a number of appraisals at different times and in different settings so that we can arrive at an understanding of his typical behaviour patterns rather than be misled by unusual incidents. Furthermore, if we are to understand the child, it is necessary to tap all relevant sources of information, among the more important of which might be mentioned the following:

The Child: Obviously, no other source can give us as good an understanding of the child as the child himself. There is, therefore, need for the teacher to get acquainted with him—in connection with the formal situation prevailing in the classroom and especially under conditions of free atmosphere such as might be found in the homeroom or on the playground. Of course, he does not understand himself too clearly so there is no point in expecting him to give a psychiatrist's explanation of his underlying motives and unresolved conflicts, but his behaviour will provide the competent teacher with the means whereby he can be understood. Informal contacts and interviews conducted in an atmosphere of permissiveness and acceptance can be most valuable: allowing the child whose behaviour has been undesirable to give his side of the story, for example, can give the teacher valuable insights into what makes him tick. Useful information can also be obtained from such instruments as the Money Problem Check List and the various personality and interest inventories available commercially, although these should not be necessary in a grade school where teachers have the same children all day for a whole year.

The Home: The child cannot be understood apart from his home. Therefore, the teacher needs to know the general status of the home, and especially the attitudes which parents and siblings and even the community hold toward the school, toward the teacher, and toward education. He needs to know the parent's views toward such things as discipline, their system of values, their goals, and their general expectations from the child. But most of all he needs to know something about the emotional climate of the home for very often the child's problems at school are very closely related to his problems at home, and, if he is having troubles there, he has all the more need for understanding at school, lest he is sour on all adults.

It is also important that the teacher appraise the socioeconomic and cultural status of the home for, when the home and the school subscribe to different cultural and economic values, the child may be involved in conflict to the extent that accepting the school may appear to him as the equivalent of being disloyal to his home and to his peers. In fact, the teacher needs to remember that no matter how bad the home situation, the child has certain loyalties which he cannot violate without conflict and that he, therefore, needs to be careful in his attempt to reach him and guide his growth toward higher cultural standards.

The Child's Former Teachers: The teachers who have had the child in class should have in their possession considerable data accumulated through observation and other means. In most schools, for instance, teachers are encouraged to write anecdotal records on the children in their classes and, when they are conscientious in the matter, anecdotal information of considerable value in understanding individual children can generally be found in their folders. Unfortunately, anecdotal records tend to be time-consuming and busy teachers often report only the unusual and the negative rather than the more typical aspects of the child's behaviour. Where this is the case, their use should be discouraged, for, unless they are a fair sample of his behaviour and are objective and accurate, they can do him more harm than good. Even at best, care must be taken that they do not prejudice future teachers against certain children and Rogers questions the keeping of records from this standpoint. The same comment can be made with respect to gossip and general impressions often exchanged among teachers.

Tests and Other Formal Instruments: Much of the information we need about the child as, for instance, his intellectual capacity, his special abilities and talents, his academic status, and perhaps his interests and personal adjustment cannot be obtained with sufficient precision by the usual observational and anecdotal techniques just discussed and recourse must be made to more formal and technical instruments. Of course, these instruments have to be used cautiously and with due awareness of their limitations but they provide objective evidence that is certainly indispensable to the classroom teacher, particularly as it is used to confirm data from other sources. There is need for a formal testing programme consisting of standardised tests that will give a broader basis for evaluating progress to supplement the data obtained through the informal, and even the incidental, appraisal made by the teacher, as well as those obtained through rating scales, questionnaires, and inventories.

Of primary interest from the standpoint of the school are the child's motivation, his values, goals, aspirations, and interests as well as his attitudes—for these are the prime determinants of what he will do. Most of these things are, unfortunately, rather difficult to appraise except by means of subjective judgment. Interests, of a vocational nature, for instance, can be measured through a number of standardised interest inventories but other interests have to be appraised through observation of his leisure time activities, or through the analysis of the themes he is asked to write on such topics as 'My Hobbies.'

Probably no more important aspect of this area can be found than the child's attitudes toward the school itself. The attitude of the individual child can usually be determined by observation and interview but when it comes to group attitudes, a more valid appraisal of the morale of the student body and pupil reaction to the various aspects of the school programme can probably be obtained by means of an unsigned questionnaire such as that suggested by Hand, a few sample questions from which are reproduced below.

I In general, how well do you like your school? (Check one).
- (1) I like it very much.
- (2) I like it.
- (3) About half and half.
- (4) I dislike it.
- (5) I dislike it very much.

II How proud of your school are you? (Check one).
- (1) I am very proud of my school.
- (2) I am proud of my school.
- (3) I am not proud of my school.
- (4) I am ashamed of my school.

III If you are proud of your school tell your main reason why.

IV If you are not proud of your school, tell the main reason why. In general, are you satisfied or dissatisfied with the way you are treated by teachers and other school officials? (Check one).

(1) Very well satisfied.

(2) Satisfied.

(3) Half and half.

(4) Dissatisfied.

(5) Very much dissatisfied.

V Do the pupils in your school treat one another fairly and kindly? (Check one).

(1) Yes, practically all of them do.

(2) Yes, most of them do.

(3) Yes, about half of them do.

(4) No, most of them do not.

VI All in all, how well satisfied are you with your school? (Check one).

(1) I am very well satisfied with my school.

(2) I am pretty well satisfied.

(3) About half and half.

(4) 1 am dissatisfied (not satisfied).

(5) I am very much dissatisfied (not satisfied) with my school.

The personality of the child, his emotional balance, and his habitual traits are of immediate concern to the teacher for the bearing which they have on the other aspects of his behaviour and growth. Much of the information which the teacher needs in this area can be obtained by observation, particularly in the grade school. Of course, the teacher needs to be alert to the limitations of observation but, very often, observation is the only means available for obtaining data regarding the child's personality, and all that can be done is to strive to make observation as valid and reliable as possible. Whenever feasible, one's observations should be supplemented by other techniques or confirmed by the observations of others: research in the area of intragroup relations, for instance, has shown the relative inadequacy of teacher observation as a means of appraising the social composition of the classroom.

Additional information can be obtained from having children write themes on such topics as 'My Biggest Problem.' A number of standardised inventories are also available such as the California Test of Personality, the Bell Adjustment Inventory; and others; but most of the more common inventories are rather easy to fake and it is essential that the student be convinced that the only reason for his filling out the inventory is to enable the teacher or counselor to be of greater help to him and that, therefore, it is in his best interest to give candid answers. Even then some faking will take place and the results should be interpreted rather cautiously. At the more advanced level, such tests as the Minnesota Multiphasic Personality Inventory and the projective techniques are relatively more adequate for appraising the personality of the individual but, on the other hand, they require special competence in interpreting the results.

These data should be incorporated into a cumulative folder made available to all teachers who have contact with the child. This folder must be complete, accurate, and concise; otherwise, it will not be worth the teacher's time to consult it. Clerical assistance should be provided for such purposes as putting these data on a profile which will tell at a glance many of the things which an interested person wants to know. Such clerical tasks can be time-consuming and take the teacher away from other things for which he is paid and for which he is better qualified. Unless such help is provided, many teachers will not cooperate or will do only a perfunctory job. A good cumulative record system should provide the teacher with the basic information he needs in dealing with the vast majority of his students. On the other hand, special cases will occur in which he will want to consult with the principal, the counselor, the doctor, or the social worker in order to get new insights into the problem of a given student. At times, it may even be necessary to carry out a case study in which the teacher, the doctor or nurse, the psychologist, the social worker, and perhaps others will each contribute what he knows about a given child. Unfortunately, such detailed studies are extremely time-consuming and can be carried out for a few advanced cases only—often too far advanced for any major improvement to be effected.

8

Exceptional Kids

Meaning of a Slow Learning Child: In the words of Prof. T. N. Birkett, "A slow learning child is one whose capacity for learning the kind of material which is taught in the ordinary school is limited by some deficit in intellectual capacity. Limited intelligence, however, is the chief characteristic of the slow learning child.

Categories of Slow Learners: Following are the main categories of slow learners:

Children, whose capacity for education or training is limited by low intelligence, cover a fairly wide I.Q. range from approximately 40 to 80 or 90. However students whose I.Q. ranges between 50/55 and 85/90 are capable of benefiting from the kind of education which is offered within the normal school system. These may be subdivided into two groups:

(a) The Educable Mentally Retarded (I.Q. range 50 to 70).

(b) The Dull Normal (I.Q. range 70 to 85).

Students whose I.Q. range is between 35/40 and 50 are usually termed as Trainable Mentally Retarded. Provision for education of such children may be made outside the normal school system.

Important Features

Sullivan summarises the characteristics of these children as follows:

1. Short attention and concentration span.
2. Slow reaction time.
3. Limited ability to evaluate materials for relevancy.
4. Limited powers of self-direction.
5. Limited ability to work with abstractions and to generalize.
6. Slowness to form association between words and phrases.
7. Failure to recognise familiar elements in new information.
8. Habits of learning very slowly and forgetting very quickly.
9. Very local point of view.
10. Inability to set up and realize standard of workmanship.
11. Lack of originality and creativeness.
12. Lack of ability to analyse, to do problems solving or think critically.
13. Lack of ability to use higher mental processes.

Identification of Slow Learners: Following methods are usually employed to identify the slow learners.

1. Achievement Tests.
2. Intelligence Tests (Individual)
3. Intelligence Tests (Group)
4. Observation by teachers and others including the school counsellor.
5. Diagnostic Tests.

Prevailing Facilities

Diagnostic Tests: Diagnostic tests should be employed in working with slow-learning children.

Curricula According to Interests: Courses and curricula should be selected by the students with the help of their counsellors on the basis of aptitude, interest and need.

Vocational Programmes: Vocational programmes should not

be forced upon slow-learners. Such children do not always have the necessary aptitude to acquire vocational skill.

Special Classes: Special classes for slow-learning children should be organized. However, partial segregation is preferable to total segregation.

Partial Segregation: It has been stated, "These children should be included in the total school set-up, regularly participating in assembly programmes, organised play, and other activities enjoyed by all children."

Short Assignments: Assignments given to the students should be broken up into short and simple units. The problems should be clearly explained.

Drill Work: Sufficient drill work should be done.

Summaries: Frequent summaries of the important points of discussion should be used.

Praise: Slow-learners should be praised occasionally when they have done their assignments properly.

Proper Evaluation: Good set of tools should be used.

Close Supervision: Supervision should be very close.

Use of Audio-visual Aids: Auditory and visual aids facilitate their learning.

Opportunities for Creative Expression: Opportunities for expression of creativeness with their hands for slow-learning children should be provided.

Equality of Opportunity in Recreational Programmes: The whole programme of recreational activities, athletics, music, art, dramatics, etc., should be opened to all on an equal basis. Mones summarizes the advantages which the slow-learners will get as, "When these pupils are accepted in secondary schools, the school clubs, the bands, the patrols, the clean-up squads, the down and ground squads, the cafeteria patrols, athletics teams-are all possible instrumentalities of their education. If they can find educational outcome as a means of developing traits, attitudes, purposes, and satisfactions, that will give them a sense of integrated personality.

Remedial Teaching: Remedial teachers who meet such students twice a week may be appointed.

Cooperation of All Agencies: All agencies engaged in the children's welfare work should cooperate.

Extraordinary Children

Meaning of Socially Disadvantaged Children: According to the National Policy on Education, the socially disadvantaged children are those children who belong to the following categories:

1. Scheduled Castes Children.
2. Scheduled Tribes Children.
3. Other Backward Classes (OBC's) Children.
4. Tribal Areas Children.

Legal Safeguards

Article 15: Prohibition of Discrimination on grounds of religion, race, caste, sex or place of births sub-section (4) states, "Nothing in this Article or in clause (2) of Article 29 shall prevent the State from making any special provision for the advancement of any socially and educationally backward classes or for the Scheduled Castes and the Scheduled Tribes.

Article 46: It reads, "the State shall promote with special care the educational and economic interests of the weaker sections of the people, and in particular, of the Scheduled Castes and Scheduled Tribes and shall protect them from social injustice and all forms of exploitation.

Article 338: It makes provision for the appointment of a Special Officer for SCs and STs.

Article 390: It envisages the appointment of a Commission to investigate the conditions of the Backward classes.

Learning Development

The Education Commission 1964-66, in chapter VI entitled 'Equalisation of Educational Opportunity and Social Change' very aptly observed, "One of the important social objectives of education is to equalise opportunity, enabling the backward or under-privileged classes and individuals to use education as a lever for the improvement of their conditions. Every society that values social justice and is anxious to improve the lot of the common man and cultivate all available talent must ensure progressive equality of opportunity to all sections of the population. This is the only guarantee for the building up of an egalitarian and humane society in which the exploitation of the weak is minimised." The Commission further stated, "The education of the backward classes in general and the tribal people in particular is a major programme of equalisation and of social and national integration. No expenditure is too great for this purpose." Alas! We have not paid heed to these words of wisdom. Non-implementation of this vital recommendation has led to disintegrative tendencies, hatred and strife.

Policies on education-the National Policy on Education, 1968, 1986 and modified Policy Formulation 1992-all stress upon speedy action for the promotion of education of the deprived sections.

The Identification: Children belonging to the four categories of sections of population as mentioned above automatically come under the category of socially disadvantaged children. Such children cannot be treated inferior on the basis of I.Q. They may not show the desired results on account of lack of facilities. They may have the potential to show good results provided ancillary facilities are made available to them.

Teaching Methods

Preparatory Classes and Compensatory Instruction: Many children belonging to the Scheduled Castes and Scheduled Tribes come from a comparatively poor environment. They may not be neat or smart. Their usage of standard language may be poor. Their vocabulary is underdeveloped as compared to their peers. They may not have formed the initial mathematical concepts. On the other hand they may be more enthusiastic to learn. Because of the lack of a congenial home environment, these children may not be in a position to complete their home assignments. Their parents are usually employed as landless labour or in other manual or agrarian activities. Therefore, such children are not able to conceptualise their future as educated persons.

There is the need to conduct some preparatory classes for

children coming from the Scheduled Castes and Scheduled Tribes. The primary objective of conducting such classes is to raise the school entry ability level of such children. This is also helpful in having a somewhat homogeneous grouping in the class. The classes may be conducted two to three weeks in advance of the general admissions. Classes may be conducted on healthy habits, personal and environmental cleanliness, eating habits etc. The children may also be helped in improving the pronunciation of the words and picking up standard language. For this, they may be motivated to participate in discussions, recitation and story-telling etc. Initial concepts of mathematics may also be introduced.

Remedial Instruction: Students coming from Scheduled Castes and Scheduled Tribes are also likely to be deficient in the scholastic areas. The school may provide some remedial education programmes. Adoption of instructional strategies, such as peer group learning, monitorial assistance, diagnostic testing and tutoring would help to improve the educational levels of these learners.

Provision of outdoor games and activities, co-curricular and work experience activities will also help in the retention of such children in the schools and create an interest in them for continuing schooling.

Monitoring of Programmes: A Standing Committee of the Central Advisory Board of Education (CABE) under the Chairmanship of Minister of Human Resource Development may be constituted to monitor and review implementation of all educational programmes for the deprived sections.

Incentive Schemes: Incentive schemes in operation for the promotion of the education of the deprived sections may be evaluated and appropriate strategies evolved in the light of such studies.

Role of the Teacher: Following are the important points which a teacher should take into account while teaching the students.

1. The teacher should take interest in meeting the needs of every type of child.
2. The teacher should ensure that his own behaviour and behaviour of students is free from bias.

3. The teacher must ensure that the interaction amongst the students is normal.
4. The teacher should understand the learning process in the context of characteristics of learners.
5. The teacher should appreciate that the special educational needs of the students reflect the special requirement of a learner calling for specific adjustment in regular educational programmes.
6. The teacher should keep in view that special needs can arise from physiological, intellectual, social and economical reasons.
7. The learner should be given importance as an individual rather than as a disabled or as a scheduled caste or scheduled tribe or a girl.
8. Educational adjustment has several dimensions like curriculum decision, class-room organisation, special teaching techniques and aids etc.
9. A teacher should be sensitive to the needs of socially disadvantaged learners.
10. The teacher should have a close link with parents to ensure regular attendance.
11. The teacher should make the parents aware of the special educational and otter facilities in the school and the neighbourhood and impress upon them to make use of them.
12. The teacher should find out specific areas of deficiency in learning.
13. The teacher should take all possible steps to develop self-concept and positive image among such learners.
14. Special incentives be provided to such students.
15. The teacher's own example in his behaviour towards students belonging to these castes is the most effective and powerful way to build up a congenial climate.
16. The school staff should ensure non-discrimination between the children of Scheduled Castes, Scheduled Tribes and other communities.

17. The school staff should avoid the use of the caste names or derogatory words while calling roll calls or naming children.
18. Teachers should provide equal opportunities to all the children to participate in the curricular and co-curricular activities of the school, including games.
19. Frequent meetings between the staff, school teachers and parents of Scheduled Castes and Scheduled Tribes children should be arranged. The details of the schemes for promoting education amongst Scheduled Castes and Scheduled Tribes should be explained to the parents at these meetings. It should be impressed upon them that they must continue the education of their children.
20. Special attention should be paid to motivating parents to educate girls.
21. Teachers should suggest to illiterate parents the advantages gained by attending functional literacy classes in the adult education centre.

Emotional Facets

There are learners with socio-emotional problems of varying intensity. Most of such learners can be identified and tackled with ordinary means and with a little more special attention.

It is observed that at some point in their school career, between 2 to 5 per cent of children become so disturbed socially and emotionally that they experience great difficulty to make desirable progress in studies and to adjust to the demands of the society in acceptable ways, unless they are given special guidance, either through psychological services or by placement in special units.

1. They are emotionally immature.
2. They do not possess a balanced self-regarding sentiment.
3. They are not able to face failures bravely.
4. They do not have a rational attitude towards sex.
5. They are over anxious.
6. They have inferiority complex.
7. They are withdrawn.

Causes Leading to Socio-emotional Problems

Family Circumstances	*Personal*	*School*	*Teachers*	*Peers*
	Some physical defect	1. Unattractive School Environment	1. Unsympathetic teachers	1. Undesirable interests and activities of peers
		2. Unsuitable curriculum or wrong choice of subjects	2. Uninspiring methods of teaching.	2. Non-acceptance in the group
		3. Lack of curricular activities		
		4. Lack of discipline		

Economic	*Psychological*	*Social*
(i) Problem of unemployment or semi-employment	(i) Over possessive parents	(i) Loss social status of the family
(ii) Low economic status	(ii) Unrealic expectations from childrens	(ii) Broken homes
	(iii) Faulty home discipline	(iii) Fear of insecurity
	(iv) Use of abusive language	(iv) Some anti-social stigma to the family
	(v) Lack of role model parents	
	(vi) Unequal parental treatment to siblings	
	(vii) Fear of insecurity	

8. They find it difficult to adjust to and within the self.
9. They find it difficult to everyday social requirements and relationships.

Diagnosis of Problems

Projective Techniques: Following types of projective techniques may be used to find out the problems if they are very acute.

(i) Play situations.
(ii) Story telling and story completion.
(iii) Incomplete sentence technique.
(iv) Original drawings and paintings.
(v) Free association and dream analysis.
(vi) Thematic Apperception Test (TAT)

2. Sociometric Tests.
3. Situational Tests.
4. Personal Documents
5. Parent's information.
6. Case conference.

The Curriculum

Following measures may be adopted to meet the socio-emotional needs of the learners:

1. Provision of normal curriculum.
2. Provision of normal co-curricular activities.
3. Sympathetic attitude of the teachers to understand the needs of such children.
4. Provision of an environment of security.
5. Protecting them for 'bully' students.
6. Career guidance.
7. Vocational guidance.
8. Counselling.
9. Cooperation of all agencies in the welfare of children.

It may be observed that usually the learners with socio-economic problems are at par with normal children in intelligence and capacity to learn. It is only their socio-emotional state of affairs that hinders their growth. They are not to be segregated from normal children.

Physically and Mentally Challenged Children : A physically handicapped child is one who is affected with a physical impairment that in any way limits or inhibits his participation in normal activities. Impairment implies abnormalities of body structure and appearance. It represents disturbance at the organ level. The impairment may be of a serious type or it may be slight in degree. For instance, a person hit by polio may be having only 15 per cent impairment on a certain part of the body or may have a total loss of mobility. Similarly, the visual defect may be total and it may not be restored. Other visual impairments may not pose serious problems and may be overcome with some aids.

Generally speaking, the physically handicapped may be classified as

1. The cripple.
2. The blind or near blind or partially blind.
3. The deaf or hard of hearing.
4. The language handicapped.
5. Cerebral palsied.
6. Orthopaedically handicapped.

In addition, the chronically ill children who may have health problems like heart defects or cardiac problems, epilepsy, allergies, diabetes, rheumatism, muscular and tuberculosis etc. also fall in the category of physically handicapped children.

Objectives of Education: Following are the chief objectives of the education of the physically handicapped children:

1. To reach the maximum level of effectiveness in school subjects.
2. To pursue those curricular matters that strategically determine effective living for specific type of handicapped school children.
3. To consider the mental as well as the physical hygiene of handicapped school children and to take suitable measures.

4. To develop rational patterns in the handicapped that will produce achievement in school and out of school.
5. To produce in the handicapped a desire to participate in the activities of non-handicapped persons.
6. To develop a realistic self-concept in handicapped children.

The education of handicapped children has to be organized not merely on humanitarian grounds, but also on grounds of utility. Proper education generally enables a handicapped child to overcome largely his (or her) handicap, and makes him a useful citizen. Social justice also demands it. It has to be remembered that the Constitutional Directive on compulsory education includes handicapped children as well. Very little has been done in this field so far on account of several difficulties. There is much in the field that we could learn from the educationally advanced countries which in recent years has developed new methods and techniques, based on advances in science and medicine.

The primary task of education for a handicapped child is to prepare him for adjustment to a socio-cultural environment designed to meet the needs of the normal. It is essential, therefore, that the education of handicapped children should be an inseparable part of the general educational system. The differences lie in the methods employed to teach the child and the means the child uses to acquire information. These differences in methodology do not influence the goals of education. This form of education is, therefore referred to as 'special'.

Pattern of Education of the Physically Handicapped Children: Following are the usual patterns of education of the handicapped:

Integration: Integration implies that the education of the handicapped should be so organised that they freely mix up with normal children. This can be achieved in various ways:

(a) Having regular classes for all children.

(b) Deliberate architectural planning to allot space for regular classes and special classes separately but in the same building.

Partial Integration: The brightest and the handicapped children join with regular groups for carefully selected experiences, games and play.

Total Segregation: Under this system, the handicapped children are completely separated from other children. They are taught in special schools.

Fundamental Principles for the Education of the Physically Handicapped Children are :

1. Recognition of the handicap of the child by the teacher as early as possible.
2. Taking all available correctional measures.
3. Development of favourable attitude towards the child.
4. Diagnostic and remedial work by the guidance counsellor.

Effects of Physical Handicaps on Children: A physical handicap may directly or indirectly create the following types of problems for the children and their parents:

Academic Performance: (i) Physically handicapped children generally work below their capacity in several areas. (ii) Some of the physically handicapped children find it difficult to deal with abstract concepts.

Emotional Reactions or Social Relationships: (i) Quite a large number of physically handicapped children suffer from feelings of inferiority. (ii) They also suffer from feelings of failures. (iii) Normal children are at times not only indifferent to the handicapped but also make fun of them. Thus the handicapped children are withdrawn. (iv) Aggressive feelings and tensions get accumulated in the handicapped as they have fewer opportunities for expressing their feelings. (v) Sometimes parents', teachers' and students' attitudes may make a physically handicapped child feet 'unwanted' or 'rejected'. (vi) Handicapped children are more prone to accident and injury. Thus, they are not in a position to participate in several co-curricular activities. This also creates a feeling of disgust in them.

Consequent Problems

The handicapped child is unable to participate in desirable normal activities of the daily life. He, therefore, needs satisfying substitute interests.

The physically handicapped child also faces emotional problems as he feels that others have a low opinion about him and develops a feeling of hatred for others or of self-pity.

The physically handicapped child is not necessarily mentally deficient. In the majority of cases, he possesses normal intelligence. it is, therefore, very necessary that the mental powers of the handicapped are exploited fully and suitable opportunities provided to generate hope in life and compensate for his physical disability.

The major problem of the physically handicapped is to identify at the earliest the impairment and make arrangement for adequate adjustment. The handicap that is obvious at birth is easily identified. Other impairments take time to be identified.

Following points may be considered while providing educational facilities for the handicapped children:

1. *Normal Curriculum:* The majority of the physically handicapped children are just normal except for their physical handicap. Such children should be provided all those educational activities which are meant for the normal children, keeping in mind, of course, their physical disability.
2. *Special Classes:* For the partially sighted students, special classes may be organised.
3. *Special Equipment and Methods of Teaching:* Blind children need special equipment and medium for their education. They also need special teaching, methods like the following.
   (i) For the teaching of mathematics, stress is laid on mental work.
   (ii) Embossed diagrams are used in geometry.
   (iii) Relief maps and globes may be used for the study of geography.
4. *Special Subjects:*
   (i) Modelling may be substituted for drawing and painting. Blind children derive pleasure from working with clay and plasticine.

(ii) Dramatic art may be cultivated.

(iii) Music may be given adequate encouragement.

5. *Physical Education:* Corrective posture work, gymnastics, running, wrestling and sports etc. should form part of the physical education programme.
6. *Vocational Education and Handicrafts:* A variety of handicrafts may be taught to the physically handicapped.
7. *Therapeutic Assistance:* Special programmes in the form of speech-therapy, physiotherapy, play therapy should be undertaken to help physically handicapped children make the correct and maximum use of whatever abilities and capacities they possess.
8. *Education for Living in Society with Handicap:* Handicapped children have to live in a world of normal people. They, therefore, should be provided all types of education, training and guidance which enable them to face their disability realistically and make suitable adjustments accordingly and live without bitterness and meet unpleasant situations boldly.

Learning Provisions

Prof. K. C. Panda (2000) mentions the following types of education services to be provided to the exceptional children, depending upon the nature and intensity of the handicap.

1. Regular class-room with minor in-class support.
2. Regular class-room with weekly 'itinerant' teacher.
3. Regular class-room with daily resource room supplemental programming.
4. Resource room with several hours of daily regular class-room instruction and non-instructional activities.
5. Regular room with limited hours of weekly non-instructional activities with regular classmates.
6. Self-contained special class-room.
7. Special day school.
8. Homebound or hospitalization.
9. Residential.

Diverse Mechanism

Integration implies the existence of following elements:

1. Sharing the same class-room, resources and opportunities by the handicapped as well as the regular students.
2. Providing special services needed for the exceptional (handicapped) students in the regular schools.
3. Having handicapped (disabled) students follow the same schedule as normal (non-disabled) students.
4. Involving disabled students in several academic courses and co-curricular activities including art, field trips, music and exercises etc.
5. Enabling disabled students to use library, playground and other facilities at the same time as normal students use.
6. Encouraging friendly relation between disabled and normal students.
7. Arranging for disabled students to receive their education in the regular environment of the community when feasible.
8. Advising all students to understand the limitations of the disabled students and accept human differences.
9. Enrolling children with disabilities in the same schools they would have attended if they were not disabled.
10. Attending to parents concern about their disabled children seriously.
11. Providing an appropriate individualised programme.

To sum up; integration approach is a particular orientation towards providing education to the majority of the handicapped children.

It is estimated that nearly 10 per cent of handicapped students receive most of their education in regular schools. An additional 20 to 25 per cent students are enrolled in special classes located in the same building.

1. He should learn about the students handicapping conditions.

2. He should understand the common characteristics of the handicapped children.
3. He should appreciate the common difficulties that the handicapped children experience.
4. He should learn about the special materials the handicapped children use, e.g., pushing a wheel chair up or down stairs etc.
5. He should meet the special education teacher to chalk out appropriate strategies to meet the special needs of the handicapped children.
6. He should accept appropriate behaviour in order to stimulate continuous effort.
7. He should seek the cooperation of normal students to improve the psychological climate of the class so that the disabled students are encouraged to put in their best.

Role of the Teacher

1. He should identify the academic or physical adaptations needed in the class-room for the disabled students.
2. He should develop programmes to prepare disabled students for entry into regular classes.
3. He should involve parents in setting appropriate goals for their students.
4. He should prepare a variety of activities that will involve the entire class in grouping patterns that are flexible.
5. He should design a variety of alternative teaching strategies.
6. He should prepare a flexible time schedule for learning as well as physical and social needs of each student.
7. He should fully cooperate with the regular teacher.

Significant Tools

1. Braille writer for the teacher.
2. Braille books.
3. Braille slates and stylus for students.
4. Abacus for the teaching of mathematics.

5. Braille sheets of paper.
6. Low vision aids.
7. Large print books.
8. Braille bulletin boards.
9. Equipment for teaching industrial and other arts.
10. Tape-recorders and cassettes.
11. Braille type duplicating machines.
12. Teaching aids.
13. Class-room furniture.

In the special programmes the handicapped children are isolated from the normal ones and placed in special institutions. In the educationally advanced countries, however, a great deal of stress is now being laid on the integration of handicapped children into the regular school programmes. This has two important advantages: reduction of costs and promoting mutual understanding between handicapped and the non-handicapped children. This has also its disadvantages. For instance, many handicapped children find it psychologically disturbing to be placed in an ordinary school.

To develop integrated programmes adequately, attention will have to be paid to the following matters:

1. The preparation of teacher will need emphasis and attention. This will necessitate a considerable increase in the capacity of existing training institutions and the establishment of new ones.
2. It is necessary to coordinate the efforts of different agencies working in the field.
3. It is also necessary to develop adequate research in the problems of integrated programme.

Statutory Provisions: With the coming into force of the 'Persons with Disabilities Act, 1955, there is now a statutory responsibility of the Central, State and Local Governments in India, to provide free education in an appropriate environment to all disabled children upto the age of 18 years.

Centrally sponsored Scheme for the Disabled Students: The Department of Education, Ministry of Human Resource Development, Government of India has been implementing the Scheme for Integrated Education of Disabled Children (IEDC) since 1974.

Important Features

Following are the important features of the scheme:

1. The scheme includes pre-school training for disabled children and counselling for their parents.
2. Cent per cent financial assistance is provided as per prescribed norms for facilities for disabled children. This covers cost of books and stationery, uniforms, transport and escort allowance for severely handicapped children, reader allowance for blind children and equipment which includes educational aids and assistive services.
3. The scheme also provides assistance to non-governmental Organisations (NGOs), engaged in the field of integrated education.
4. *Polytechnics:* Two polytechnics for disabled students have been set up at Mysore and Kanpur.
5. *Curriculum for Teacher Training:* The NOTE (National Council for Teacher Education) has developed curriculum for teacher training and orientation so that both general teachers as well as resource teachers are trained to handle disabled children.
6. *NCERT Programmes:* The NCERT has also taken up several programmes in this area.
7. *India-Australia Training and Capacity Building Project (IACBP):* The programme includes:
   (i) Intensive training of 10 teacher educators in Australia to turn them into Master Trainers.
   (ii) Further training by the Master Trainers along with three Australian experts in various places in India.
   (iii) A study tour of 6-10 Officers of the Government of India and State Governments as well as educational

institution to have first hand experience in Australia in the field of IEDC.

(iv) Technological exchange programme in this field.

Coverage: The IEDC scheme is being operated in 26 States/ UTs through nearly 15,000 schools and over 55,000 children are being benefited under this scheme.

How to Teach the Blind ?

Children whose vision is so impaired that they can see objects at a distance of 20 ft. which a normal eye can see at a distance of 200 ft. are legally blind. The totally blind children read Braille. Blindness affects the life of the individual in the physical, mental, social, educational and vocational aspects.

Usually for blind children, going to school implies admission to a residential school for the blind (Braille classes). Of late some attempts have been made to integrate them with the normal children by admitting to them to normal schools but the coverage of blind population of the students in this respect is not significant. A blind school aims at assisting the blind child, through the use of special methods and aids, in his adjustment to the world in which he has to live as an adult.

Schools for the blind usually provide for activities such as dancing, scouting, and dramatics.

Special equipment and methods of teaching are employed for the education of the blind.

Particular attention is given to practice on type writer because it permits written communication with the seeing.

(i) As many as concrete experiences as possible, either by letting them observe the object as such or by providing replicas, may be provided to the blind students.

(ii) Blind children at least during the primary classes, should be taught by a unit plan of instruction.

(iii) Topics of the units may consist of everyday experiences such as provision shops, post offices etc.

(iv) Self-activity should be made an integral part of the education of the blind.

The Disabled Ones

Several children do not have sufficient vision. They find it difficult to read the writing on the blackboard clearly. There are partially sighted children also. Some can read only large print. Visual impairment results in several learning problems. Children with visual impairments may have enormous capacity to work. However, this depends upon the nature of the impairment.

Identification of Children with Visual Impairments: It is very necessary to identify each category of children with visual impairments. Medical treatment may become necessary in some cases. Parents also need to be informed.

Children with visual impairment may be identified from the following:

1. Having watery eyes.
2. Rubbing eyes frequently.
3. Reddening of eyes frequently.
4. Covering one eye and titling the head forward.
5. Holding objects and books close to the eyes.
6. Asking help from others when taking notes from the blackboard.
7. Blinking frequently-squinting eyelids together.
8. Complaining about headache following close eye work.
9. Bumpening into people or objects.
10. Skipping words or lines while reading.
11. Having poor eye-hand coordination.
12. Moving head forward and backward while looking at distant objects.

Visual handicap is defined in terms of visual acuity, field of vision and visual efficiency. Snellen chart, developed by Herbart Snellen, a Dutch doctor, is used to assess the visual ability. The chart starts with a big 'E' which a normal eye can at a distance of 200 ft.

Visual acuity is not the only criteria for measuring acquision of basic skills. Following tests are used for measuring intellectual abilities.

1. The Blind Learning Aptitude Test.
2. The Haptic Intelligence Scale for the Adult Blind.

Role of Teacher

1. Children with visual impairment may be seated in the front rows so that they can read the writing on the blackboard without any difficulty or pressure.
2. Such children may be given training in listening with comprehension.
3. Books with bold letters may be provided to such children.
4. Radio and T.V. broadcasts may be arranged for to such children.
5. Efforts may be made to procure cassettes in different curricular areas. State Institutes of Education or State Councils of Educational Research and Training or District Institutes of Education and Training or Centres or Institutes of Educational Technology may be approached for this purpose.
6. Blind children need Braille script books.
7. School doctor may be consulted from time to time.
8. Cooperation of the parents be sought in the follow-up work.

Method for Differentiation

Listening plays an important role in academic learning. Hearing problems interfere with the achievement of the students. It is, therefore, desirable to identify such children and take steps to meet their educational needs. Such children may be identified as under:

- Some observable deformity of the ear or ears.
- Frequent complaints of pain in ears.
- Frequent scratching of ears.
- Frequent discharge from ears.

- Turning head on one side to hear better.
- Frequent requests to teachers to repeat questions and directions etc.
- Making errors in taking dictation or notes.
- Displaying speech difficulty.

Guidelines

1. Children with hearing problems may be given front seats.
2. While speaking, the teacher may use a reasonable level of pitch.
3. The teacher should avoid mumbling.
4. The teacher should avoid speaking too fast.
5. Students should be encouraged to speak gradually and steadily.
6. Other students of the class may be asked to give due consideration to such students.
7. A lot of visual aids may be used in the class-room.
8. Some of the hearing problems can be corrected through drill and practice.
9. Medical help may be needed if speech disorder is due to an organic defect in speech mechanism.

Identification: Such children can be easily identified as their impairment is usually observable.

1. Deformity may be observable in fingers, hands, legs, neck or waist etc.
2. Showing difficulty in sitting, standing and walking.
3. Showing difficulty in picking up and holding objects and putting them on the ground.
4. Frequently complaining of pains in the joints.
5. Experiencing difficulty in holding the pen to write.
6. Walking with jerks.
7. Experiencing difficulty in the movement of limbs.
8. Amputated limbs.

Locomotor Impairment

1. The teacher should accept such children as he accepts other children.
2. The teacher should avoid sarcasm for the disability of the child.
3. Other children should be advised to appreciate the disability and show due regard to such children. They should be made to understand the disability.
4. Seating arrangement in the class may be adjusted to the specific needs of such students.
5. Reasonable opportunities for participation in recreational activities, sports and games should be provided to these children.
6. Remedial teaching may also be arranged for them.

9

Physically Challenged

Exceptional children refer to those children whose needs are very different from the majority of the children in the society and who differ from the majority in their emotional, mental, physical and social characteristics. Such children cannot develop themselves under normal classroom conditions and special environment has to be created for them.

In the words of W. M. Crunchshank, "An exceptional child is he who deviates, physically, intellectually, emotionally and socially so marked from normal growth and development that he cannot be benefited from a regular class-room programme and needs special treatment in school."

According to Kirk, "An exceptional child is one who deviates from normal or average child in mental, physical and social characteristics to such an extent that he requires a modification of school practices or special educational services or supplementary instruction in order to develop to his maximum capacity."

Crow and Crow have observed, "The term a typical or exceptional is applied to a trait or to a person possessing the trait if the extent of deviation from normal possession of that trait is so great that because of it the individual warrants and receives special attention from his fellows and his behaviour responses and activities are thereby affected."

Salient Features

1. He is markedly different from the normal child.
2. The difference may be emotional, mental, physical or social.
3. An exceptional child needs a special environment.
4. The special environment may be provided in the normal system of schooling or in a special school. In case of some categories of exceptional children, only special schools can meet their needs.

Broad Classification of Exceptional Children

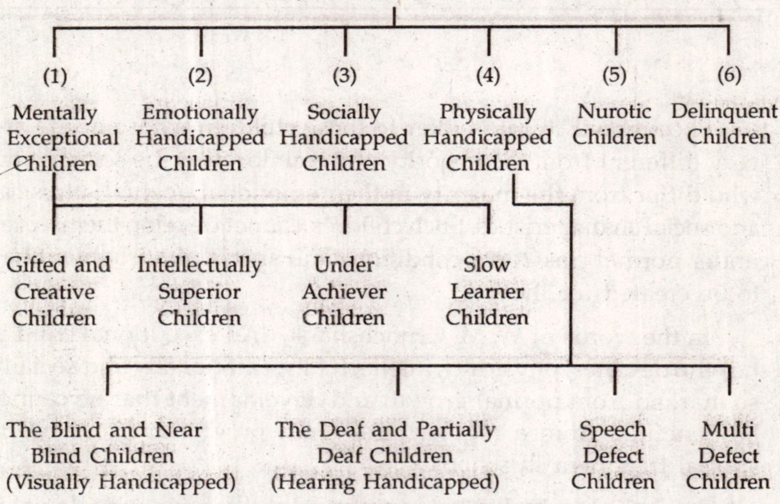

Categorisation of Children on Intelligence Quotient (IQ) on Stanford Revision (USA)

IQ	*Percent*	*Classification*
160-169	0.3	
150-159	0.2	Very Superior/Gifted/Creative
140-149	1.1	
130-139	3.1	
120-129	8.2	Superior/High Average
110-119	18.1	

Contd...

IQ	*Percent*	*Classification*
100-109	23.5	Average
90-99	23.0	
80-89	14.0	Low Average
70-79	5.6	Borderline Defective
60-69	2.0	
50-59	0.04	
40-49	0.02	Mentally Defective
30-39	0.03	

Source : Terman and Merril

The Working Group on the Education of the Disabled Children (1981), set up by the Government of India recommended that the following categories of handicapped children should be served:

1. The blind or the virtually handicapped.
2. The deaf or the hearing handicapped.
3. The orthopaedically handicapped.
4. The educable and trainable mentally retarded.
5. The cerebral palsied.
6. The neurologically handicapped, including epileptic.
7. Children with speech and language disorders.

Dr. V. V. Karnath's Classification of Indian Children

I. Q.	*Category*
140 and above	Near genius or Genius
130-139.9	Extraordinary
120-129.9	Very superior
110-119.9	Superior
99-109.9	Average or Normal
80-98.9	Backward
70-79.9	Very Backward
60-69.9	Borderline
40-59.9	Moron
20-39.9	Imbecile
Below 20	Idiot

Education for Them : Following are the important considerations for making provision for the education of the gifted children:

1. Regular classes for normal children do not meet the needs of exceptional children. Hence they need separate classes.
2. Under normal conditions, exceptional children may develop behaviour problems.
3. The principle of equalisation of educational opportunities highlights that exceptional children should have opportunities to develop themselves to the maximum.
4. Proper opportunities will make them economically self-sufficient.
5. Special categories of children like deaf, dumb, blind, etc. require special school's learning.

Developed Children

Meaning of the Gifted and the Creative: In simple language a gifted child is one who can make outstanding contribution in any area of national life. Giftedness generally speaking includes actual or potential qualities of creativity, emotional stability and social adaptability. Following are the important definitions of gifted children:

James Drever is of the view that "children possessing high intellectual ability, generally or in a particular field are gifted children."

Terman and Oden state, "Gifted children are far above the average in physique, social adjustment, personality traits, school achievement, play, information and versality of interests."

In the words of Hillingworth, "By a gifted child we mean one who is far more educable than the generality of children are. The greater educability may lie along the lines of one of the arts, as in music or drawing, it may lie in the sphere of mechanical aptitude, or it may consist in surpassing power to achieve literacy and abstract knowledge."

Paul Witty states, "Those whose performance in a worthwhile human endeavour is constantly remarkable as well as those who are academically superior."

R. J. Havighurst observes, "Gifted children are those individuals from kindergarten to high school age who show unusual promise in some socially useful area and whose talent might be stimulated."

Broadly speaking 'gifted children' should include all those children who give promise of creativity of a high order in any worthwhile line of human endeavour. They have superior ability that can make them contribute to the quality of living in society. Therefore, we include not only the intellectually gifted but also those who show promise in music, the graphic arts, creative writing, dramatics, mechanical skills and social leadership. Nevertheless, here we are dealing with children having gifted intellectual ability.

While discussing education of the gifted, the creative and the intellectually superior, it may be observed, that in essence, all these three types of children may be placed in the same category. In practice, it is very difficult to formulate separate policies. These categories differ in degrees only and not in kind.

Wide Variety : In the words of Hollingworth, "By a gifted child we mean one who is far more educable than the generality of children are. The greater educability may lie along the lines of one of the arts, as in music or drawing, it may lie in the sphere of mechanical aptitude, or it may consist in surpassing power to achieve literacy and abstract knowledge." Paul Witty, Ruth Strang, Havighurst and many others think that the term gifted children should include all those children who give promise of creativity of a high order in any worthwhile line of human endeavour. They have superior ability that can make them contribute to the quality of living in society. Therefore, we include not only the intellectually gifted but also those who show promise in music, the graphic arts, creative writing, dramatics, mechanical skills and social leadership.

Specific Qualities

1. Very high I.Q.
2. Ability to apply knowledge to unfamiliar situations.
3. Ability for abstract and symbolic thinking.
3. Annoyance with details.
4. Attention span long for age.
5. Curiosity indicated by asking serious questions.

6. Dislike of rigid time schedule.
7. Energy level (physical and intellectual) very high.
8. Exposure needed limited and fewer repetitions to learn.
9. Intense interest in one area.
10. Knowing a lot about things of which other students are unaware.
11. Learning commensurate with that expected of older students, often start of reading at an earlier than average age.
12. Memory very extraordinary.
13. Often thinking faster than they write (can result in sloppy work).
14. Spontaneous and diverse interests.
15. Standards and goals unusually high.
16. Vocabulary very high and mature expressive ability enormous.

Those students who show some or several of the characteristics mentioned above are referred to by many adjectives such as 'genius', 'gifted' and 'talented' etc.

Categories of Gifted Children: Usually following are considered as the categories of the gifted on the basis of Intelligence Quotient (I.Q). (Stanford Revision-USA).

I. Q.	*Percent of Population*
160-169	0.3%
150-159	0.2%
140-149	1.1%
130-139	3.1%
120-129	8.2%

On the basis of Dr. V.V. Kamat's classification, 120 I.Q. may be considered as the lower limit of giftedness.

Usually it is said that nearly 2 to 3 per cent of the population may be placed under the category of the gifted children.

Special Attention on the Education: It is of great importance to bring out the hidden 'gem-like' potentialities in pupils not only for the interest of such students but for the interest of the humanity as a whole. The following lines fully illustrate this:

"For many a gem of purest ray serene. The dark unfathomed caves of the ocean bear. Full many a flower is born to flouriest unseen. And waste its sweetness on the desert air."

We are interested in the gifted on account of the following considerations:

1. There is a limited pool of ability and special talent in every country. This must be identified and developed to save it from loss.
2. The gifted individuals have played an important role in the preservation and advancement of civilization.
3. Values of democracy will be realized in the fullest sense when we recognize the full range of ability within our total population.
4. Many gifted children languish in educational institutions simply because they are not aware of their 'gifts' and the school programmes do not provide them enough motivation and challenge.
5. We need leaders for our business, education, research and government etc. These leaders are provided by this class of gifted children.

Adjustment Problems: A gifted child may become a problem for the parents and the teacher if he is not handled properly. Following problems may arise:

1. When he is not properly guided, he utilises his superior intelligence in mischief, indiscipline, gang-formation and revolts against his elders. He becomes a nuisance.
2. Because of lack of opportunities and lack of recognition, he sometimes develops inferiority complex.
3. Too much of recognition or applauses by the parent or teacher also develop in him boastful conceit.
4. There is lack of stimulation for him in the subjects of his interests when he does not get opportunities of progressing according to his own pace.

5. He revolts against the parents and teachers when they do not recognise him, and sometimes creates mischief in order to catch their attention or to show his superiority.

Identification: For identifying the gifted children, following techniques are employed:

1. Intelligence Tests (Individual)
2. Intelligence Tests (Group)
3. Achievements Tests and Batteries.
4. Observations by Teachers and others.

It may be observed that reliance should not be made only on one technique.

Enrichment Programmes: Enrichment consists in giving the gifted child the opportunity to go deeper or to range more widely than the average child in his intellectual, social and artistic experience. Such a programme may be characterized by :

(1) emphasis upon the creative or the experimental;
(2) emphasis on the skill of investigation and learning;
(3) independent work, stressing initiative and originality;
(4) high standard of accomplishment;
(5) cooperative planning and activity that provides opportunity for leadership training and experiences in social adjustment;
(6) individual attention given by teacher to student;
(7) first-hand experiences;
(8) flexibility of organization and procedure;
(9) extensive reading; and
(10) concern with community responsibility.

The Triple Track Plan: In this type of learning plan, there are three tracks:

(a) The first is for the dull child who may cover it in a longer duration of time.
(b) The second one is for the average child who covers it in an average period of time.

(c) The third is for the child of superior intelligence. He covers the entire work in a shorter period of time due to his intelligence, efforts and initiative.

Such a system has been adopted in most of the schools in the United States.

Rapid Promotion: Gifted children should be promoted to the next higher grade as soon as they achieve the target of a particular grade.

Special Schools: In some countries special schools are organised for gifted children. Some educationists have pointed out some limitations in organising such schools.

Acceleration: Acceleration offers opportunity for a gifted pupil to move at a pace appropriate to his ability and maturity and to complete an educational programme in less than the ordinary amount of time. It involves advancing the gifted child rapidly from grade to grade in school so that he enters college earlier than others.

Segregation or Ability Grouping: The gifted pupils may be placed in special groups for all or part of the school day. The purpose of ability grouping is usually to provide for enrichment of children's experiences in both depth and breadth, and to permit the children to stimulate one another.

Summer Programmes: Special cultural and educational programmes may be organised for gifted children during the summer season. This approach is being tried in U.S.A. and in a limited measure in our country as well.

Scholarships: Gifted children should be given special scholarships for pursuing their studies. This will lead the gifted child in the right direction.

Special Visits: Groups of gifted children may formally visit places of historical, industrial, geographical and economic interest. This would enable them to understand and appreciate important places of social value also.

Contact with Eminent Persons: Gifted children may show interest in any special field of activities. Their meetings may be fixed up with persons of eminence of that particular field.

Vocational and Personal Guidance and Counselling: The gifted children should receive proper guidance in all areas of life so that their total development is of an optimum level.

The role of the counsellor in the promotion of talent can be very important. The counsellor with his detailed knowledge of each talented student is in a unique position to formulate a programme of enrichment for him and to suggest the necessary modifications in the curricular and extra-curricular requirements. Where special counsellors are not available, this task will fall on the teachers. It will, therefore, be necessary to train teachers for this responsibility through in-service seminars and special courses. It should be impressed on them that the class-room atmosphere and the attitudes of teachers is of considerable importance. In a social and educational set-up like ours where the relationship between the teacher and the taught is still largely authoritarian, the general tendency is to suppress any urges and interests that deviate from the class norm. The first requirement for the promotion of talent, therefore, is for the teachers to create an atmosphere of free expression in the class-room and to provide opportunities for creative work.

Summary: We may remember these words of wisdom said by AX Whitehead, "Any race which does not value trained intelligence is doomed."

The Deprived Ones

We usually hear parents and teachers making such remarks as "Sohan is bright and intelligent. We do not understand why he gets so poor marks," or "Lata could do much better if she really tried and took an interest in her studies. She has the ability." Such remarks indicate that most of us are aware of the fact that many school children work far below of their expected level of intellectual development. If such situations are not corrected, students gradually lose interest in academic work and may generally drop-out from school. They become a liability not only to themselves and their parents but also to the society. It is, therefore, very necessary to identify under-achievers early. We must help them to progress in their work.

Meaning and Characteristics of the Under-achiever Children: There is no set definition of the under-achiever children. Several writers and experts do not refer to under-achiever children as a special category of children. They club this category with the slow learning children. Some authors and experts use terms like mentally retarded children and backward children. Hence there is a lot of confusion regarding the use of terms. An underachiever child generally speaking is one whose achievement falls below the level of his natural abilities.

Some experts regard an under-achiever child one who compared with other children of the same chronological age shows marked educational deficiency. The generally accepted meaning of under-achievement implies that a student's academic achievement is below on certain norm or standard which is expected of him on the basis of his potential ability. This means that we consider a student an under-achiever when his achievement is not at par with his intelligence.

From a broader point of view, an under-achiever child is one who has high potential in fields other than intellectual also but he is not using his potential adequately.

According to John Holt, an under-achiever child fails to develop more than a tiny part of the tremendous capacity for learning, understanding and creating with which they was born.

(i) An under-achiever with superior intelligence but having average performance in school subjects.

(ii) An under-achiever with average intelligence but whose achievements are significantly below a reasonable level of age and who does not appear to be making much progress.

(iii) The dull and the slow learner who is not working up to his capacity and is capable of improvement.

(iv) One who is highly creative and talented in fields other than intellectual but has not been able to develop his creative powers and talents to the full.

(v) An under-achiever who has lived under deprived, restricted and un-stimulating conditions for prolonged periods during early childhood and therefore, shows low scores on an intelligence test. His achievement is usually unsatisfactory in the school situation.

Factors Responsible for Under-achievement

(1) *Physical Factors*	(2) *Intellectual Factors*	(3) *Emotional Factors*	(4) *Factors Relating to Home*	(5) *Factors Relating to the Community*	(6) *Factors in School*
1. Poor physique of the child. 2. General disability of the child. 3. Chronic illness 4. Lack of stamina etc. These present a child from doing his best in the academic field.	1. Weakness in some specific area of cognitive functioning. 2. Poor power of attention and concentration. 3. Lack of aptitude for a particular subject. 4. Lack of curiosity 5. Lack of eagerness to learn	1. Emotional insecurity Emotional 2. immaturity.	1. Unfavourable physical conditions. 2. Un favourable parental relations leading to tension and worries. 3. Inconsistent disciplinary methods. 4. Siblings relations and perental fondness for some children and indifference to others. 5. Lack of encouragement by parents to child's school work. 6. Frequent transfer of parents.	1. Neighbourhood social group norms. Peer influence	Discussed separately

Unhealthy School and Class-room Environment: This refers to the following:

1. Absence of social security.
2. Absence of emotional security.
3. Faulty curriculum.
4. Ineffective and uninspiring methods of teaching.
5. Authoritative and unsympathetic attitude of the teacher.
6. Faulty class-room organisation.
7. Lack of co-curricular activities.
8. Lack of equipment.
9. Overcrowded classes.
10. Lack of effective guidance and counselling.

The Difference

1. Use of intelligence tests.
2. Achievement tests.
3. Observation.
4. Parents view.
5. Socio-metric techniques.
6. Participation in co-curricular activities.

The Evaluation

Role of the Teacher: Curriculum would be the same for the under-achiever and the normal child. In the case of the under-achiever, the role of the teacher assumes special significance, He is expected to take the following measures to bring about achievement in the under-achiever:

1. All possible efforts should be made by the teacher not only in detecting of under-achievement but also in trying to understand the nature of the problem in each individual case. A child may be carefully observed in different situations. Relevant information about his development may be found out. Parents may also be contacted and consulted. The school counsellor, if any, may be approached to study the under-achiever. Thereafter a remedial programme suitable to child's needs may be prepared and implemented.

2. At the early stages, attempts should be made to lay the foundations of good work habits and attitudes in children.
3. Emotional support by teachers should be provided to children. This will help them in meeting the developmental tasks which are a part of their normal growth.
4. Tensions in child's environment should not be allowed to build up. Sympathy and patience should be the watch words.
5. Genuine interest in the welfare of the students should be taken.
6. A few periods per week should be set apart for a small group of under-achievers for solving their problems.
7. One or two periods per week may be devoted for individual counselling to such students.
8. The under-achiever should be encouraged at his performance and thus helped in building his self confidence.
9. Outlets for children's tensions through provision of play in the form of dramatics, games, sports and a varieties of other self expressive and creative activities should be provided.
10. Assignment should be adapted to the needs of students.
11. Special care should be taken to accept the under-achiever child as a unique individual. His particular needs should be immediately attended to.
12. Efforts may be made to re-establish child's confidence in himself.
13. Remedial work for the under-achievers should be undertaken.
14. Class teacher should seek the cooperation of other teachers and the parents of the under-achievers.
15. In case of deep-rooted emotional problems which lie at the root of under-achievement, referral may be made to a child guidance clinic after taking the parents into confidence.

10

The Younghood

The term adolescence is derived from a Latin word 'adolescence' meaning 'to grow', 'to mature'. Now this term primarily implies to emerge or to 'achieve identity'. It is very difficult to define exactly the period of life which constitutes adolescence. No sharp chronological boundaries may be fixed to this period. Generally speaking, it covers a period of seven or eight years, normally from 12 to 18 or 20 with large variations in many cases. Some children may manifest traits of its advent as early as the 10th year while others may manifest it till the fifteenth or sixteenth year. Twelve or thirteen may be considered as the normal period for boys in India and even for girls when adolescence begins.

Meaning and Concept

Adolescence is best defined in relation to puberty. This is the period which begins with puberty and ends with the general cessation of physical growth; it emerges from the later childhood stage and merges into adulthood.

According to G. R. Medinnus and R.C. Johnson, "Adolescence begins when signs of sexual maturity begin to occur in both physical and social development and ends when the individual has assumed adult roles and is concerned in most ways as an adult by his reference group."

A. T. Jersild observes, "Adolescence is that span of years during which boys and girls move from childhood to adulthood mentally, emotionally, socially and physically."

According to Dorthy Rogers, adolescence is "a process rather than a period, a process of achieving the attitudes and beliefs needed for effective participation in society."

The Hadow Report in England has described this stage as, "There is a tide which begins to rise in the veins of youth at the age of eleven or twelve. It is called by the name of adolescence. If the tide can be taken as flood, and a new voyage began in the stream and along the flow of its current, we think it will move on to fortune."

WHO defines adolescence both in terms of age (spanning the ages between 10 and 19 years) and in terms of a phase of life marked by special attributes. These attributes include:

- Rapid physical growth and development
- Physical, social and psychological maturity, but not all at the same time
- Sexual maturity and the onset of sexual activity
- Experimentation
- Development of adult mental processes and adult identity
- Transition from total socio-economic dependence to relative independence

To distinguish adolescents from other similar (and sometimes overlapping) age groupings, which however differ in these special characteristics, WHO has also defined youth and young people.

- Youth—persons between 15 and 24 years
- Young people—persons between 10 and 24 years

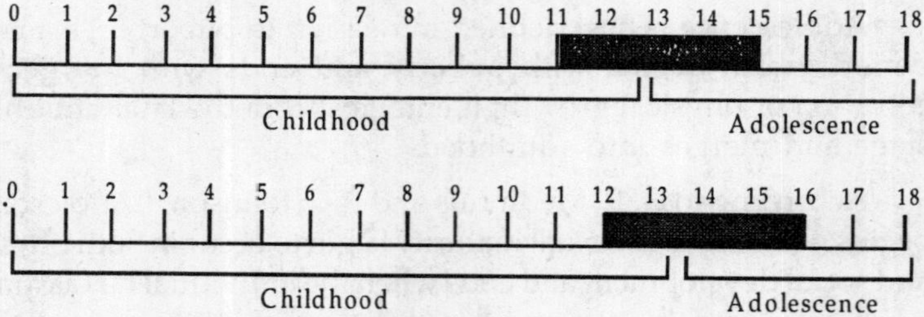

Fig. Puberty overlaps the end of childhood and the beginning of adolescence

Salient Features

1. The adolescent is a combination of opposites. Sometime he is an altruist and sometimes a miser. On the one hand, he behaves like a child in many ways and on the other hand he likes to be treated as an adult. He wants to have the privileges of adulthood but does not want to undertake its obligations and responsibilities.
2. The adolescent of lacks experience though he may exhibit a 'know-it-all' attitude.
3. He regards himself as more suited than the adults and grown- ups to frame rules, laws, codes and morals which will be just and true.
4. He is intensely emotional. He fluctuates between two extremes. He may be active and happy at one time and moody and dull at another.
5. He is seeking his own place in the life around him.
6. There is a strong tendency of self-assertion which is prominent owing to the new orientation which sets in life.
7. The adolescent wants to free himself from bondage. There is a tendency to revolt against authority.
8. The growth of intelligence reaches its maximum during this period.
9. The adolescent is extremely passionate for expressing his own opinions and appreciation.
10. A group of adolescents sets to practical work with Great zeal and works patiently.
11. He responds more readily to the influence of the teacher than of the parents.
12. There is unlimited admiration for some adult whom he considers to be outstanding. An adolescent is essentially a hero-worshipper.
13. There is interest in and emphasis on physical attractiveness and good grooming.
14. Girls are more interested in boys than boys are in girls; of course both are interested in the opposite sex.

15. In extreme cases, homosexuality (association with the same sex) is established.
16. An adolescent exhibits exuberant imagination. This period is characterized as a period of day-dreams.
17. He wants to form small groups or gangs.

·Specific Needs

Although in many respects, several needs of adolescence stage are similar to the needs of the other stages but they are quite different in the matter of intensity and forcefulness. The following chart illustrates the specific needs of the adolescence.

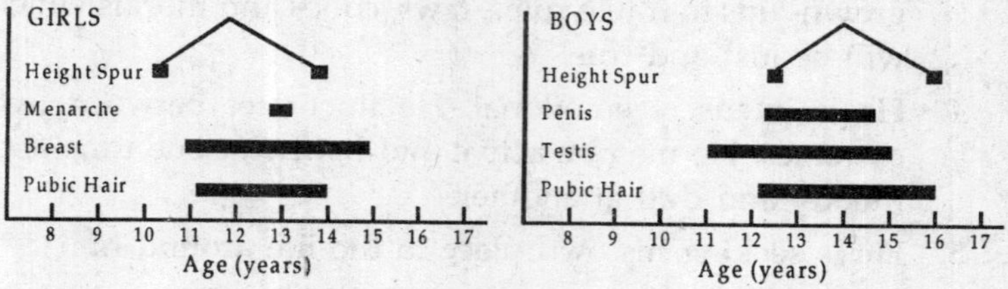

Fig. Pattern of Development of Secondary Sex Characteristics in Boys and Girls

Significant Specific Needs of the Adolescence

Physical Needs	*Social Needs*	*Emotional Needs*	*Intellectual Needs*	*Moral Needs*
1. Enough nutrition for physical development.	1. Acceptance in the society. 2. Suitable peers.	1. Heightened emotions. 2. Recognition of self identification.	1. Heightened curiosity. 2. Independent thinking.	1. Search for values. 2. Equality
2. Channels for the utilisation of abundant energy.	3. Adjustment in the group and society. 4. Equal treatment	3. Arousal of sexual emotions. 4. Development of confidence.		
3. Acquaintance with body development aspects.				
4. Sex				
5. Security				

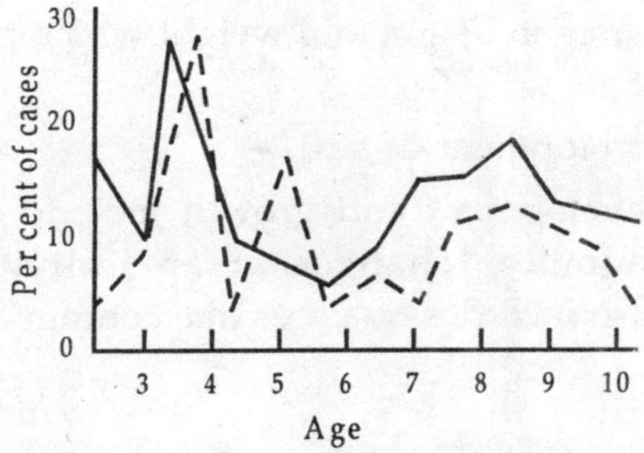

Fig. Irritability tends to increase early in puberty and then to decline

General Needs

Hall has very emphatically observed, "A ton of knowledge, bought at the expense of an ounce of health which is the most ancient and precious form of wealth and worth costs more than its value." Similar views have been expressed by Carlyle when he writes, "We manufacture clever devils by the thousand because health is not the object of party politics." Great seer Swami Vivekananda has also stressed the importance of well-built bodies when he remarks, "What India needs today is not the Bhagwad Gita but the football field." Our schools must give due importance to this aspect of education. W.M. Ryburn remarked "We need in Indian Education-a general philosophy of physical education-we need a conception of education in which physical education takes its rightful place and in which its vital importance is recognised."

A properly directed physical development programme should result in health, happiness, efficiency and character.

Health based Education

Physical education relating to physical development is that field of education which deals with muscle activities and their related responses. Physical development includes the following aspects:

(i) It is growth of nervous system.

(ii) It is growth of muscles.

(iii) It is functioning of glands.

(iv) It is change in height and weight which people normally observe.

(v) It is development of sex.

Physical development and growth include the physical as well as psychomotor changes in an individual. Physical development also includes qualities like courage, endurance and self-control.

Concept of Developmental Growth

At the adolescent stage, marked changes take place in the following domains:

(i) Height and weight.

(ii) Bodily proportions.

(iii) Change in voice.

(iv) Increase in motor performance.

(v) Sexual changes.

Sexual Changes: Sexual changes are very prominent during the period of adolescence.

(a) *Primary Sex Features*

1. Boys develop their sex organs.
2. Sex glands-the gonads-start producing sperms. Boys may suffer from night dreams.
3. The growth of sex glands among girls is not visible. The first menstrual flow is indicative of their sexual growth.

(b) *Secondary Sex Features*: These features are not related to sex organs but are indicative of sexual maturation which is a part of adolescence. These are different in the case of males and females. Among the males the features are:

(a) Growth of public hair around the sex organ,

(b) Hair in the arm pit, legs, arms and the chest,

(c) The growth of beard, and

(d) The tone of the voice deepens.

Among the girls the growth of sex organs is not visible. Other changes are:

(a) The development of breasts,

(b) Increase in the width of lips,

(c) A rounded appearance of body and limbs,

(d) Growth of pubic hair, and

(e) A shrill voice.

Sexual identity includes the expression of sexual needs and feelings and the acceptance or rejection of sex.

Adolescence period is the onset of puberty. Puberty implies a series of physical changes that make the organism capable of reproduction.

Puberty leads to sexual activity, erotic fantasy, experimentation and masturbation.

The period of puberty is a difficult one for most of the adults.

Physical Growth and Development: A programme of physical growth and development is not confined to the playground but should pervade the class-room and in fact the entire school programme. Physical development in the class-room may take the following forms:

1. Direct instruction emphasising the necessity of having a good physique may be given.
2. Suggestions regarding the maintenance of good health are very helpful:
3. Emphasis on right postures should be laid.
4. Provision of good seating and lighting arrangements in the class-room, thereby impressing upon them the importance of studying under healthy surroundings should be made.
5. Providing ample opportunities to the children for physical activity should be given its due importance.
6. Medical examination of school children by the school doctor should be made at suitable intervals.

7. Physical exercise for every child should be compulsory in the school.
8. Various activities promoting physical development should be well planned and children should be encouraged to take part in these activities.
9. Activities like woodwork, spinning and weaving, book binding, gardening etc. may be introduced in the school as a group project. Such activities will lead to motor development as well as promote cooperation, and emotional adjustment among students.
10. At this stage students also have sexual development. It is necessary for us to impart them sex education.
11. Teachers should be conversant with norms of motor development of the child.
12. A variety of co-curricular activities should be introduced to provide outlets for the development of emotions and instincts which have a close link with physical growth and development.

Summary: Montaigne has very aptly remarked, "Physical education does neither train up the soul nor body, but the whole man." Froebel rightly stated, "Early education must deal directly with the physical development and influence the spiritual development through the exercise of senses."

Mental Development and Emotions

Emotional development is one of the major aspects of adolescence growth and development. Not only adolescent's physical growth and development is linked with his emotional make-up but his aesthetic, intellectual, moral and social development is also controlled by his emotional development. To keep one's emotions under control and be able to conceal them is considered a mark of strong and balanced personality. Therefore, adolescents must be trained to control their emotions and achieve a mental balance and stability which will lead to individual happiness and social efficiency.

The term emotion is derived from the Latin term, 'emovere' which means 'to stir,' 'to agitate,' 'to move' or 'to excite.'

Woodworth, by making use of this explanation defined emotion in the following way: "Emotion is a 'moved' or 'stirred up' state of an organism. It is a stirred up state of feeling-that is the way it appears to the individual himself. It is a disturbed muscular and glandular activity-that is the way it appears to an external observer."

Crow and Crow have defined emotion in the following way: An emotion 'is an affective experience that accompanies generalized inner adjustment and mental and psychological stirred up states in the individual, and that shows itself in his overt behaviour.'

According to Kimball Young, "Emotion is the aroused psychological state of the organism marked by increased bodily activity and strong feelings directed to some subject.

How Emotions Work? All of us observe a large number of persons and objects in the world. We have some feelings for them in our mental make-up. Sometimes our feelings become strong either in favour or against the object or individual or an occasion. This disturbs our mental balance. This disturbance is known as Emotion. It not only disturbs our mind, but the entire organism. It is expressed in various movements and expressions of body and it tries to adjust to face the situation.

Important Factors

1. We have emotions due to our intensity of feeling. The depth of intensity differs from individual to individual.
2. The expression of emotions is universal in nature, i.e., it is found in all living beings.
3. Every individual has his own outlet of emotions in his own way.
4. Our expressions of emotions are related to a person, object, idea or work.
5. Sometimes the expression of emotion leads to the loss of thinking power.
6. Our emotional expression is related to our instinct.
7. Our emotions persist for sometime and then they disappear.

8. Expression of emotions leads to changes in our behaviour.
9. Emotions rise abruptly but die slowly.

A suitable educational programme needs to be developed to enable the adolescents to control their emotions and obtain a mental balance and stability which will mark for individual happiness and social efficiency.

Emotions can be suitably modified by the following mechanisms:

(i) Redirection
(ii) Sublimation
(iii) Catharsis
(iv) Inhibition

Active Forces

Some of the important factors which disturb the emotions of adolescents in school are:

1. Lack of security.
2. Economic disparities.
3. Faulty methods of teaching.
4. Fearful atmosphere in school.
5. Emotionally unbalanced teacher.
6. Traditional concept of discipline.
7. Poor physical conditions in schools.
8. Disregard of individual differences.
9. Lack of co-curricular activities.
10. Lack of sex education.
11. Faulty examination system.
12. Faulty curriculum.

Role of the School and the Teacher in satisfying the Needs of the Emotional Development of the Adolescent. Following are the ways for meeting the needs of the adolescents:

1. Providing equal treatment irrespective of considerations of wealth, status or gender of the adolescents.

2. Using dynamic and progressive methods of teaching-learning.
3. Love and affection on the part of the teacher to be made the basis of work.
4. Balanced emotional behaviour of the teacher himself.
5. Creative and democratic classroom and school discipline.
6. Healthy physical conditions in the school.
7. Due regard to individual differences of the adolescents.
8. Due regard to the individuality of the adolescents.
9. Adequate provision for a variety of co-curricular activities.
10. Provision of sex education.
11. Rich and varied curriculum.

Social Facets

Meaning of Social Development. Educators have defined social development in a number of ways.

Freeman and Showel observe, "Social development is the process of learning and conforming to group standards, mores and traditions and becoming imbued with a sense of oneness, inter-communication and cooperation."

H. E. Garret states, "Socialization or social development is the process whereby the biological individual is converted into a human person."

E.B. Hurlock thinks, "Social development means the attaining of maturity in social relationships."

Herbert Sorenson writes, "By social growth and development we mean increasing ability to get along well with oneself and others."

Thus social development refers to the process of development by which a child acquires the necessary attitudes, skills and values that make him an acceptable member of the group to which he belongs.

Characteristics of Social Development: Following are the important characteristics of social development during adolescence:

1. Adolescence is marked with too much sex consciousness resulting in sexual social relationships.
2. During adolescence loyalty becomes very much pronounced and adolescents are in a mood to sacrifice their selfish interests for the greater cause of the group, society and nation.
3. Adolescence stage is often marked with increased friendly relationships.
4. Emotional behaviour of the adolescent dominates his social characteristics and qualities.
5. There is too much diversity in the adolescents regarding their social interests.

To sum up, we may say that the adolescence is a period of maximum social awareness, increasing and intimate social relationships.

Factors Affecting Social Development: Important factors are given below:

Personal Factors: These include:

(i) Physical strength and health,

(ii) Level of intelligence,

(iii) Emotional set up.

Environmental Factors: These comprise :

(1) Family environment,

(2) Social and physical environment of the school,

(3) Peer group relationships and gang influence,

(4) Community environment,

(5) Social clubs,

(6) Mass media.

According to T.P. Joseph, an adolescent wants a friend 'someone to be trusted', 'someone to talk', 'someone who is dependable.'

Harrocks and Benimoff observe regarding the peer influence on the adolescence as, "The peer group is the adolescent's real world, providing him a stage upon to try himself and others.'

Atmosphere in School

The function of the school has considerably changed in the rapidly changing civilizations. The traditional function of imparting the basic skills of the three R's is now no longer considered to be adequate to meet the present challenge. The present day school has also to perform some of the functions of the family. It must develop certain desirable social habits. It is through co-curricular and extracurricular activities that the task of social development can be achieved more successfully. It is only the sympathetic understanding and sincere desire of the teacher to act positively in an un-prejudicial manner that can help.

Class in the Process of Socialization: Class provides innumerable opportunities to the adolescents to move and mix with other groups. This is the beginning of the social development of the child. Here children get many chances to mix without any distinction of caste, colour or creed. The teachers are expected to be vigilant to ensure that the students do not think in terms of untouchability, caste distinction and other prejudices.

Role of the Teacher in Social Development: A teacher can play a vital role in the social development of adolescent under his change. He exerts a great influence upon the development of the personality of the adolescent.

Following are the important suggestions for the social development of the adolescent:

1. Adolescents may be taken from time to time to public places like museums, courts and places of historical importance etc. to observe social interaction.
2. People engaged in different economic activities or vocations may be invited to school for giving a description of what they do and how useful their work is to the nation. This will enable the adolescents to be acquainted with those around them in the society.
3. Work experience will enable the adolescents to have first hand experiences of the activities pursued in farms and factories.
4. Adolescents should be acquainted with the social events like the celebration of the birthdays of leaders.

5. The school programme should be full of numerous co-curricular and curricular activities in which adolescents meet, cooperate and learn from each other's personality.
6. The introduction of common school dress, common lunch, etc., in the schools will prevent adolescents of poor and lower middle classes from facing inferiority complex due to the ego of the children of the well-to-do families.
7. Teachers and parents may encourage the adolescent to mix in inter-caste and regional groups.
8. The teachers and the parents should respect the personality of adolescents.
9. The mechanism of praise and blame, reward and punishment should be carefully used for the social development of the adolescents.
10. Appropriate social education may be provided to the parents so that they understand the significance of the social development of the adolescents.
11. The teachers should demonstrate democratic outlook.
12. Community activities like camps, common meals, social services etc., should be frequently organised.
13. There should be a close cooperation between the teachers and parents on matters relating to the proper social development of the adolescents.
14. Adequate stress may be laid on group activities.
15. Stories depicting self-sacrifices made by great men for the cause of general good may be told to adolescents so that they are motivated to rise above petty gains and work for the betterment of the humanity.
16. The teachers should not show any discrimination. They must ensure a safe and healthy social development in which the adolescents may imbibe desirable values of freedom, equality, integrity, honesty, patriotism etc.

Concluding Remarks: The task of social development of the adolescent is not an easy one. The educational thinkers point out very emphatically that certain conditions in the learning-teaching situation must be created and made available in the school so that it may become an effective instrument of social development. These conditions are:

(i) A democratic social climate in the school;
(ii) Effective interpersonal relationships;
(iii) Motivated learning situations;
(iv) Group methods of teaching;
(v) Social discipline;
(vi) School-community inter-relationships;
(vii) Student participation and involvement in the school management;
(viii) A rich programme of co-curricular activities.

Requirements

Meaning of Intellectual Development: Mental or intellectual development implies the growth and development of those abilities and capacities of the adolescents that enable them to accomplish a task that needs complex cognitive abilities and enable them to adjust their behaviour to the ever changing environmental conditions. Cognitive abilities include abilities like sensation, perception, imagination, memory, reasoning, understanding, generalisation, interpretation, problem-solving and decision-making etc. In fact the most part of the school programmes relates to mental developments.

Characteristics of the Mental Development of the Adolescents: The adolescents learn to reason and seek answer to 'how' and 'why' of every thing rationally and scientifically. Power of critical thinking and observation is much developed. They are more creative and inquisitive. They are almost critical of everything. They develop a lot of imagination. This becomes the beginning of the artist, inventor, philosopher, poet and writer etc. in the adolescent. An adolescent tends to become day-dreamer.

Factors Affecting Intellectual Development: Intellectual development of the adolescent in the school is affected by curricular and co-curricular programme, teaching-learning environment, and the role of the teachers.

Measures for the Satisfaction of Intellectual Needs or Intellectual Development of the Adolescents: Among the important factors are:

(i) Provision of rich curriculum.
(ii) Provision of streaming.
(iii) Provision of varied activities like debates and discussions.
(iv) Provision of socialised teaching.
(v) Project work related to subjects.
(vi) Subject related educational tours.
(vii) Library and reading room facilities.
(viii) Problem solving teaching-learning.
(ix) Challenging questions.
(x) Exploratory activities.

Moral Development

***Meaning of Moral Development*:** By morality we mean conformity to the moral code of the social group. The term comes from the Latin word 'mores', meaning manners., customs or folkways. To act in a moral way means to act in conformity to group standards of conduct. Morality also includes a sense of right or wrong-a behaviour which has to do with the conscience of the individual. Moral behaviour is learnt. Moral standards vary from group to group depending upon what has been accepted by the group as the socially approved behaviour. True morality comes from within the individual. It is internal in nature and not imposed by external authority. Immoral behaviour is that behaviour which is unfavourable to the group.

Bowley and others are of the view that a person of moral character has the following qualities:

(i) Self-control,
(ii) Reliability,
(iii) Persistence in action,
(iv) Industry,
(v) Feeling of responsibility,
(vi) Consciousness.

Several thinkers equate morality with character.

B. N. Jha has stated that character is "a mental factor of the individual, which determines his social behaviour. It is a mental organisation which lies at the back of all his connotations."

A person of character has the following characteristics in his behaviour:

(a) He is firm and not impulsive in his behaviour.

(b) He is not dominated by others in his actions.

(c) He has a strong sense of self-respect and is governed by his self-regarding sentiment.

(d) He is intelligent and cheerful in his behaviour.

(e) He is hard working and faces difficulties with courage and optimism.

(f) He is idealistic in his approach. His inner and outer self is dominated by some ideals.

Role of the School Environment: Behaviours and norms adopted in the immediate environment influence the adolescent in shaping his moral behaviour. It is very unfortunate that generally elders observe double standards of morality. We hardly practice what we preach. These double standards are observed by adolescents. It is, therefore, very essential that elders set high standards of morality.

Role of the Teacher: It has been stressed again and again that nothing can be more helpful in moulding the adolescent's moral behaviour than the teacher's own conduct. A teacher has to set a high standard of moral behaviour before the adolescent.

The school plays a very important role in the moral development of the adolescent. Through the organisation of various curricular and co-curricular activities, teachers can foster among children various moral qualities. In the teaching of different subjects like languages and social studies etc., teacher may stress moral qualities like love, sacrifice, self-control, truthfulness and uprightness, etc. Social service programmes should be undertaken on a large scale. Self government may be organised.

A comprehensive programme of guidance and counselling needs to be organised.

11

Motivational Approaches

Motivation as a term is both a fascinating and frustrating subject in the field of educational psychology. It is fascinating because all of us are engaged in something or the other most of the time. A child is playing, a girl is singing, a medical student is preparing to be a doctor, a social worker is helping his fellow men, a philosopher is discussing and thinking and a politician is planning for elections. The reason for such acts is motivation. Motivation makes a fascinating game in which all individuals are engaged, though sometimes it is right and sometimes it is wrong.

Motivation is also frustrating because we at times wonder about our own motives. How many times have we all had the sad experience of having to say to ourselves, "Why did I do that?" "It's not like me; I don't do things like that". We may have been unaccountably rude to the bus driver on the way to town; we may have spent some of our savings foolishly; or on a hard day, the cat got in our way and we kicked it. We realize that we must have been motivated to act as we did but what were our motives and why?

Salient Features

In vocabulary of psychology, we come across hundreds of words which refer to motivation: "wants", "striving", "desire", "need", "motive", "goal", "aspiration", "drive", "wish", "aim", "ambition", "hunger", "thirst", "love", "revenge", etc. If we try to define we can define them differently, but their meanings overlap so much that it is difficult to maintain uniformity. It is a process by which an individual is "inspired, goaded or coaxed to do something". It is one of the most important conditions which aid learning. The psycho-physiological construct implies the individual to achieve his predetermined goal(s). Bhatia confirms: "To motivate is to induce movement". Motivation, then, must be considered as the process by which a child may be prepared to respond to situations which are directed towards the achievement of objectives. Motivation is a broad-based term and encompasses many aspects of behaviour. It might be designated as "the tendency for the direction and selectivity of behaviour to be controlled by the conditions to consequences and the tendency of this behaviour to persist until a goal is achieved". Motivation is purposive; without the presence of goals this process may not start at all.

Learning in Classroom

Every human behaviour is motivated. Without motive a living being cannot move even a step ahead. In other words, behaviour of men is controlled by some motives. The teacher, in order to make his teachings effective should have a good knowledge of motivation and its effect on learning. Science of motivation teaches a teacher how to motivate a student to learn. It also helps him to study individual difference among students. Learning is a behaviour which is aroused by a wish of fulfilling a necessity. In the same way learning is also a goal-oriented activity. Several factors contributing for its success are - environment, mental set-up of the learner and skill of the teacher. Teaching is fulfilled in a disciplined environment, backed by a strong motivation of the students. It is difficult to teach without any knowledge about motivation. It arouses interest of learners and makes them attentive and interested.

Motivational Aspects

The word motivation has been derived from the Latin word 'mover' meaning to put into action or to move. So it is the process of arousing movement in the organism. The process that puts the organism into physiological or psychological action, and by which man is able to fulfill his needs and desires is called motivation. According to psychologist Woodsworth, "motivation is the activity in progress."

Motivation supplies the human being with energy to act. Discussing from this point of view we know that learning is impossible without motivation. Motivation is an internal process. We can understand the nature of motivation by observing the behaviour of an organism. According to McDonald, motivation is change of a power structure in a human being which is related to stimulus and reaching a goal. From this definition we come to know about three dimensions of motivation.

Motivation takes its origin from the change in energy level.

Motivation is an inspiration that affects the personality. By it, psychic tension is aroused.

Motivation is backed by a desire to reach a goal.

Other psychologists have also tried to define motivation in their own way. They are mentioned below:

Atkinson defined motivation as, "the arousal of tendency to act to produce one or more effects". D.O. Hebb holds that the term motivation refers:

(i) to existence of an organised phase sequence.

(ii) to its direction and content.

(iii) to its persistence in given direction or stability of content.

Maslow has advanced the theory of hierarchy of needs ranging from basic physiological needs to self-actualization. According to him, "motivation is constant, never ending, fluctuating and complex and that it is an almost universal characteristic of particularly every organismic state of affairs".

According to H.W. Bernard "motivation refers to all those phenomena which are involved in the stimulation of action towards particular objectives where previously there was little or no movement towards these goals".

Motivation refers to a definite set of mind of the child which inspires him to reach his goal. So it is the duty of the teacher to motivate the student to develop in the learning process, that would enable him to reach a higher goal in his future life.

The Ramifications

Motivation begins with drives and ends with adjustments. The *Oxford Dictionary* defined a motive as "that which moves or includes a person to act in a certain way, a desire, fear or other emotion or a consideration of a reason which influences or tends to influence a person's volition, also often applied to a contemplated result of object, the desire of which tends to influence volition." In ordinary sense motivation is an internal energy which enfuels us to carry out an intention. Our intentions may be varied and one's intention may differ from another. Hence motives have been used in different senses. It has broadly been classified into two categories. They are:

1. *Primary Physiological Motives:* They are hunger, thirst, pain, sex, impulse, etc.
2. *Secondary Psychological Motives:* This includes wishes for social status, approbation, authority over others, etc.

But this two way classification is not final and universal. Psychologists have put forth their own classifications. Again this classification is not clear cut. For example, though sexual drives are included in the first category, it depends much on social status and social consciousness of the individual. Some other psychologists have classified motive into three categories such as:

(i) Physiological motives,

(ii) Social motives,

(iii) Personal motives. Shatter has divided it into four classes. They are motives of security, motives to reply, motives of agreement and motives of new experience. In another classification motives have been divided into self-respect, security, social value, self-importance, social identification and socialisation etc.

Diverse Dimensions

Needs, drive and incentives are the building blocks of the structure of motivation. It is a complex phenomenon which is influenced by multiple variables operating within the organism and in the environment. A number of psychological and physiological factors are involved in motivation. Emotion also affects motivation. Emotional states act as drives and they can reinforce motive in progress. Likewise, habits, mind-set, values and attitudes of the individual also influence motivational process. We will discuss what role the three important factors (needs, drives and incentives) play in motivating an individual to act.

(a) *Needs:* Men have countless needs and most of them have to be met with in order to make the existence of a human being possible on the earth. Some needs such as love, pity, anger, affection, etc, are emotional. In the same way, social needs are there and they include social status, fame, respect, etc. Man adopts various methods to fulfill his various social needs. For example, a hungry man strives for food, and adopts various methods to get food for himself. Here changes occur in his behaviour. Psychologist Maslow has categorised the needs into six groups.

1. *Physical Needs:* They are bare necessities of life like food, water, air, rest, house, work, etc.
2. *Security and Needs of Self-defence:* Endeavours to do away with misery, helplessness, incapabilities etc.
3. *Emotional and Mental Requirements:* Love, affection, pity, sympathy etc.
4. *Social Needs:* To establish one's ownself in society.
5. Aesthetic needs
6. Needs of self-realisation.

(b) *Drives:* Man lives in an uncertain stage, if his needs are not fulfilled. He tries to get rid of such a situation. He tries one method or the other. The stage of uncertainty supplies him with energy, drive and skill to get over his difficulties. Drives help man to be active.

(c) *Incentive:* Every organism is influenced by his environment. Many factors of environment that attract him and others leave a distaste in him. These factors also control his behaviour. They fulfill various physical needs and brings internal satisfaction to a human being. While teaching new lessons the teacher should take into cognizance the necessities of the students and should take the help of incentives, because in order to be effective the teaching process should be interesting. So this method should be applied in classroom teachings. The factors of environment which enables the learner to learn better are called incentives.

Diverse Methods

Learning is not possible without motivation. For better learning, the teacher should arouse interest in the students. Motives make a work to be started. When the student completes a task, he becomes satisfied. Then he argues and at times receives advice from others. It is because success in one learning experience motivates him to take into hand another task. He wants to master it and wants to become an expert. He is motivated to learn values. Hence some steps should be adopted in the classroom teaching to motivate the students. They are discussed below.

1. *Reward and Punishment:* Reward is the best incentive to make the student an expert. It arouses interest in him and motivates him to master the skill. But educationists differ on this point. Some of them opine that reward deviates students from their goal. They forget it and act in their own way. Reward is an outer factor, and self-actualization is not possible by it.

   Some educationists profess punishments to be the better method to correct the wrong behaviour of students. Correcting a wrong behaviour leads to learning of correct behaviour. But mere physical punishment is harmful and hence should be avoided. The teacher should be aware of that. The student should know the cause of his punishment. Only by this can he try to correct his wrong behaviour.

   Reward is a tool of motivation, not its aim. But in schools

teachers often use it as the goal and that is why aims of education are not met with any success. Reward leaves a negative effect on the child. Overuse of the method of reward makes the child think that he is coming to school only to get reward and not to learn.

2. *Praise and Insult:* Praise is a commonly used motivation in classroom teaching. Praise works better than insult or blame. All types and all grades of students gain from it. But the teacher should be cautious about it. In case of small children, criticism and insult works better.

   Praise is required more for average students than for a genius. Again it works better in case of girls than in case of boys. Psychologists view that workability of praise or insult depends upon how the teacher manipulates these. But it is the duty of parents and teachers alike to motivate the child to learn by praising and appreciating his right moves and achievements. Blame or insult is generally negative in character. It hampers learning of all types of students. The extroverts often succumb to insult and show better results by its application. But it should never be applied to introvert students. Here loss is more than gain. To apply this principle, the teacher should come personally in contact with the student, and then find out the way to steer his behaviour by applying praise or insult.

3. *Competition:* Competitive attitude is advantageous both inside the classroom and outside it. It is a powerful source of motivation. It makes the child not only to reach his destination sooner, but also to show a better performance beyond expectation. Competition is of two types; individual or personal competition and group competition. The first yields better result than the second. But over-competition gives rise to pride and egoism. Emotions like jealousy, hatred, aggressiveness take their origin from it. There is no doubt that competition accelerates learning process but over-competition makes the student deviate from social norms. From this point of view group competition is encouraged in school curriculum. Above all, the teacher should be careful in handling this method to motivate students.

4. *Knowledge of Progress:* It is an important source, of motivation. When the student knows about his success and progress he is motivated to learn more and better, because his interest is heightened. It also helps him in correcting his mistakes. So progress of the child should be intimated to him from time to time.
5. *Knowledge of Achievement:* The student should set his own goal in learning. Again they should know the nature and aim of the subject they are taught. In modern educational system, aim of education is fixed by the education committee and students toil for it. Their achievements are judged by teachers and the committee. But this achievement should be informed to the students. They should know the outcome of their labour. It supplies them with inspiration and motivates them for further learning. So in every school progress report of examinations are supplied to the students. In these reports the ultimate limit of their progress should be mentioned. Again, for periodical evaluation of students, a standard should be adopted in schools. Questions for such evaluations should be objective and purposeful. After evaluation the student should know his result.
6. *Novelty:* Analysis and change in age old curriculum is necessary to bring novelty to it. Children love to see new things. So instead of changing the subject matter in toto, something new can be added to it. It arouses their interest. Mixture of something new with old materials brings satisfaction to life process of human beings. This truth should not be forgotten by the teacher. Not only the books should be novel in appearance, but also the method of teaching should be changing in nature. The child becomes interested and his attention is centered when he finds a new thing in his subject He is motivated to learn the whole of the subject for the sake of that small new portion.
7. *Audio-visual Apparatus:* Teaching, solely by lecture method is not so much effective as teaching by audio-visual aids. Teaching must be interesting all the time So in modern

teaching system, the scientific tools are considered a great help to motivate students.

8. *Interest:* It is the most interesting factor of motivation. Children are curious by nature and want to know everything they come across. Their interest sometimes bores and irritates the elders. But the teacher should have patience and describe the things they want to know. Teaching and learning should not be exclusively book-oriented. Writing, singing, and acting should accompany reading books and listening to lectures of the teacher. This is known as multidimensional activities of the teacher.
9. *Self-importance:* Every individual is aware of his self-respect and so he does not allow his personality to be run down before others. If anything hampers his respect his mental stability becomes imbalanced. Feeling of self-importance is a social requirement. The teacher should take necessary steps to secure this in the student. If the student is aware of his own self he is motivated to learn better in order to maintain the standard of his personality.

An analysis of the above methods shows that motivation plays an important role in learning. But it depends a lot on the teacher who studies the environment, energy, calibre and choice of the students. There are some suggestions put forth by psychologists in order to motivate the students.

1. The students should be aware of what he is learning and what is the practical applicability of the learning material.
2. New method of teaching should be based on old system of education. It should not deviate from the old norms of education.
3. The learning material should be arranged in order and organised in a definite way. It should be in the ascending order of difficulty.
4. The student should not be under pressure and he should not be compelled to master a particular lesson.
5. Reward should not be given in terms of any object. It should be symbolic and signify his development.

6. A student should not be punished for his wrong response. The teacher can explain him his error and show him the right way. Punishments should be given only at the time of changing a particular behaviour.
7. The teacher should intimate the student about all his achievements.
8. Competition should be conducted groupwise. It should not touch personal life.

Above all, the role of the teacher is the most important. He is the friend, philosopher and guide to the student. So he should try his best to motivate students which will ensure their journey to the goal of their life.

Psychological Approach

A course in educational psychology can be justified as part of the teacher-preparation sequence only as it leads to an improvement in the effectiveness with which the teacher carries out the work of promoting the growth and development of the child. Throughout the chapters of this text, various psychological principles have been considered against the background of the work of the classroom. This chapter will attempt to pinpoint some of the more important applications and implications of these principles particularly as they relate to the organisation of educational experiences by means of which the maximum self-realisation of the whole child is to be promoted. The student must not expect prescriptions and rules of thumb: this book promised none, will give none! Further—more, it must be understood that the present chapter makes no claim to a complete coverage of the implications of psychology for educational practice. The discussion will be restricted to a few of the highlights and the student is urged to review the material covered in the various chapters not as something to learn for a final examination but rather as a foundation upon which educational practice must be based.

Potential Perceptions

Education has undergone drastic changes since the turn of the century. Great progress in both educational thought and educational practice has resulted from such influences as (a) the contribution of educational psychology, especially in the area of a greater understanding of the nature of the learner and of the learning process, and (b) sociological changes leading to a new concept of the role of the school in modern democratic society. The net results, although not amenable to a succinct synthesis, are probably best reflected in the reorientation of educational practice toward the all-around growth of the child as opposed to an emphasis on any given aspect at the expense of the others as was characteristic of the school of yesteryear. What is more, modern schools—and modern teachers—here and there throughout the country not only exemplify the latest philosophical and psychological thinking put into practice, but also earn public recognition and respect through the caliber of the services they provide and of the product they turn out.

Yet along side this modernism that characterises certain schools and certain teachers, there exist throughout our country, schools and teachers whose Rip Van Winkle organisation and procedures are not only woefully ineffective but—worse—are definitely detrimental to the all-around growth of the unfortunate children who are subjected to their influence.

Ironically, much of the harm done to children comes at the hands of teachers and administrators whose sincerity cannot be doubted—who are fully convinced that they are acting in the child's best interest—but whose lack of under-standing of the basic principles of psychology and of education makes them, nonetheless—and no less—an undeniable hazard to the maximum self-realisation of countless children. Thus, daily, well-meaning teachers force children to participate in exercises in which they have no interest, push children to do things which are completely beyond their abilities, who berate, scold, nag, and fail them because students cannot meet their unrealistic standards, and who punish them when, in final desperation at this constant frustration of their needs, children misbehave. All this, because of a firm belief that hard work is good for anyone and that "if they tried hard enough, they could do it." Anyway, the content of the curriculum has to be covered—regardless of the cost! These teachers are apparently unfamiliar with such fundamental psychological concepts as the difficulties imposed by intellectual and experiential limitations, the complications caused by emotional blocking, and the negative attitudes that result from coercion, to name but a few.

In the same way, many teachers (perhaps not entirely well-meaning) are apparently under the impression that, unless children are driven with a whip like tigers in a circus act, the quality of their performance will be impaired, and that children will neither work nor behave unless kept under the constant threat of failure and punishment. So they would never think of giving a compliment for work well done, for fear the child will immediately rest on his laurels; but, on the other hand, they never miss an opportunity to criticise (presumably, as a way of building moral fiber and a striving for perfection). And the sad part is that these teachers feel they are doing their duty. That they might accomplish more by trying to understand the child and his problems and by encouraging him to do his best than by trying to crush him and to downgrade his self-concept, it seems, hasn't dawned on them!

Paralleling these inexcusable violations of the principles of educational psychology—or perhaps, more correctly, because of this failure on the part of certain teachers, who are supposedly psychologically trained persons, to comply with the principles of educational psychology in dealing with the child—our schools have not been overly successful in promoting his growth. As we have seen in the chapters on adjustment and mental health as well as in the discussion of social and emotional maturity and the concept of enlightened self-interest, the products being turned out of our educational institutions considered as a whole fall considerably short of perfection. However, since the school cannot be expected to shoulder the whole blame for failure in these areas, we may more appropriately evaluate the extent of its relative success in promoting academic growth since this is one area where whatever credit or blame is due can, to a greater extent, be attributed to the efforts of the school.

Empirical evidence points rather conclusively to the fact that, no matter from what point of view we look at the work being done in the classroom, we invariably find little cause for rejoicing. This, of course, does not pertain to all teachers, or even to all schools, for some are doing an outstanding job: it does, however, apply to the majority and this is the standard by which parents and the general public measure our worth. Many critics have lambasted our educational institutions for their ineptitude and, whereas these criticisms are not always completely warranted, they are, nevertheless, not entirely without foundation. In fact, even such objective observers as Mursell and Burton mince no words in pointing out that our efforts have been anything but successful. Thus, Mursell not only gives examples of teaching in direct violation of the principles of educational psychology but goes on to say that these examples are, unfortunately, typical of many of our present educational practices.

Among the many examples of inefficiency and malpractice in the classroom which can be noted by any impartial observer who looks into the problem, one might mention the following:

(a) Much of the activities of the classroom consist of verbal discussions and descriptions with a heavy reliance on abstract and technical language. The logical outcome in too many cases is verbalism piled on verbalism, frustration, gradual disinterest, apathy, and misbehaviour. Thus, the child's knowledge of grammar does not lead to an improvement in his oral and written work, the teaching of science is often formalised and systematised into intellectual units which have no relation to his daily experience and interest, mathematics is rarely brought down to the level at which he can understand it let alone use it in living, and social studies are often taught in the abstract so that it is completely foreign to the problems he faces in everyday life.

(b) The unsuitable curriculum which dominates some of our schools interferes with promotion of the maximum self-realisation of the child both directly through the nature of the learning experiences it contains and indirectly through the shackling of the teacher and the consequent encouragement of ineffective teaching methods. The curriculum in the great majority of our schools is a subject curriculum; in many cases, according to Burton, it is a textbook curriculum "tragically unrelated to life needs" not only for children but also for adults, "for immediate and remote needs of anyone, anywhere, at any time." Under such conditions there can be no good teaching. Page assignments to a single text followed by a verbal quiz and drill aimed at the memorisation of facts— with no other aim than covering the text—is used by the "great majority" of secondary school teachers even though, again to quote Burton, "It would be difficult to devise an educational practice so grossly ineffective, so certainly calculated to interfere with learning..." Many of our schools still rely on such potentially damaging measures as coercion, competition, and punishment as a means of pushing meaningless material on defenseless children. As a result, the things that stand out in too many of our schools are lack of motivation, satisfaction with mediocrity and getting by, a great interest in "cinch" courses, and "goofing-off."

Schools exist for the purpose of providing meaningful experiences through which the growth of the child can be promoted most effectively. No one denies the fact that the child can—and does—learn many useful and important things out of school. However, such out-of-school experiences tend to be haphazard, uncoordinated, and not sufficiently organised and concentrated for society to be able to depend upon them for educating the child. School cannot be like life: it is precisely because of the failure of ordinary life experiences to provide a suitable education that schools have been established. Schools exist for the purpose of selecting those experiences that are worthwhile and meaningful to the child, of bringing them into vital relationship with him so that he can integrate them in a functional way, and guiding him in his reactions to these experiences so that they will be effective from an educational point of view.

The Syllabus

The sequence of experiences through which the school attempts to promote the growth of the child is known as the curriculum. Ideally, the curriculum should incorporate the best experiences one could devise to further his growth and development and its importance in the promotion of this growth can, therefore, not be minimised. In fact, a poor curriculum (in the sense of emphasising the unimportant at the expense of the essentials, of emphasising the unattainable and the useless, of being unrealistic) would automatically negate the very purpose for which the school exists.

Most, if not all, experiences are educative in the broad sense of the word. However, some experiences, even though educative, are detrimental from the standpoint of long-term growth of the learner. Also to be considered is the fact that a great many experiences which are educative in the beneficial sense can be found and that, if time were unlimited, the child could become educated by simply being exposed to them all— or at least to a large proportion of them. But time is not unlimited and the school, if it is to fulfill its responsibility to society, must choose among the many experiences to which the child could be subjected those that are likely to result in the maximum growth at the minimum expense in terms of his time and effort. Just what these experiences are is, of course, a matter of considerable disagreement.

The experiences incorporated into the curriculum are simply the vehicle through which desirable learning takes place and it is the learning that counts rather than the experience through which it is achieved. Yet, for all the talk about teaching the child (and not subject-matter), it is still a psychological fact that children learn only through the medium of subject-matter, *i. e.*, through the experiences to which they have reacted, for learning takes place as a result of the learner's responses and the latter occur only as a result of stimulation. Thus, subject matter is incidental to learning and the study of history or algebra is worthwhile to the child only to the extent to which it enables him to do something which is purposeful to him. The question is not one of teaching the child algebra or any other subject but rather of choosing the sequence of experiences that will promote in the most effective way the learning he needs for self-realisation. In this area, the science of psychology can make a definite contribution.

What to include in the curriculum is first of all a problem of educational philosophy as we have pointed out. Educational psychology also has a definite role to play in determining this curriculum: whether or not Latin or physical education should be emphasised in our schools, for example, centers around the extent to which the disciplinary and direct values of each in promoting child growth are greater than those of other experiences competing for inclusion in the curriculum. Likewise, whether the curriculum should be oriented toward the more formal aspects or those more closely related to the childs' experience cannot be considered apart from the effectiveness with which such learnings can take place.

Generally speaking, the long term goals of education, *e. g.*, ability to think clearly, a scientific attitude, tolerance, and social competence are a matter of educational philosophy. On the other hand, the more immediate goals and the means whereby both short-and long-range goals are attained are more properly the province of educational psychology. Thus, whether the teacher conducts a unit on sanitation, transportation, or city government as a means of promoting learning in the area of number work, reading comprehension, or civic responsibility is probably best decided on the basis of psychological rather than philosophical considerations simply because the extent to which an experience is truly educative depends upon such psychological factors as the child's interest, goals, and needs. Likewise, if one has to choose between two equally important goals to be achieved through the curriculum, preference might be given to the one which, according to the principles of educational psychology is relatively more attainable or functional—or both.

The school must constantly reevaluate not only its methods but also its curriculum in the light of changing social and philosophical thought and especially in the light of new discoveries in the area of educational psychology. On the other hand, it must not initiate changes simply for the sake of change. Teachers are not believers in doing things by halves: when convinced that a suggested procedure is better than a present one, they are likely to make a complete shift without realising that perhaps the solution lies in a middle-of-the-road position—and educational procedures have a long history of pendulum like shifts over the years—from a completely phonetic approach to a total disregard for phonics, from rigid drill procedures to an easy going curriculum dictated by the whims and fancies of immature children, from a rigid teacher-controlled classroom atmosphere to a pupil-dominated state of classroom disorganisation.

Some of these changes have come in response to the demands of the public that certain courses be offered in the school (*e.g.*, sex education) or that a greater or lesser emphasis be placed on a certain phase of the curriculum because of its alleged importance or unimportance. Thus, statistics on the physical inadequacies of the American youth inducted into service during World War II led to an increased emphasis on physical education in schools only to have it cede to science and mathematics as a result of the clamor of scientists that accompanied the Russian Sputnik. Generally, Americans consider themselves practical and, in contrast to the European idea of the finishing school and the gentleman scholar, tend to emphasise the practical and even the vocational as opposed to the cultural and the theoretical. Likewise, there tends to be a more or less persistent demand for the specific and the tangible as opposed to the general—a trend which has met with considerable favour among harried teachers eager to meet the demands of still another emphasis in American education, namely, adequate objective performance on various tests of academic achievement.

Some of the demands made upon the school have come from professional educators and psychologists and have been based on sound research evidence. Thus, a greater emphasis on the "life adjustment" curriculum more closely related to the everyday life of citizens in a democracy—as opposed to the more abstract and classical curriculum has roots in the thinking of such educational and psychological leaders as Dewey, Thorndike, and others. On the other hand, pressures have also been applied by various groups for a return to a curriculum or to methods which do not make psychological or pedagogical sense. And, unfortunately, rather than attempt to educate the public, schools have at times given way to these demands despite the fact that, in the final analysis, the only important consideration is the welfare of the child. The effect of public pressures is evident in many classroom procedures and methods: thus, fear of public censure has made schools cautious in their adoption of newer techniques of classroom management, of teaching, reading, of dealing with the whole child, and of differentiated treatment of children with different abilities and background.

Indeed, the fact that we still grade children and report their progress on the old-fashioned report card, that we regulate our assignment of homework to the wishes of parents whom we have never bothered to educate is hardly indicative of professional status on the part of the teacher who ought to know what is in the child's best interest and who ought to be willing to exercise leadership in school matters rather than relinquish it to the school board, the PTA, or the general public. This is not to imply that all public pressures have been misdirected and that the school should not be sensitive to the needs of society as reflected in public opinion. It is simply that teachers need to be reasonably convinced of the desirability of the changes advocated before making them.

The Concept of Traditionalism vs. Progressivism : The curriculum represents the content by means of which the school stimulates the child's growth. It is, however, necessary for the curriculum to which the child is subjected to be broken down into units for, obviously, it cannot be assimilated as a whole. This breakdown can be done in various combinations of two major ways:

(a) the subject-matter organisation in which learning is arranged around some central topic logically organised and generally selected in advance by the curriculum-maker to fit the school on a local or even a statewide basis;

(b) the experience organisation centering on problems related to the desire of students in a class to satisfy some need or achieve some purpose.

These two approaches are not entirely independent and separate: certainly all curriculum units incorporate both subject-matter and experience. Likewise, both can result—and have resulted—in desirable outcomes. Since these approaches in their extremes represent extremes in philosophical and psychological orientation, a study of their major contrasts is of interest and value here.

Whereas the differences in the two approaches involve many facets that defy easy synthesis, the major difference lies in their orientation. The subject-matter approach is teacher-centered; it is predicated on the assumption that it is the function of adults to (a) select and organise the content, (b) present the material, (c) direct the learning, (d) measure the results, and (e) diagnose difficulties and provide remedial work where indicated. There is an implict assumption that unless teachers organise, teach, prod and test, the child will learn little or nothing. By contrast, the experience school is pupil-centered and the work of the teacher lies in (a) setting the stage and utilising the student's purposes in selecting the experiences by means of which they are to learn, (b) giving moral support and whatever help students need to achieve their purposes, and (c) cooperating in the evaluation and in the planning of the next step.

A great deal of discussion of the relative advantages and disadvantages of these two approaches can be located in textbooks and professional journals under such headings as traditional and progressive, conservative and modern, teacher-centered and pupil-centered, and even autocratic and democratic, all used more or less synonymously. In addition, the progressive method has, at various times, been called the project or the activity method or the experience curriculum. Unfortunately, much of the writing on the subject has simply reflected the opinions of writers with a bias in one direction or the other; it is not uncommon, for instance, to find the discussion casts one method in its best possible light while, at the same time, emphasising the shortcomings of the other. Therefore, as we turn to a discussion of the two approaches, the student is cautioned against letting his prejudices on the subject obscure the real issues and to distinguish between what is an inherent strength or weakness in a method and what is more correctly an abuse—or perhaps an abuse to which the method is prone.

Evaluation Process

The primary weakness of the teacher-centered approach stems directly from the fact that it is oriented toward adult goals and relies on adult direction, a situation which can easily run counter to the principle that an experience is educative to the extent to which it is brought into vital relationship with the needs, goals, and purposes of the learner. It is based upon the philosophical view of education as a preparation for life, a position which Snygg and Combs (354) show to be psychologically unsound since the child cannot solve problems he does not have—and cannot have. Because he would have to be an adult to have the self-concept of an adult, the only possible outcome of a curriculum based on such a premise is a childish response to an adult problem. As they very aptly point out

> ... the process of equipping children with a repertoire of specific facts, skills, and techniques which will enable them to meet specific situations in adult life proves as impractical in theory as many generations of frustrated teachers have found it to be in practice.

With the advance of educational psychology and the clarification of the nature of the learner and of the learning process—out of which the pupil-centered approach evolved— it has become increasingly evident that more effective learning is likely to result out of letting classroom experiences grow out of the child's purposes and goals than having them preselected and preplanned in detail by the curriculum-maker. Of course, with a certain degree of psychological insight, the curriculum-maker can make a reasonably valid attempt at relating the curriculum to the purpose and development of the average child; he would certainly agree, for example, that the introduction into the curriculum of the Magna Carta, the Bill of Rights, and other historical events of man's struggle for independence should coincide with the adolescent's need to gain emotional independence from adults. However, it takes considerable ingenuity for the curriculum-maker to devise a curriculum that will fit all children of a given grade, regardless of ability, interest, and experiential background. It also takes considerable ingenuity for the teacher to promote the readiness and the motivation for whatever topic comes next in the curriculum sequence. In other words, the traditional preplanned curriculum does not lend itself well to taking advantage of the spontaneous interests and purposes of the class and of the opportunities for effective learning that sometimes present themselves.

An obvious question arising out of the discussion of the preceding paragraph concerns the continuity of the experience from which the child is to learn. In the teacher-centered school this continuity is provided automatically by the expert curriculum-maker who plans the whole sequence. The experience school, on the other hand, guided as it is by the interests and purposes of the child, has no such inbuilt guide toward its ultimate goals and, in extreme instances, can degenerate into the aimless wanderings for which the project method was often ridiculed with the much-repeated "Teacher, I wish we didn't have to do what we want to do, today." Obviously, when the planning of the curriculum is put into the hands of children, their education is likely to be fragmentary and incomplete. But proponents of the pupil-centered method do not advocate that the curriculum be left to the whims of children. They are as fully convinced as anyone else of the absolute necessity of having the general curriculum sequence—and particularly the overall goals—planned in advance by experts. The freedom they allow children under the direction of the teacher is in the choice of particular experiences by means of which the objectives of the curriculum are to be attained. (Parenthetically, it should be noted that this puts the teacher in a key position, a professional person in a position to do a professional job. And it allows no room for incompetence.)

It is, of cours true that the experiences planned by children often lack the tidy organisation which an adult can give them and, at times, the teacher may feel a concern for the muddle in which children can get and a compulsion to step in and direct the learning along the lines common to the traditional method. However, the emphasis upon logical organisation, often accepted as the greatest strength of the teacher-centered method, needs to be questioned. It rests upon the assumption— obviously false— that the material can be absorbed ready made from a structural standpoint in much the same way as impressions of wet ink are absorbed by a blotter. Organisation, continuity, and meaning lie in the learner, not in the material, and it is the learner who must organise his experiences. They cannot be organised for him and, although the arrangement of the material by adults may facilitate the process of reconstruction by means of which he can obtain meaning out of his experiences, the process is certainly not automatic. In fact, the beautiful (adult) organisation of the material may have no meaning for the child with his particular background of ability and experience, as many teachers have realised as they despairingly read on the examination the child's garbled renditions of the explanations so clearly stated in the book or given in class.

Of primary importance in connection with any learning situation is the matter of the motivation of students and this is one area which has a definite bearing on the relative effectiveness of the two methods. To the extent that the traditional curriculum is selected by adults and oriented toward the attainment of adult goals, it has to rely on the ability of the teacher to sell these goals to children. This, certain teachers are able to do effectively in at least a good percentage of the time for a good percentage of the children, especially since certain topics and subjects have a certain inherent appeal to the children for whom they are intended. Teacher approval is an important aspect of the total situation and many good teachers are able to have children gradually develop interest in the subject-matter as well as a positive self-concept as it relates to academic work.

The situation is not always so ideal, however. Since the goals are adult goals, often related only remotely to the goals of a good fraction of the members of the class, it is not surprising that, for many children, their attainment or unattainment is a matter of relative indifference. As a consequence, motivation has to be extrinsic, and an excessive emphasis on competition, grades, and other external incentives is more or less a natural adjunct of the traditional school, as a number of pupils, denied the satisfaction which stems from striving for meaningful goals, work to avoid punishment or for a grade as something to salvage out of an otherwise distasteful activity. Very often students have as their primary goal the circumventing of the goal set by the teacher. The latter, on the other hand, uses whatever means his ingenuity enables him to devise. Some teachers are relatively restricted in imagination and can think of nothing beyond sarcasm, scolding, failure and punishment, and various forms of threat in order to force the class toward the prescribed goals— presumably on the assumption that (a) learning is learning, regardless of the means used to promote it, and (b) if children are made to comply long enough, they will continue to comply through the operation of habit motives. Very effective learning actually occurs in many cases. However, for many other children, whatever learning does take place is often relatively meager and superficial, but there is certainly nothing superficial about the negative attitudes that are promoted.

The pupil-centered classroom, on the contrary, by using the student's purposes and background as the starting point and by placing on his shoulders a greater share of the responsibility for his education, is more likely to stimulate ego-involvement and whole hearted acceptance of the goals toward which he is to strive. Since it is his problem in the sense that he had a hand in choosing it and planning its execution, he is not only more likely to work effectively in carrying it out but also to derive a greater degree of satisfaction at its solution. (Note, for example, the difference between the learning of the student preparing a speech to hand in to his teacher as an assignment and that of the student preparing a speech in connection with his campaign for election to office in the student government.) As a result, the need for external incentives with which to goad him is correspondingly reduced and the likelihood of a virtuous circle of success, interest, and self-actualisation is correspondingly increased.

The fact that apathy, misbehaviour, and ineffectiveness in learning are more or less direct resultants of the unsuitability of its goals and the unrealistic demands it makes upon children was not fully appreciated by the traditional school. Rather, as pointed out by Beaumont and Macomber, it considered motivation and misbehaviour as appendages extraneous to the business of the school to be dealt with through external incentives and, where necessary, through punitive disciplinary measures. Many teachers today are equally shortsighted and much of the difficulty still to be found in our schools with respect to motivation and discipline is the direct outcome of their failure to relate their procedures and their curriculum to the needs and purposes of children. This is well stated by Snygg and Combs in the following quotation:

> It is quite likely that much of the conflict between pupils and teachers which still occurs in school is due to the fact that the schools are run by teachers who are chiefly concerned with preparing the student for his function in adult life and are filled with students who want to satisfy their needs here and now.

Thus, whereas the student-centered classroom, by adapting the work to the group and to the individual child and, thereby, providing him with the opportunity for continuous satisfaction for his needs, undercuts the child's need to misbehave, the traditional school often has to resort to repression. However, repressive discipline does not make the curriculum any more suitable: it merely increases the tensions associated with the frustration of the child and, whereas it makes for order—and a certain amount of learning—it often has a detrimental effect on his overall growth.

The practical significance, to those who would guide the growth of children, of the point discussed here cannot be overestimated. No matter from which aspect of his self-realisation it is viewed—academic growth, personal and social adjustment, attitude and character formation—it is evident that the individual, whether a child in school or an adult at work, must find satisfaction for his needs out of meeting the demands of the job or the classroom rather than have to rely on extrinsic incentives such as grades or salary or the satisfaction of such side activities as the after-school athletic programme, the after-work bowling league, or the coffee-break friendships. As it pertains to the school child, this means that the organisation of the classroom and its curriculum must have inbuilt satisfactions, *i. e.,* it must make it possible for the child to derive his major satisfactions, not out of getting a grade or misbehaving, but rather out of solving meaningful and challenging problems, and out of contributing to the attainment of group goals. The fact that the student-centered approach tends to have greater possibilities from this standpoint constitutes one of the strongest arguments in its favour.

The advantages noted so far of relating the curriculum to the goals and purposes of the learner are of obvious importance but we still have to consider what is to the average layman the most crucial question, namely, the extent to which experiences so organised lead to effective and desirable learning outcomes. Critics of the progressive school, on the thesis that work is work and play is play (Tom Sawyer to the contrary notwithstanding) have, at times interpreted the fact that children have a good time or enjoy school, that they do "what they want to do" as evidence supporting their contention that little learning is taking place. They fear that giving children a say in the choice of activities will result in their selecting what is easy and pleasurable (another instance of soft pedagogy) and that, as children flit from one pleasant activity to another, little will be learned. They fear, for example, that children in the progressive schools will be weak in the fundamentals which are more difficult to integrate into an experience unit.

Two factors prevent the learning in the pupil-centered classroom from being oriented toward the easy and the pleasurable but useless. One of these is the fact, previously stated, that the general curriculum and the over-all goals of pupil-centered schools are set by adults and not by children so that, except in cases of teacher incompetence in the use of the method, the danger is relatively small. The second consideration is even more fundamental: children want to grow, to be challenged, to explore new areas. To fear that children will seek easy task, is to fail to grasp the central theme of the concept of the phenomenal self, advanced by Snygg and Combs:

> Such criticism would fail to take into account the fact that in shifting the major purpose of education from the acquisition of subject matter to the development of an adequate phenomenal self, we have shifted to an activity for which the child does not need to be motivated. Building a satisfactory phenomenal self is the primary motive of his every act. His basic need

is for the preservation and enhancement of his phenomenal self.

It is only when the child is under threat (due to unrealistic demands, failure, and punishment) that the student plays it safe: normally, the fact that they do not lead to self-enhancement will prevent him from seeking easy tasks. Furthermore, new and more mature interests come easy to the child whose curiosity and initiative have not been blunted so that he will want to forge ahead toward new conquests.

Also related to the question of the effectiveness of the progressive school in promoting desirable learning outcomes is the criticism often heard of the time allegedly wasted by students as they select and plan an activity (by comparison with the traditional approach in which the teacher comes fully prepared with the work of the day). There is, of course, in any procedure calling for group planning, a danger of having endless and pointless discussion.

There is the further danger that the final plans and products will be not nearly as perfect as they would have been had the teacher taken a more active part. All of this may be frustrating to the perfectionistic teacher—and even to the brighter members of the class. The highest degree of efficiency and perfection would probably be attained when the teacher did it all by himself or appointed the best students to carry out the project in the name of the class but this would hardly result in much learning on the part of children. The important thing is not the product but the learning that takes place in the process. Group selection and planning of classroom activities are essential aspects of the pupil-centered approach and they are at the very foundation of its success. Far from being wasted, the time taken results in the selection of an activity which is realistically related to the needs, goals, capacities, and interests of the group, in the ego-involvement of the various members in the cooperative attainment of group goals, and in the clarification of the part each is to play. The outcome is not only a more effective contribution on the part of each individual child but a greater degree of satisfaction and self-fulfillment. Cooperative selection and planning of units spell the difference between the child going aimlessly and apathetically toward a goal known only to the teacher and one working on an activity which he sees as real and potentially satisfying. As pointed out by Wingo

> ... the most fruitful kind of learning experience is one in which a person or group evolves a plan for dealing with a meaningful situation, puts the plan into action, and then evaluates the outcome of the plan in terms of its original purpose.

The fear that student participation in the selection and planning of classroom activities will lead to their becoming "happy morons" whose learning is meager and fragmentary has not been borne out by research. Comprehensive studies such as the Eight-Year Study (2) and many others have invariably shown students of progressive schools to be at least up to par on the fundamentals and considerably superior in ability to reason critically, to apply what they know, and to integrate their experiences. They also tend to be superior in cooperation, self-confidence, sociability, effectiveness of expression, breadth of interest, and creativity.

It is particularly worthwhile to note that the superiority of the pupil-centered approach is largely from the standpoint of the functionality of the learnings it promotes. The teacher-centered method is reasonably effective in promoting the learning of isolated facts and skills (provided it can deal with the motivational problem) but psychology is not interested in knowledge per se unless it is reflected in behaviour. When all is said and done, the activities of the school, its curriculum, and its methods must be evaluated in terms of the difference it makes in the life of the learner: the employer, for example, is more interested in whether the graduate can do the job than he is in the number of facts he can reproduce for an examination. This is actually a fundamental distinction: whereas the traditional school with its subject-matter orientation stresses the acquisition of knowledge as an end in itself, the modern school is interested in knowledge only as it becomes an integral and functional part of the learner's life. Or, stated differently, whereas at times the old school seems oriented toward making the pupil a "cyclopedia of useless information", the aim of the modern school is not merely to "engender information and skill but to guide his purposes, attitudes, and interests..."

Since the activities of the pupil-centered classroom stem from the existing motives of the child and are, therefore, more in line with his background of ability and interest, they are more likely to be functional in guiding his further purposes. Thus, a child working on a unit on city government which involves him in interviews with the city commissioners is more likely to appreciate the working and importance of city government—and also more likely to develop civic attitudes, effectiveness of expression, and social graces—as a result of having lived the experience rather than having merely studied about it in his civics book. Such an approach is also more likely to be effective in fostering self-reliance, pupil initiative, habits of independent study, or problem-solving techniques. In other words, an experience unit is more likely to originate from the whole child and to be reflected in changes in the whole child, *e. g.*, understandings, applications, appreciations which go beyond the confines of subject-matter.

Contributing to a considerable extent to the ineffectiveness of the conventional school from the standpoint of the functionality of the learnings, it promotes the fact that, with its compartmentalisation of subject-matter, it often cuts across real experiences and reduces education to the memorisation of isolated facts along a narrow and artificial path. This is not a necessary accompaniment of the traditional method but definitely a weakness to which it is prone. Because it is defined in terms of subject matter, it encourages the development and use of a text designed to incorporate said subject-matter as decided upon by the curriculum-maker. In the absence of a more meaningful guide to the learning of the child who, in many cases, has no great interest in it anyway—in a series of easy steps—the subject-matter approach often becomes a textbook approach and, in its extreme form, degenerates into a chapter-at-a-time or page-at-a-time routine devoid of any purpose beyond that of covering the book before the end of the year. On the contrary, the ultra-flexibility of the pupil-centered approach, if nothing else, at least discourages the exclusive use of a 'prescribed' text and encourages the development of resourcefulness and proficiency in locating and integrating information from multiple sources.

Also vitally involved in the relative success of the teacher-centered and the pupil-centered methods is the extent of their adaptability to individual differences among children. Generally speaking, the former, with its preplanned curriculum, does not permit easy adaptation of the work of the school to individual differences in ability, interest, and experiential background. This is especially so when it gets tied down to a textbook which is then followed slavishly on a page-by-page basis despite the fact that, being pitched at a certain level, it frustrates both the duller and the brighter child. For successful operation, without undue departure from its basic procedures and its preplanned curriculum, it has to place considerable emphasis on development of the required pupil readiness.

However, pupil failure and retention are often too useful a crutch for teachers who are accustomed to fight unmotivated students, and wholesale retardation is rather typical of the old school's attempt at dealing with individual differences. Equally, if not more objectionable from the standpoint of effective education, is its emphasis on drill oriented toward the attainment of limited objectives. By the very nature of its curriculum and the apparent assumption that the same lesson is equally educative for all, the traditional subject-matter approach tends to make unrealistic demands upon many children. Probably its most effective measure from the standpoint of actual reduction in the range of individual differences—and one of the most vicious—consists in encouraging the dropping out of frustrated and bored students. In more recent years, "social promotions" have replaced retention and state laws have curtailed the incidence of drop-out, but these have hardly made the traditional curriculum and methods any more adaptive to differences among children.

The pupil-centered method, by contrast, is more flexible: not only is the class likely to select units that are more realistically in line with its interests and resources; but it can also make adjustment for individual differences in the allocations of responsibility for the various aspects of the project among members of the group. This enables each child to derive the benefit and the satisfaction of making a contribution in keeping with his talents and interests.

Of major significance from a modern psychological point of view is the much more effective use made by the student' centered approach of the fact that the classroom involves a social situation and, as such, constitutes the teacher's best ally in promoting the all-round growth of the child. Whereas the traditional school with its emphasis on competition and individual assignments discourages the development of group spirit and group cohesiveness and often promotes a pupil-versus-pupil (and pupils-versus-teacher) situation, the pupil-centered approach encourages the development of a social situation in which each member contributes to the cooperative attainment of group goals and in which the teacher is a resource person helping children toward self-realisation. As a result, not only does it tend to make possible greater academic gains through the inter-stimulation of members and a greater degree of ego-involvement of the individual child but, through its group organisation, it provides practice in the democratic resolution of group problems through group discussion and group planning.

On the other hand, one must not make the volume of discussion going on in a classroom the criterion of its quality. Certainly, discussion is often futile and, at times, most undemocratic. Not only can it become essentially a pooling of ignorance, but it can degenerate into an endless verbiage on the part of a few empty-heads, endless arguments over inconsequentials, and domination by a few demagogues within the group. The teacher needs to be particularly skillful in moving discussion along and keeping it on the right track and in preventing a few individuals from monopolising the conversation or from making a mockery of democratic processes. It would seem logical to assume, for example, that if someone has to dominate the group, it might as well be the teacher who is at least better informed and better trained.

The child-centered approach is also generally more effective in promoting wholesome attitudes. The fact that it gets children involved in cooperative activities in which each member contributes to the attainment of group goals is conducive not only to the development of cooperation, consideration for others, social and civic responsibility, enlightened self-interest—all of which are of prime importance in a democratic society—but it is also conducive to the actualisation of these attitudes through active participation in worthwhile and meaningful activities. This is one area in which the traditional school is often lacking: on the assumption that knowledge is sufficient for the development of desirable attitudes and behaviour, it is, in many cases, concerned almost exclusively with the imparting of knowledge. If the child develops negative attitudes toward the school, toward learning, toward persons in authority, that is too bad—as long as he learns. This is, of course, not to imply that it invariably produces negative attitudes; for the nature of the attitudes developed would vary with the nature of the atmosphere of the class, the relative success of the individual, and other factors. It would be ridiculous to suggest that these are always, or even generally, unsatisfactory. On the other hand, it is probably true that the progressive method is more oriented toward the importance of attitudes in the determination of the individual's behaviour and, because of its emphasis on group participation toward the attainment of meaningful goals, it tends to be more effective in promoting positive attitudes.

The Admixture

The previous discussion has pointed to the relative superiority from the standpoint of psychological theory of the pupil-centered over the teacher-centered approach. The evidence also points to its superiority from an empirical point of view, although considerable variation may be expected from situation to situation. The former lends itself more readily to the promotion of the major objectives for which the modern school exists but, as may be expected, the extent to which its potential advantages are realised depend in no small measure upon the capability and the ingenuity of the teacher and other aspects of the local situation. Thus, as we have stated, a project on city government which calls for interviewing city officials might be expected to produce a better understanding and appreciation of city government than the study of it in a book but this would not necessarily be so. It is entirely possible that the child might get little beyond the name of one or two of the commisioners and a few minor details while missing out completely on seeing the complete picture in perspective. It seems reasonably clear that a combination of the traditional and progressive approaches, depending on the suitability of one or the other for a particular unit of the curriculum would result in more effective learning than would complete adherence to one alone. Certainly not all tasks are amenable to the group project approach, for example.

Likewise, one or the other of the two methods may tend to be more suitable for certain students. Thus, the traditional method by making fewer demands on the child in terms of self-direction, ingenuity, initiative, and originality may provide a more reassuring atmosphere for the emotionally insecure child—and teacher. Also, it is likely that the logical organisation of the subject-matter approach is more effective for the bright or mature student or for the college situation and that the activity method is better suited to the elementary school. Thus, Burton expresses the view that:

> The education of little children, or beginners... is believed to proceed better when experience units are used by competent teachers.

The education of students who have more adequate reading ability and who have achieved sufficient maturity to be able to learn through verbal abstraction... is believed to proceed better when the assign-study-recite-test procedure as currently improved is used by competent teachers.

Generally the elementary school is more oriented toward the use of the activity method than is the high school. This may stem in part from the fact that teachers-in-training choosing the elementary level are perhaps more oriented toward children whereas those going to the secondary level are more oriented toward subject-matter. It may also be, of course, that arithmetic is more adaptable for inclusion in a project than is solid geometry, for example. Yet the Eight-Year Study was conducted—with considerable success—at the high school level, and therefore the question may be raised as to whether some of the ineffectiveness of our high schools may not be related to their use of antiquated techniques. On the other hand, the grade school must be cautioned against exclusive reliance upon projects and activities: the young child needs contact with concrete experiences but experiences are useful and usable only when synthesised into generalisations—and the subject-matter approach may well be an effective way of integrating these experiences, once he has had them.

The pupil-centered approach is not without its critics. Some of the criticisms to which it has been subjected are ill-founded and based on a lack of understanding of what the school is trying to do, the psychological principles underlying its techniques and procedures, and the role of the school in modern society. This may perhaps be blamed on a failure of the school to communicate with the public. Many critics have used the schools as a scapegoat in connection with their frustrations over the prevalence of juvenile delinquency, over international tension and the cold war, and hurt pride that "practical and scientific America" should have 'allowed' Russia to launch the first rocket to the moon.

Criticisms can also be expected in as much as some people are against any change and are likely to resent any departure from the "good old days" when they went to school. And, of course, the fact that those who did graduate from the old school (with the drop-outs and the repeated grades eliminated from the discussion) did know how to spell, read, and compute, and that, as a group, they are now successful in the community, only adds strength to their conviction that the progressive school is "off the track". (On the other hand, some people will accept anything simply because it is new—in the case of education, perhaps unconsciously feeling that any change from the old school which they attended would have to be an improvement.) Other criticisms, however, represent valid objections to what may be considered misuse or abuse of the method—or perhaps objections to the price the progressive method may have to pay in order to reap greater benefits in other directions. Educational psychology, of course, does not have all the answers and certain techniques which it apparently endorses may actually be in considerable error.

As we have also seen, the teacher-directed approach is not

without certain merits, particularly as it applies to the promotion of academic growth and if this were the only consideration, it could probably be modified rather than abandoned. Its greatest weakness lies in the area of promoting the all-round growth of the child where, to be effective, it would generally have to undergo considerable modification from its present organisation. This is not to say that the traditional method is incapable of dealing with the whole child. Whereas it is often associated with the teaching of facts and skills by methods that are frequently dull and boring, reinforced by coercion, there is no denying that many teachers who have used the method with ingenuity and insight into its possibilities have not only made the subject-matter approach exceedingly interesting and challenging but have also turned out graduates educated in the best sense of the word.

There is reason to suspect that the superiority of the progressive method stems from the type of teacher it attracts almost as much as it does from any superiority inherent in the method. Many of the teachers in traditional schools, upon which criticism of the method has been based, are perhaps not as well qualified and as familiar with the principles of educational psychology as those who, by training and experience, want to experiment with a new method and to apply psychology to the classroom, and who are also more apt to be understanding and flexible in dealing with children. Also involved may be an important personality difference: the teacher who is secure and who displays competence, initiative, and resourcefulness tends to be more willing to experiment—realising that the progressive class, being more loosely organised, might result in bedlam if things go wrong. The insecure teacher, on the contrary, is likely to stick to the safer subject-matter approach. It should also be noted that whereas a dull, unintelligent, and incompetent teacher may be able to go through the motions of using the traditional method, on an autocratic, page-assignment basis, such a teacher could not handle the experience method. In fact, a definite weakness of the progressive method lies in the demands which it makes upon the ingenuity and competence of the teacher. In the hands of the wrong teacher—or even the inexperienced teacher—it can lead to disastrous results. Both methods lead to good results in the hands of the competent teacher—the pupil-centered approach merely allows more freedom for the competent teacher to display his competence.

Effective Plan

The classroom depends for its effectiveness upon its compliance with the principles of psychology. The list of these principles is, of course, too long to be reviewed here. Therefore, this section will attempt simply to give a very brief overview of the major ideas of this text, an understanding of which is essential to the teacher interested in effective classroom procedures.

The author, being unaware of any particular virtue in ignorance or incompetence, does not wish to minimise in any way the importance of the knowledge of subject matter, of methods, and other aspects of teaching: a teacher lacking in these areas is simply unqualified. Nevertheless, this text has consistently emphasised the view that an understanding of the why of the child's behaviour is the key to guidance of his growth and development. It is the author's contention that the greatest source of failure in the classroom stems more from the teacher's inability to deal effectively with the motivational and personal aspects of teaching than from any other cause (as indeed it does in any situation involving people as they interact with each other). It is not uncommon for a supervisor to find that a beautiful lesson plan has been worked out by a teacher who has a good grasp of the subject, who has also brought in a nice balance of audio-visual aids and other illustrative materials, and who is fully prepared to teach—the only thing that is missing is an appropriate answer to the question: "Specifically what would make the children in the class interested in the material to be presented?" Many an otherwise good lesson has floundered on that question. Accordingly, the following points may bear reconsidering:

(a) The key idea which any prospective teacher must never lose sight of is that behaviour is purposive: it always occurs in connection with the satisfaction of the individual's needs;

(b) However, as a result of his previous experiences, the individual learns to satisfy his needs in a specific way, i.e., not only to seek the satisfaction of his needs but to do so through the attainment of specific goals. Thus, motives rather than needs determine the individual's behaviour: not only will the individual satisfy his needs but he will satisfy them in ways consistent with his past experiences, his habits, his values, his self-concept.

(c) In the face of the multitude of unsatisfied motives with which the individual is invariably confronted (some of which are reinforcing, others conflicting, each with a certain vector strength in a given situation), behaviour is the net resultant of relevant motives. Thus, behaviour is oriented toward the satisfaction of dominant motives. Conversely, the individual can be relied upon to take whatever steps within his power he needs to take, in order to attain the purposes which are important to him. He can do no more and no one can expect him to do more!

(d) Since behaviour results from unsatisfied motives, a certain degree of tension is conducive to learning. On the other hand, excessive tension is likely to result in anxiety and ineffective, if not deviant, behaviour. Probably no other developmental concept has greater implication for effective living than that of the development on the child's part of security, *i. e.*, relative freedom from anxiety.

(e) Every experience the individual undergoes is potentially satisfying or frustrating depending on the degree of readiness he brings to bear upon the situation. Every aspect of his development has a bearing on the attainment of his goals and he cannot be considered except in his totality.

(f) Maturity implies behaviour that is effective in the attainment of goals and constructive from the standpoint of the welfare of others. Any educational system must not only orient the child toward the concept of enlightened self-interest but must also provide him with practice in social living, i.e., practice in making decisions involving the welfare of the group of which he is a member.

(g) Not only does the social group provide the maximum opportunity for satisfaction of the individual's needs but, indeed, only through the group can the individual attain maximum self-realisation.

(h) The school, as an agent of society, has no greater mission from the standpoint of the welfare of both society and the individual than the development on the part of the latter of sound character based upon a foundation of positive attitudes and ideals of integrity, morality, and consideration for others.

The same concepts apply to the classroom: the key to effective educational experience lies in the motives of the child. The child will exert himself with whatever capacity he can muster when he is working toward goals that are real and meaningful in terms of his needs, motives, and purposes, on one hand, and his background of ability and experience, on the other. His need for self-enhancement will not permit him of do otherwise. Such experiences, in turn, will make for (a) maximum learning, retention, and functionality from the standpoint of successful living; (b) success and maximum tension-reduction and self-fulfilment; and (c) desirable attitudes and values. On the contrary, to the extent to which the child is forced to participate in experiences which are not related to the attainment of his goals and purposes, aversive effects-apathy, superficial learning, frustration, negative attitudes, misbehaviour, maladjustment—are bound to follow.

The implementation of this principle into actual classroom practice is obviously too comprehensive a matter for complete coverage here. The discussion will, therefore, be restricted to a listing of the following as minimal essentials of such a programme:

(a) An understanding of children:

1. In general: the teacher needs to understand children in terms of the psychological principles that govern their growth and development, of the particular characteristics and problems of children, of the role of readiness and maturation.
2. Individually: the teacher cannot provide meaningful experiences for a child whose ability, interests,

background, values, goals, or purposes he does not know.

(b) A suitable curriculum:

1. There is need for a good selection of educational experiences designed to promote desirable behaviour changes in individual children in the most efficient way. These experiences must not be standard for all children in a given grade or class but must, on the contrary, be tailor-made with respect to content and method of presentation to fit the particular child.

(c) A social situation conducive to the maximum self-realisation of the child:

1. The children of the class must be integrated into a cohesive group characterised by unconditional acceptance of individual members, effective communication among members and between members and teacher, commonness of purpose, and enthusiasm in the attainment of worthwhile goals.
2. The teacher, as a group leader, must be one who can communicate with and inspire children.

(d) Effective guidance of the process by means of which the child is to achieve his potentialities:

1. Guidance is needed if experiences are to be satisfying to the child and effective in promoting his growth. At the same time, the teacher must realise the necessity of having the learner actively involved in the learning process and must provide for ego-involvement through the operation of realistic and clear-cut goals.
2. Effective learning centers around such concepts as problem solving and meaningfulness and implies experiences that are real in terms of the child's purposes, interests, abilities, and background. It must, in turn, be reflected in functional behaviour and in more mature interests, goals, and purposes.
3. The school programme should capitalise on the child's natural desire to grow and be synchronised with his

natural pattern of development so as to promote his maximum self-realisation.

4. Meaningful group participation in the pursuit of realistic and worthwhile goals is one of the best means of (a) promoting the development of personal and social adjustment and of sound attitudes and character, and (b) of having them reflect in positive behaviour.

(e) A competent, sensitive, and dedicated teacher:

1. The teacher is certainly the most important cog in the educative machine and, although we cannot list all the characteristics and traits which would be desirable for a teacher to have, we may at least mention the following: (a) a thorough grasp of subject-matter; (b) ingenuity and competence in setting the stage for the maximum growth of the child, in guiding the learning process, in welding students into a cohesive group working toward common goals; (c) sensitivity to the needs and problems of children, a firm conviction in the inherent dignity of the individual, and a dedication to the cause of promoting his maximum growth; and (d) an awareness of his responsibility as a leader of youth, of the importance of personal integrity, and a sincere interest in the welfare of children.
2. Ability to relate to children and inspire them toward the moral values and democratic ideals of our society.

The education of the child is obviously a complicated task which does not allow for quick solution or easy prescription. Society has a general idea of the type of person a graduate of its schools should be; it can even list tentatively the requirements and perhaps describe the process for educating such a person as we have attempted to do, in part, in this text. And on the surface, it would seem that these are not only necessary but reasonably sufficient conditions for the promotion of an educated person. Education, however, may be likened to housebuilding—whether we get an effective and livable house out of the required quantity of cement, lumber, and other materials depends to a large extent on the professional caliber of the architect and the builder, so also does the quality of the final product turned out of our schools depend to a large extent on the professional competence of the curriculum maker who devises the programme and of the teacher who puts his plans into action. An error on the part of either can negate the best efforts of all concerned.

There is not complete agreement as to what to include in the curriculum and—within limits—perhaps it is not necessary that there should be, since it is the growth that results from a given experience rather than the experience itself that counts. But there should be reasonable agreement as to what constitutes an effective—and an ineffective—teaching method. The technological progress which has put America in a position of world leadership has not been achieved through procedures that were "good enough". It is time we begin to expect from our schools the same degree of efficiency that characterises other areas of scientific endeavour. We need to reevaluate our schools and their procedures, not for the purpose of labeling them 'traditional' or 'progressive' but rather for the purpose of identifying those that bring about results and those that do not; not with a view toward immediate implementation of a panic sponsored crash programme, such as the Sputnik-inspired increased emphasis on science and on stiffer grading, but rather with a view toward bringing educational practice in line with sound philosophical and psychological considerations. When this is done, we shall no longer have to apologise for our failures, and our students will be as adequate as per their potentialities.

12

Guidance and Counselling

The Counselling

Webster's Dictionary defines counselling as "Consultation, mutual exchange of opinions, deliberating together."

Wrenn says, "Counselling is personal and dynamic relationship between the two individuals-one of whom is older or more experienced than the younger, who together approach a more or less well defined problem of the younger or less experienced or less wise, with mutual consideration for each to the end that the problem may be more clearly defined and that the one who has the problem may be helped to a self-determined solution of it."

Counselling is a process in which a pupil is approached by the counsellor on an individual basis and is helped in arriving at a decision or making choice finding a direction.

Types of Counselling: There are three types of counselling:

1. Directive Counselling
2. Non-Directive Counselling.
3. Eclectic Counselling

Directive Counselling: E.G. Williamson favours this type of counselling. It is counsellor directed counselling. Counsellor is the leader or it is he who dominates. It is the counsellor who discovers the problem, diagnoses it and provides a solution to it. Majority of the talking is done by the counsellor. In this type of counselling, the emphasis is upon the problem. What caused the problem? How can it best be solved?

According to Andrews and Willy, the basic assumptions of the directive counselling can be:

1. Counsellor has superior training, experience and information and is competent to give advice about how a problem is to be solved.
2. The maladjustment of an individual does not entirely impair the intellectual ability of the client, hence counselling is primarily an intellectual process.
3. Because of such factors as bias, the client is not always capable of solving his problems.
4. The objectives of counselling are achieved primarily through a problem solving situation.

Role of the Counsellor in Directive Counselling: The role can be portrayed by presenting the various steps the counsellor uses:

(a) *Analysis:* The collection of pertinent data by a variety of tools and techniques.

(b) *Synthesis:* The mechanical and graphical organisation of the data.

(c) *Diagnosis:* Drawing a conclusion about the causes of disturbance.

(d) *Prognosis:* A prediction of the future development of the student's problem.

(e) Counselling and Treatment

(f) Follow-up and Evaluation

Merits

1. It takes less time and is economical with respect to time.
2. The counsellor comes to the solution soon. This gives him happiness.
3. Directive counselling gives more significance to the intellectual rather than to the emotional aspect of individual's personality.

Demerits

1. It kills the initiative of the child and as such it makes him somewhat helpless.
2. It does not guide the counselee to be efficient and he cannot express himself freely.
3. There is lot of regimentation in it because of the dominant role played by the counsellor. It is undemocratic.
4. Lastly, the counselee is made dependent upon the counsellor.

Non-Directive Counselling: Non-Directive Counselling is also known by various other names such as permissive counselling or counselee or client-oriented counselling. Carl Rogers is the leading exponent of this type of counselling.

This type of counselling is totally opposite to directive type of counselling. In non-directive counselling, the counsellor remains silent to the maximum and allows the counselee to speak freely about the problem. The counsellor passes an occasional remark as to keep his client on the track. The counsellor asks a few questions. In this way the counsellor helps the pupil to think out the solution of the problem himself. Complete responsibility is placed on the individual and the counselee plays the primary role.

Significance of Counsellor : Carl Rogers has outlined the role of the counsellor by listing down the following steps in the said type of counselling:

The individual or the counselee comes for help.

The helping situation is usually defined.

The counsellor encourages the counselee to express his feelings freely.

The counsellor accepts and clarifies negative feelings.

Negative feelings or impulses are followed by tentative expressions of the positive impulses.

Counsellor accepts and recognizes positive feelings of the counselee.

This provides a basis on which the counselee can go ahead to the new level of integration.

Counsellor clarifies possible course of action.

Counselee develops further insight, a more complete and accurate understanding of the problem.

Merits

1. In the present day personnel work, the non-directive counselling movement may be linked to the progressive movement in education. Both stress the freedom of the individual.
2. As therapy, it has indisputable values.
3. Non-directive counselling can be compared to confessions made in the church and as such when one is allowed to talk, one brings one's repressed thoughts to the surface and relieves one's tensions.
4. This facilitates integrated positive action.
5. This develops a feeling of increased independence on the part of the counselee.

Demerits

1. It is a time consuming process. The counselee may begin a never ending dialogue.
2. In view of above, it may deprive many other counsellor to seek necessary counselling.
3. The resources, judgement and wisdom of the client cannot be relied upon.
4. How most problems be solved by simply talking out things in the interview situation is a big limitation.

Eclectic Counselling : Eclectic counselling is a combination and synthesis of directive and non-directive types of the counselling or viewpoints. As stated earlier, the two extremes forms of (Directive and Non-Directive) are combined. Here both the counsellor and the counselee are active and cooperative. Both do the talking turn by turn. The problem is solved jointly.

This also raises one problem-how much freedom should the counselee be allowed? Answer is simple-fifty per cent. But the factors of the personality of the counselee and the situation should also be taken into consideration.

To Conclude: In the absence of any clear-cut indication of the superiority of one counselling method over another, the eclectic approach seems justified provided it is coupled with the positive concept that counselling is essentially a learning process for both the counsellor and the counselee.

The Method

So whatever be the type, it has been found out that counselling process has the following five characteristics:

1. Counselling is a professional service.
2. Counseling is centred upon the problems of the client.
3. Good counselling results in client-made decisions.
4. Counselling is one to one process.
5. Counselling must be on the accuracy of the counsellor's prediction.

Vital Issues

It is sometimes said that guidance is the heart of education and counselling as the heart of counselling.

Guidance is relatively a broader term and counselling is one of the services under the guidance programme.

Need for guidance arises when an individual is confronted with some problems. Problem may be solved by providing information. This is the initial phase of guidance. The individual having the problem may be charged with emotion. It may be unable to adjust himself with the environment on account of emotional tension. In such a situation he needs counselling to overcome tension.

Diverse Views

There are two methods of guidance: (i) Individual guidance, (ii) Group guidance.

Group guidance includes the following techniques:

1. Talks by teachers, school counsellor and experts on educational matters.

2. Use of audio-visual aids, including electronic media to disseminate career information.
3. Career conferences and exhibitions.
4. Group discussions.
5. Orientation courses.
6. Parent-teacher meets.
7. Commercial and industrial visits.
8. T.V. talks and panel discussions.
9. Counselling.

Individual Guidance includes the following techniques:

1. To tell an individual about his potentialities.
2. Orientation to the individual to educational, vocational and avocational opportunities and requirements.
3. Assisting individuals to adjust themselves to various situations.
4. Assisting the individual to assess himself what he is.
5. Assisting the individual to appreciate where he is.
6. Assisting the individual to become aware of his assets and limitations.
7. Assisting the individual to find his own path in accordance with his assets and limitations.
8. Assisting the individual to follow his chosen path.
9. Assisting the individual to promote his career.

The Guidance

Fundament Need : The need for guidance is based on the fact that every individual needs help. Jones has very rightly observed that everyone needs assistance at some time in his life, some will need it constantly and throughout their entire lives, while others need it only at rare intervals at times of great crisis. There always have been and will continue to be people with an occasional need for the help of the more experienced persons in meeting problem situations.

The need for a comprehensive programme of guidance has become imperative in view of the following considerations:

1. Complex nature of society.
2. Individual differences.
3. Changed agricultural, commercial and industrial patterns of the country.
4. Changed occupational pattern of the country.
5. Changed occupational structures.
6. Changed educational pattern of the country.
7. Need for conservation of human energy.
8. Vocationalisation of education.
9. New researches in educational psychology.
10. More leisure and the need for its proper utilisation.
11. Impact of electronic mass media.
12. Impact of press media.
13. Juvenile delinquency.
14. Urbanisation and congested cities.
15. Growing tension on account of increased stress.
16. Changed family structure and lack of guidance and counselling at home.
17. Employment of women in large numbers.
18. Need for correct understanding of religious matters.
19. Political exploitation.
20. Population explosion.
21. Industrial psychology and its requirements.
22. Search for identity of the youth.
23. Need for wholesome relations
24. Need for making educational choices.
25. Need for effective learning.
26. Need for proper involvement in co-curricular work.

Earlier Events

During the late 1920s and early 1930s, in the U.S.A. for example, education and guidance were considered almost synonymous. During the same period, psychologists like Binnet, Cattell, Terman and Tbomdike introduced psychological testing in the field of guidance. About the middle of 1930s, the emphasis shifted and more attention was given to economic problems, placement or employment and occupational trends. More and more of assistance was given to the employer in order to make him more effective in his work. This trend was described by some writers as 'personal movement.'

Modern meaning of guidance concept, however, does not restrict itself to any one discipline. It is being influenced by sociology, psychology, economy and education etc.

The Meaning

Following are the important definitions of guidance.

1. Chisholm states "Guidance seeks to help the individual discover his own talents in comparison to the opportunities of the world and help him prepare himself so that he can find or develop a place in which he can live a well balanced life and contribute his part to the welfare of his fellow men."
2. In the words of Ruth Strang, "Guidance is a process of helping every individual, through his own efforts, to discover and develop his potentialities for his personal happiness and social usefulness."
3. Dr. J.A. Humphreys and Dr. A.E. Traxler, define guidance as: "At any level, guidance implies that the individual attains self-direction just as fast and as far as his mental, social and emotional abilities permit. Guidance of the younger or less mature individual, of course, calls for closer direction than does guidance of the older or more mature individual. The term guidance, moreover, aptly applies to working with an individual all along the lines from early childhood into adulthood."
4. According to Jones, "Guidance involves personal help given by someone; it is designed to assist a person in deciding where he wants to go, what he wants to do, or how he can best accomplish his purposes; it assists him in solving problems that arise in his life. It does not solve

problems for the individual, but helps him to solve them. The focus of guidance is the individual, not the problem, its purpose is to promote the growth of the individual in self-direction."

5. According to the Secondary Education Commission, "Guidance involves the difficult art of helping boys and girls to plan their own future wisely in the full light of all the factors that can be mastered about themselves and about the world in which they are to live and work. Naturally, therefore, it is not the work of a few specialists, but rather a service in which the entire school staff must cooperate under the guidance of some person with special knowledge and skill in this particular field. Guidance in this sense is not confined to the vocational field only. It covers the whole gamut of youth problems and should be provided in an appropriate form at all stages of education through the cooperative endeavour of understanding parents, teachers, headmasters, principals and guidance officers."

Significant Features

From above mentioned definitions, we conclude:

1. Guidance is assisting the individual to find his own place.
2. Guidance is assisting the individual to know his assets and liabilities.
3. Guidance is assisting the individual to find his path through his own efforts.
4. Guidance is assisting the individual to help himself for promoting his self-direction.
5. Guidance is assisting the individual to adjust himself.
6. Guidance is a point of view that reflects a positive towards oneself and others.
7. Guidance is assisting an individual to develop his potentialities and talents to the optimum level.
8. Guidance is helping the individual to make appropriate educational, personal, recreational and vocational choices.

9. Guidance is assisting the individual to establish harmonious relations with his parents, neighbours, peers etc.
10. Guidance programme is organised.
11. Guidance programme has a structure, system and personal.
12. Guidance consists of specialised services-testing, counselling, educational and vocational information, placement and follow-up.
13. Guidance programme is an integral part of the school programme.

The Motives

The aims of guidance are :

1. Optimum development of the potentialities of an individual.
2. Orientation to the individual to educational, vocational and avocational opportunities and requirements.
3. Assisting individuals to adjust themselves to various situations.

The Practice

An effective guidance programme comprises the following functions:

1. Assisting the individual to assess himself what he is.
2. Assisting the individual to appreciate where he was.
3. Assisting the individual to become aware of his assets and limitations.
4. Assisting the individual to find his own path in accordance with his assets and limitations.
5. Assisting the individual to follow his chosen path.
6. Assisting the individual to promote his career.

Different Standpoints

1. Career Guidance.
2. Civic Guidance.

3. Community Guidance.
4. Cultural Guidance.
5. Educational Guidance.
6. Emotional Guidance.
7. Family Relations Guidance.
8. Health Guidance.
9. Human Relations Guidance.
10. Leisure Time Utilisation Guidance.
11. Moral Guidance.
12. Personal Guidance.
13. Physical Guidance.
14. Professional Guidance.
15. Psychiatric Guidance.
16. Recreational Guidance.
17. Religious Guidance.
18. Sex Guidance.
19. Social Guidance.
20. Spiritual Guidance.
21. Vocational Guidance.

In fact there is no aspect of life which does not need guidance.

Meaning of Educational Guidance: Following definitions of educational guidance bring out the meaning of educational guidance.

In the words of G. E. Myers, "Educational guidance is a process concerned with bringing about between an individual pupil with his distinctive characteristics on the one hand, and differing groups of opportunities and requirements on the other, a favourable setting for the individual's development or education. If there is a single group, of opportunities and requirements, as is the case with a fixed curriculum, the problem is simply one of the education by the best methods possible in a setting already determined and not one of educational guidance."

Jones defines educational guidance as the assistance given to the pupils in their choices and adjustments with relation to schools, curriculum's, courses and school life.

Ruth Strang observes that educational guidance is positive. It is a developmental programme concerned with the questions. What is this boy or girl good for? What kind of education will reveal his capacities and help him to develop them? According to the same author, educational guidance is intended to aid the individual in choosing an appropriate programme and in making progress in it. This involves (1) knowledge of the abilities and interests of the individuals, (2) awareness of a wide range of educational opportunities, and (3) programmes and counselling which help the individual to choose wisely on the basis of these two kinds of knowledge.

Brewer defines it as "Educational guidance is a conscious effort to assist in the intellectual growth of an individual-anything that has to do with instruction or with learning may come under the term of guidance."

Dunsmoor and Miller observe, "Guidance as a form systematic assistance whereby students are aided in achieving satisfactory adjustment to school and life."

In the words of Dr. K. G. Rama Rao, "Guidance in the wider context of a total curriculum and embracing education of everyone of the basic activity pattern-intellectual as well as social, economic as well as artistic, moral as well as spiritual, domestic as well as physical-becomes all inclusive as well as competes with instructional and testing or examining functions of the school in preparing the school-leavers for work and life in general."

Shirely, Hamrin and Clifforde Erickson write, "Guidance in the secondary school refers to that aspect of the education programme which is concerned especially with helping the pupil to become adjusted to his present situation and to plan his future in line with his interests, abilities and social needs. Guidance or personal work represents an organized effort on the part of the school, equipped with both a knowledge of the pupil and information as to opportunities, of an educational, a social and a vocational character to help the individual pupil become adjusted to his present situation in such a way as to provide the greatest development for him and to aid him in planning for his future. It is rightly said that this programme helps John see through himself and then to assist him in seeing himself through."

The Need: Educational guidance is needed to make the best use of the potential of children.

Lack of educational guidance has created what is known as the problem of 'educated unemployment.'

Lack of educational and vocational guidance has led to a dearth of suitable hands for many occupations needing a specialised training.

It has been rightly said, "Nothing but a well-organised network of guidance services throughout the country will save us from the impending tragedy."

Almost every system of education is based on two assumptions. The first is that every student should strive for maximum self-development and the other is that every student should take his place in the society as its useful member. These two assumptions imply that the school and community activities of a child should be based on some definite pattern. Educational guidance services must assist the child to achieve this end.

For achieving above purposes of guidance, several kinds of services are organised in the school.

1. To assist the student secure information regarding the possibility and desirability of further schooling.
2. To assist the student to know the purpose and functions of the different categories of senior secondary schools and other institutions.
3. To assist the student to know in detail the offerings and facilities of the school he might attend.
4. To assist him to know the requirements for entrance into the school of his choice.
5. To assist him to adjust himself to the curriculum, the school and the social life connected with it. Under this we may include:
   (a) To help the student in the selection of the subjects at the senior secondary stage.

(b) To help him in the selection of textbooks and other instructional material.

(c) To help him in developing study habits.

(d) To help him in making satisfactory progress in various subjects.

(e) To help him in the selection of hobbies.

(f) To help him in the selection of co-curricular activities.

(g) To help him in knowing the availability of scholarships, loans etc.

(h) To help him to find out his aptitudes, interests etc.

6. To assist him in building healthy social relationship.
7. To help him in selecting subjects in accordance with his vocational choice.
8. To assist him in knowing the various openings available after.

Unique Approaches

There are two important reasons which give rise to the necessity of a specialised guidance service. The first is that there is a marked difference in the curriculum of an elementary and secondary school and that of a higher secondary school. Curriculum of a Higher Secondary school is a diversified one which involves the problem of selecting subjects in class XI.

The second reason is that much emphasis is placed upon the vocational point of view. Important decisions are to be made in class XI and class XII. In class XI the selection of subjects is largely influenced by vocational requirements. Important decisions are taken and help is needed when the students are about to leave the school, either to secure jobs or to go to college or to some other type of further training.

Expert Guidance

The distinguishing mark between the two is the character of the dominating purpose. In vocational guidance, the vocational considerations are dominating, whereas in educational guidance 'making a life' in school is more important than 'making a living' after the school stage. Educational and vocational guidance are parts of the total guidance process by which an individual's potentialities are discovered and developed through his own efforts for his personal happiness and social usefulness. The student's vocational plan and selection of courses are functionally related.

The Planning

1. Appraisal of the student by means of	(a) Tests and rating scales	
	(b) Parents ratings	
	(c) Diagnostic records	
	(d) Individual inventories	
	(e) Sociometric analysis	
	(f) Observations	
	(g) Anecdotes	
	(h) Case studies	
	(i) Cumulative records	
2. Adjustment by means of	(a) Change in the environment through	1. Socialised curriculum.
		2. Co-curricular activities.
		3. Physical surroundings
		4. Community resources.
		5. Educational and vocational opportunities.
		6. Group contacts.
	(b) Changes in the individual through	1. Interviews
		2. Developmental exercises.
		3. Instruction.
		4. Guidance.
		5. Group process.

Prevailing Facilities

Following five types of guidance services are needed in a school :

Individual Inventory Service: Compilation of individual inventory giving detailed information about each student concerning his abilities and achievements in different areas is the first essential of every guidance programme in the school. This information should be kept up-to-date and is to be used for the good of the student. It may be compiled in the form of a cumulative record.

Information Service: Students of higher secondary schools generally need three types of information which is very helpful to them in making decisions about various courses, occupations and institutions such as : (a) Information about colleges and training opportunities, (b) Information about available occupations, and (c) Information about scholarships and other financial help available during the training period. Information may be collected from papers and magazines, government notifications and bulletin's and information centers of the Employment Exchanges, etc. The usefulness of this information will be lost if the information is not kept up-to-date. This information may be supplemented by talks of people from different occupations.

Counselling Service: Counselling service is regarded as the 'heart' of the guidance programme. This service must assist an individual in identifying, understanding and solving problems that confront him. Counselling can be done by a well-trained counsellor. A detailed discussion on the role of the counsellor is available elsewhere in this book.

Placement Service: This service implies help to the individual in obtaining employment. There are three stages of this service:

(a) Assessing the abilities, aptitudes, and interests of the individual student.

(b) Analysing several occupations, particularly the ones in which the student expresses his interest.

(c) Relating occupations and abilities.

5. *Follow-up Service:* This implies continuation of the programme to check the effectiveness of the programme.

Guidance and Education: Following are the main differences between guidance and education.

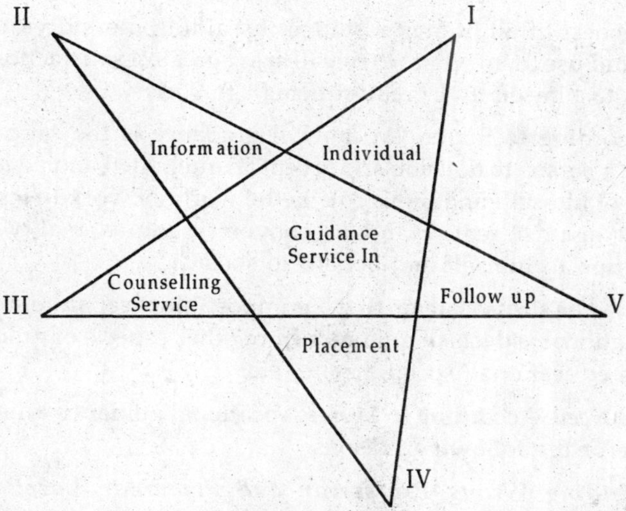

Diagram showing Guidance Services in the Schools

1. "All guidance is education but some aspects of education are not guidance, their objectives are the same-the development of the individual-but the methods used in education are by no means the same as those used in guidance," writes Jones.
2. Again the same author writes, "Education may take place, and often does, through the effort and initiation of the individual alone. This is education, but not guidance."
3. There might be some element of compulsion in education but not in guidance.
4. Guidance is present when the cooperation of the individual is secured and when help is given to him. Guidance is the outgrowth of a philosophy of education that every child in a school system should have an opportunity for all round growth and development in order to achieve his greatest potential.

Meaning and Definition of Vocational Guidance: To quote Prof. G. E. Myers, "Vocational guidance is fundamentally an effort to conserve the priceless native capacities of youth and the costly training provided for youth in the schools. It seeks to conserve these richest of all human resources by aiding the individual to invest and use them where they will bring greatest satisfaction and success to himself and greatest benefit to society."

According to Super, "Vocational guidance is the process of helping a person to develop and accept an integrated and adequate picture of himself, and of his role in the world of work to test this concept against reality and to convert it into a reality with satisfaction to himself and benefit to society."

It may be stressed again that it is impossible to separate sharply the vocational aspects of guidance from other aspects of guidance such as educational, social, health, etc.

The Need: According to Myres, Vocational guidance is needed because of the following reasons:

Avoiding Wrong Profession and Economic Loss: If an individual stays in a wrong profession for a long time, he suffers economically and there is financial loss.

Checking Psychic Loss: If an individual stays in a wrong profession, he suffers from a psychic loss. The individual is not happy. He is frustrated. His family life is also affected.

Right Profession and Economic Advantages: Vocational guidance provides many economic advantages to the employers. Their problems are less because their workers enjoy job satisfaction.

Health Point of View: Proper profession is needed from the point of health of the individuals. If the profession is such where health breaks down, production suffers and morale of individuals goes down.

Personal and Social Values: There are a large number of personal and social values of vocational guidance. Leaving aside financial considerations, the worker's happiness, his personal development, his value as a social unit and his contribution to human welfare are all involved. Right vocational guidance helps us to achieve this objective.

Maximum Utilisation of Human Potentialities: Human potentialities are utilised to the maximum with the help of vocational guidance. The nation also derives benefit as the resources are utilised very profitably.

13

School and Society

While discussing various needs and problems of development of the adolescents, it is important to keep in view the following important points.

Needs Give Birth to Problems: Problems create worries and anxieties which in turn result in fears. Satisfaction or dissatisfaction of the needs thus have a great bearing on the development of the personality of the adolescent.

Needs → a Problems → Worries → Anxieties → Fears

The interrelatedness of the various aspects of the development of the personality of the adolescent may be illustrated as under:

A proper balance has to be struck between traditional values and modern values.

Ethical, moral and spiritual values on the one hand and scientific and technological values on the other hand have to be taken note of while considering adolescence needs and problems.

Rising Trends

Far reaching changes have been taking place in recent years in all societies, Schools, as social institutions have to rethink the way they are structured. At present, by and large, they tend to be based on the 20th century. Other models for schools need to be considered if students' development, especially of adolescents is to be enhanced.

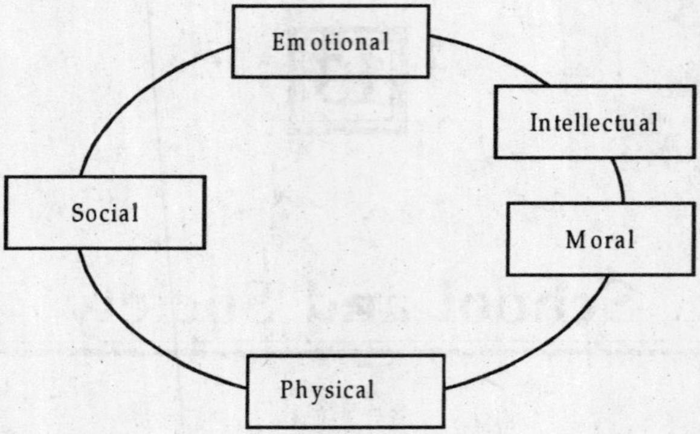

***Various Aspects of the Development* :** Following are the developments which affects adolescence growth and development and create new problems:

1. New developments in information technology including computer aided learning, interactive video and television offer important opportunities to improve the quality of many adolescents. At the same time they exercise an adverse influence also. Developments in this area, however, require a large investment of effort and finance. In many developing countries, the reality is that only a few elite schools would have such technology, thus aggravating the equity problem.
2. The current trends towards democratization in the societies will hopefully promote better understanding. In order to support such a change, we will need an education for the adolescents which enables them to live harmoniously in the plural society of today.
3. The global problems we face with the environment will acquire a new responsibility on the adolescents.
4. Human rights and dignity still be an issue at the forefront of our concern.
5. The ecological developments taking place are producing

changes in the people's work and living conditions. The adolescents need to be acquainted with these concerns.

6. The gap between the rich and the poor societies is increasing. This also reflects on the status of adolescents in educational institutions.
7. The emergence of self-concept, egoism and sex instinct during adolescence have to be considered in the light of new information technology.
8. Schools alone cannot influence the adolescents in the fast changing societies. In a world where mutual respect and cooperation is essential, it will be important to develop environment at school, at home and in wider society in which adolescent's self-esteem is enhanced.

Varied Elements

1. Support by society for the career development of adolescents and counselling.
2. School's responsibility for career development as well as moral development of adolescents.
3. Constructive and cooperative educational environment.
4. Creation of a 'pedagogy of democratic fellowship' in which adolescents collaborate and support each other in their learning.
5. Classrooms to be minisocial realities in which adolescents assume different roles including those of leadership.
6. Teachers to play the role of facilitators, organisers and managers of learning.
7. Science courses to give students the opportunity to consider the social, economic and ecological impact of scientific and technological innovations.
8. Environmental Science to play an important role in helping the adolescents appreciate the interdependence of living things and the fragile balance in the biosphere.
9. Providing equality of opportunity.
10. Technology courses to be designed in such a way as they address students' needs in their own environment.

11. Along with mother tongue, foreign language to be given greater attention in the case of adolescents whenever needed.
12. Providing suitable television programmes to adolescents.
13. Encouraging the involvement of adolescents in the mass media programmes meant for them.
14. Introducing a variety of vocational courses for the adolescents.
15. Developing skills of thinking, planning, communicating, organising, problem solving, monitoring and assessing.
16. Developing educational systems to reinforce rural development programmes.
17. Introducing non-military national service for adolescents.
18. Greater-learning opportunities at work places.
19. Programmes for balanced personal opportunities.
20. Programmes for developing in the adolescents a sense of service and the advancement of public good.
21. Developing in the adolescents skills how to learn.
22. Laying emphasis on the development in the adolescents values of self-awareness and esteem and confidence in order to deal with a rapidly changing world.
23. Developing in the adolescents a positive outlook for the future.
24. Developing in the adolescents a commitment to promote interpersonal development.
25. Promoting in the adolescents values of tolerance and respect for different perspectives and views, cultures, religious and races and towards opposite sex and to disabled people.

The Problems

Adolescence is marked by specific attitudes and behaviour patterns. Among the most important of these according to E.B. Harlock are: (i) Feeling of vague status during transitional period (ii) A period for important changes: (a) Heightened emotionality (b) Rapid sexual maturing (c) Marked physical changes (d) Major changes in adolescents interests and behaviour patterns. (iii) A dreaded attitude (iv) Unrealism (v) Threshold of adulthood.

Adolescence has been called a period of 'Challenge and Potential'. The adolescent has enormous potential-physical, ideational and intellectual. At the same time he is faced with great challenges on account of his rapid physical growth, soaring as well as falling ideals, his search for identity as he is neither considered as a child nor an adult, his growing sexual desires, heightened emotions and lack of appropriate energies for channelising his enormous energy. All these issues and problems make the adolescence period as the period of 'Stress anal Storm'. An adolescent is faced with several alternatives on account of his 'conflicts and dilemmas'. 'To do or not to do' attitude creates several problems the solution of which needs guidance and counselling. Since an adolescent, in general, has the notion of 'knowing all things', several difficulties confront him.

Salient Features

Some of the important specific characteristics of adolescence problems and worries as given by various thinkers are briefly described here.

Becoming Independent: J. A. Hadfield (1962) is of the view, "When we speak of adolescent as growing up we mean that the youth is leaving behind the phase of protective childhood and is becoming independent."

Age of Ideals: Jean Piaget defines adolescence as, "the age of great ideals and the beginning of theories as well as the time of simple adaptation to life."

Rapid Physical Growth and Development: Rate of growth is so rapid in some cases as it seems almost 'as they go to bed one night as children and wake-up the next morning as adults.'

Health and Adolescence: It has been stated, "A growing youth has a wolf in his stomach." At this period appetite for food is often enormous. There is a widespread notion that "this is physically a critical period." Various ailments that often manifest themselves are anaemia, nosebleed, nervousness, growing pains, palpitation of the heart and especially among girls, headache, etc.

Programme of Adolescents : 14-18 years Age Group

Objectives	*Context*	*Approach*
1. To help adolescents develop into a responsible adult.	Knowledge of the phenomenon of ovulation, foetal development and birth of a baby. Marriage for reproduction, need of assistance at birth.	a) Talks with the aid of audio-visual aids. b) Emphasis on leading highly moral and ethical life in the interest of family happiness and community peace.
2. To make adolescents understand venereal diseases.	Different venereal diseases. This mode of infection and their damaging effect on the patients.	Causes of these diseases, their symptoms and the conditions of the patients should be illustrated by means of films, film strips and pictures.
3. To make adults aware of promiscuity and prostitution.	Danger's of promiscuous sex relations. Its adverse influence on the family life and its being a great social evil. Prostitutes as chief sources of the spread of vene real diseases.	Frank discussion. Students to be told emphatically that all extramarital sex relations must be avoided in the interest of personal health and family happiness.
4. To make student careful of homosexuality.	Homosexual an unethical and unnatural practice. An offence under law punishable by imprisonment. Can convey vene real diseases	Adolescents must not be permitted to go out with strangers. They should be motivated to utilise their surplus energy and spare time in sports, cultural programmes, community welfare service and nation building activities. Such programmes should be systematically organised.

Sex and Adolescence: One writer has remarked, "Sex powers permeate the whole body and the entire life of feeling and thought and will."

Emotions and Adolescence: In the words of Richmond, "Adolescence is the heyday of the emotional life, the blossom time of all those feelings and emotions which depend at bottom upon sex." Masterson has observed, "Emotional disorders frequently arise during adolescence. Such disorders range from simple depression to being over anxious about health to suicidal thoughts or attempts." Many adolescents who engages in delinquent, bizarre, or self-abusive behaviour do so as a cell for help during a difficult period. Some adolescents use drugs, alcohol, or sex as a response to emotional disorders. The emotions of the adolescents drive them from one extreme to the other. At one time a boy or a girl may be shiftless, lazy or at another full of enthusiasm and energy.

Steps Required

1. A friendly, open-mindedness classroom climate, free of embarrassment to students should pervade.
2. Students should be free to ask questions which trouble them.
3. Answers given by the teachers should be honest and sensible.
4. Sex should be talked in an objective and a matter-of-fact way like any other subject.
5. A question box may be used in which adolescents may put questions anonymously if they do not feel free to ask questions in the class.
6. Films and other aids may be used to clarify concepts.
7. An adequate number of books on sex education should be kept in the open shelf school library.

Characteristic Spirit of Schooling : School ethos implies moral nature or environment of the school, its guiding principles, its distinguishing character and its sentiment.

The concept of an ideal ethos of a school has been very beautifully summed up by S. Bala Krishna Joshi, an eminent headmaster of a well managed school as, "A school is not a mere brick and mortar structure housing a miscellany of pupils and teachers; a school is not a market place where a heterogeneous crowd gathers with diverse objects; a school is not a rigorous reformatory where juvenile suspects are kept under vigilant watch, a school is a spiritual organism with distinctive personality of its own; a school is a vibrant community centre, radiating life and energy all round; a school is a wonderful edifice, resting on the foundation of goodwill-goodwill of the public goodwill of the parents; goodwill of the pupils. In a word, a well conducted school is a happy home, a sacred shrine, a social centre, a state in miniature and bewitching Brindavan, all beautifully blended into a synthetic structure."

Vital Factors

It is not without reason that the Education Commission 1964-66 observed "The destiny of India is now being shaped in her class-rooms. On the quality and number of persons coming out of schools and colleges will depend our success in the great adventure of national reconstruction."

Following factors in the school ethos greatly influence children's' learning and then overall growth and development.

Training in the Art of Living Together: "We do not visualize the school as merely a place of formal learning, whose main concern is to communicate a certain prescribed quantum of knowledge but rather as a living and organic community which is primarily interested in training its pupils in what we have called the gracious "art of living", observed the Secondary Education Commission.

Development of Child's Entire Personality: We would like the school to see if it can provide a richly varied pattern of activities to cater to the development of its children's entire personality. It has to formulate a scheme of hobbies, occupations and projects that will appeal to draw out the powers of children of varying temperaments and aptitudes.

Provision of a Stimulating Environment: The primary concern of the school should be to provide for its pupils a rich, pleasant and stimulating environment which will evoke their manifold interests and make life a matter of joyful experience.

Transformation into Activity School: The school must be transformed into an "activity school" because activity has an irresistible appeal for every normal child and in his natural path to the goal of knowledge and culture.

We do not visualize that these schools will have dull, routine ridden formal lessons in the class plus a number of independent unrelated extracurricular activities which have no intrinsic relationship with them either in contents or methods. The entire programme of the school will be visualised as a unity and inspired by a psychologically congenial and stimulating approach, the so-called 'work' being characterised by the feeling of joy and self expression usually associated with play and hobbies, and these having something of the meaningful and purpose which are normally considered a special feature of academic work. Thus by planning a coherent programme of these different activities, rich in stimuli, the school will not be frittering away either the time or the energy of the pupils but will be heightening their intellectual powers also side by side while training them in other fine qualities.

Opportunities for Self-Discipline: Discipline in the school will not be a matter of arbitrary rules and regulations enforced through the authority of the teachers helped by the lure of rewards or the fear of punishment. The students will be given full freedom to organise functions, to conduct many of the school activities through their own committees and even to deal with certain types of disciplinary cases. In this way, discipline will be maintained through the influence of the social group and it will gradually lead to the development of self-discipline.

No school can develop into an educative community, capable of releasing the students' creative capacities, if the teachers maintain a stiff forbidding attitude towards their pupils and try to maintain their authority through various kinds of punishments whilst the pupils, on their part, stand in awe of them and are not prepared to share their problems and difficulties with them.

The School as a Centre of Community Service: Another thing which will distinguish this school from most of the traditional schools is that it will be organised as a community.

Providing Work Experience and Socially Useful Work: We expect the school to devote special attention to craft and other productive work and thus redress the balance between theoretical and practical studies which have been upset for many years.

Democratic Classroom Climate	*Autocratic Classroom Climate*
1. Students are teacher-guided.	1. Students are teacher dominated.
2. The students are guided by the teacher in the choice of many activities.	2. The teacher plans activities without conferring with the pupils.
3. The groups suggests and proposes supplementary work- all of which is reviewed and appraised by the group.	3. All the supplementary work is chosen and assigned by the teacher.
4. The student aid in planning the academic work, make suggestions and proposals.	4. The students answer questions asked by the teacher.
5. The pupils share with teacher in establishing standards of achievement.	5. The teacher sets up standards of achievement without conferring with the pupils.
6. The students share with the teacher the responsibility of appraising their work.	6. The students are not conferred with in appraising their growth.
7. Students are encouraged by the teacher to make suggestions concerning their work.	7. The teacher ignores suggestions of the pupils.
8. The students can move about the room with comparative case and without disturbing the work.	8. The students can move only with the permission of the teacher.
9. Students are encouraged to correct their mistakes.	9. The teacher directs pupil activities.
10. The daily programme is elastic and can be changed as the group decides.	10. The teacher decides when pupils are to stop working on one subject and when to start on the next. Daily programme is rigid.
11. The teacher adopts an exploratory attitude.	11. The teacher gives directions in a firm manner.
12. The teacher tries to understand the child.	12. The teacher works according to set procedures.

Contd...

Democratic Classroom Climate	Autocratic Classroom Climate
13. The teacher is sympathetic.	13. The teacher springs awe and fear.
14. The teacher tries to find reasons for misbehaviour.	14. The teacher arbitrarily punishes pupils for misbehaviour.
15. The teacher takes into consideration the individual differences of the students.	15. The teacher treats all children alike.
16. Children are naturally affectionate and are encouraged to show affection.	16. Teacher is cold to child's affection and does not reciprocate.
17. Every child is provided with an opportunity to contribute and to lead a group.	17. Only the aggressive and brighter children contribute and lead.
18. Materials and books are provided for all mental levels in a grade.	18. One level of supplies is furnished for single grade no matter what the ability range.
19. Students are grouped properly.	19. Students are grouped on administrative reasons.
20. The students express themselves freely.	20. There is no such freedom of expression.
21. Curriculum is flexible to meet with the needs of each child.	21. Curriculum is definite and same goals are set for all the children.
22. Teachers cooperate with other teachers to study problem students.	22. Teacher normally does not participate in group study of pupils.
23. Teachers encourage parents to visit school for a closer relationship between home and school.	23. Teachers discourage parents from visiting school because according to them it disrupts the schedule.
24. School atmosphere is reflected by student's remark, "I like School."	24. School atmosphere is reflected by student's remark "I don't like school."
25. Students committees assume responsibility for selecting equipment and supplies needed.	25. Teacher or the principal assumes responsibility for selecting and purchasing supplies and equipment.

Comprehensive Curriculum: Curriculum should fulfil psychological and social needs of the students.

Guidance and Counselling Services: These should be adequate.

Human Relations: Students should be made acquainted with the principles of developing good harmonious relations.

Class Atmosphere

Meaning of Classroom Climate: Class-room climate implies classroom environment in which the change of behaviour or learning takes place through interaction in the group which consists of students of various shades and the teacher who is the leader of the group. In the process of learning, the mental health of the group is an important factor. As a leader, the teacher is expected to create democratic environment. His democratic behaviour in the classroom can steer constructive and inspirational individual as well as group activities in the right direction.

General Suggestions: Apart from the above mentioned factors for creating a democratic classroom climate, following suggestions should prove very useful:

1. It would be desirable for a teacher to throw some light on the qualities of leadership so that students choose their leaders wisely and the teacher is able to influence the class through its leaders. However it must be stressed that teacher must remain neutral in the selection of leaders.
2. The behaviour of the leader of the group is imitated by the members of the group.
3. Suggestion plays a big role in influencing the group behaviour. The suggestions put forward by the leader of the group are readily accepted.
4. The recent studies have made it clear that for bringing about changes to the individual, we must bring about changes in the characteristics of the group. The teachers, therefore, should adopt appropriate group methods in the class and through these influence the attitudes of the members of the group. Group training is better than individual training.

Need of a Role Model

Teacher's Personality: It has been rightly observed, "While books can teach, only personality can educate." A good personality includes:

(a) Impressive Appearance
(b) Modulated Voice
(c) High Character
(d) Effective Power of Communication.

Mahatma Gandhi observed, Woe to the teacher who teaches one thing with the lips and carries another in the heart."

Personality of the child in the desired dimension cannot be developed if the teacher who is the model to be followed lacks personality. Example is better than precept is an old saying, and it is absolutely true for the teaching profession. No amount of sermons from the teacher can make appreciable head way. A teacher teaches not only by 'What he says' but very largely by 'what he is'. Children are imitative and suggestive by nature. They imitate the dress, voice, habits and manners of their teachers. On several occasions, the likes and dislikes of teachers become the likes and dislikes of their students.

Children who are in the plastic period of their lives are easily influenced by their teachers. 'Man know thyself' is the advice given by sage Yajnavalkya in India and the philosopher Socrates of Greece. The teachers must undergo a spiritual inner training. They should try to find out their own shortcomings and remove them. Ryburn has observed, "Self-analysis on the part of a teacher is a necessary equipment" Montessori stresses that every teacher worth his salt must destroy these sins: pride, anger, sloth, sensuality and envy. He should be partly a doctor, partly a scientist and completely religious. He must acquire a moral alertness, patience, love and humility. Writing about the role of the teachers, Lauri has observed, "If a teacher has not an ideal aim, he had better to take to shop keeping at once, he will there doubles find an ideal within his capacity."

Dynamic Methods of Teaching: The Secondary Education Commission (1952-53) has very rightly observed, "Every teacher and educationist of experience knows that even the best curriculum and the most perfect syllabus remains dead unless quickened into life by the right methods of teaching and the right kind of teachers."

A wise teacher can make his class-room teaching-learning easier and effective if he can direct group dynamics into constructive paths.

Through group discussion and activity methods, the teacher would give the individual student a chance to participate actively and to contribute to group work in the class. Some specific group techniques which could be used for the improvement of the group are:

(i) Buzz session, in which a small group of five or six students participate, is organised for purposes of stimulating discussion.

(ii) Role playing, in which problems of handling a situation are dramatised for the benefit of the group.

(iii) Brain storming, in which a group is organised for stimulating discussion.

(iv) Catharsis, in which a planned group expression of problems of concern to the group is provided.

(v) Recreational experiences, in which opportunities are provided for participation in dramatics, picnics, parties, etc. to improve the morale.

Effective Interpersonal Communication: Good teaching is interpersonal communication. Teaching is a two-way communication. As the name indicates, interpersonal communication is the presence of the facility to seek reactions, information etc. One way communication i.e., telling or lecturing by the teacher denies the facility to the learner to seek clarification, confirmation etc. The learners do not get the opportunity to develop interpersonal relationships. Interpersonal communication has a built-in-system of feedback. It ensures that further information and clarification etc. are provided wherever possible. The receiver or the learner gets an opportunity to understand the message or the content of the communication.

Healthy interpersonal communication is the sound basis of sound instruction or teaching.

Ego-involvement: The personality of the child should be given its due recognition. Emerson has observed, "The secret of education lies in respecting the pupil"

Constructive and Creative Discipline: The teacher's attitude towards his children should be sympathetic but firm.

Stimulus Variation and the Teacher: It has been generally observed that children are not able to attend to one thing for a very long period. The effectiveness of the teaching- learning process in such a situation depends to a great extent on the stimulus variations used by the teacher behaviour. Some of the common teacher behaviours in the class-room which fall under variation are:

1. Teacher movement
2. Teacher gestures
3. Changes in speech pattern
4. Changes in sensory focus
5. Changes in postures.

Reinforcement: Praise and Blame "Praise like gold and diamond owes its value to scarcity", writers Robinson Johnson. It implies that this technique should be employed with great care. These may be classified as:

(a) *Positive Verbal Reinforcement:* Following a pupil's answer, the teacher verbally indicates pleasures at the pupil's response by the use of words like 'Good,' 'Fair', 'Excellent,' 'Correct', etc.

(b) *Positive Non-Verbal Reinforcement:* This includes: Nods and smiles.

Teacher's friendly movements towards pupils.

Teacher's friendly look.

Teacher writing student's response on the blackboard.

(c) *Negative Non-Verbal:* This comprises gestures, sneering, frowning, expression of annoyance, impatience, etc.

(d) *Negative Verbal:* This includes comments like 'No,' 'Wrong,' 'No good,' 'Poor', 'Of course not,' etc.

Learning combined with creative Humour and Appropriate Laughter: An experienced teacher once observed, "I consider a day's teaching-learning wasted, if we do not have a hearty laugh."

Teacher as a Guide: Sri Aurobindo writes in the regard, "The first principle of true teaching is that nothing can be taught. The teacher is not an instructor or a task master, he is a helper and a guide. His business is to suggest and not to impose. He does not impart knowledge to the pupil: he shows him how to acquire knowledge for himself."

The Evaluation

The teacher should keep an eye on the progress of every child. He should maintain a proper record of the same. He should inform his pupils about the success achieved by them. This will develop a sense of achievement among the pupils. This will also lead to achievement-motivation.

Diverse Factors

Among the social factors, other than the school, the five major groups that affect learning are: the family or the home, the class or the caste, the community and the rural-urban background. Learning is also affected by the tribal non-tribal background.

Familial Elements

American President Abraham Lincoln used to say, "Whatever I am and whatever I hope to be, I owe to my mother." Shivaji and Gandhiji expressed the same feelings. Educationists, psychologists and sociologists, all agree that the family is the most important single influence on the development and learning of the child. It has been said by Jemni, the author of 'Brahmasutra'. "The child learns the best lesson of citizenship between the kiss of the mother and care of his father."

The parents are the transmitters of the cultural and social standards Parents as the first teachers lay the foundations of the preliminary education/learning. Most of the education/ learning at this stage is at the unconscious level. While communicating or interacting with the child, the parents unknowingly impart knowledge, develop skills and inculcate values. The way in which the parents communicate with the child, and their choice of words have a lasting impact on the personality of the child.

Family is the primary school of citizenship. It is the family which teaches the child how to get along with others. The family teaches the lessons of cooperation and give and take. A family can play the role of the 'cradle of all virtues.'

Effective relationship of the child with the parents is a crucial factor in the development of the personality of the child. The parent-child bond is one of love, security and trust.

The parents must understand that no two children are alike and therefore their approach in dealing with different children must differ.

Parents can learn much about their children if they observe them carefully.

A child's natural curiosity forces him to explore new things. He wants independence and freedom. The parents must understand this fact fully.

Parents need not to be too rigid or too liberal to introduce toilet training in early years.

Parents should encourage the child to communicate. They should tell simple stories and sing songs etc. This will help the child to feel secure.

Meeting the child's physical needs is of prime importance. Malnutrition is a very common problem in India and it is to be checked. The diet of the child has to be a balanced one as it affects learning.

Food must be nutritious. Efforts should be made to develop regular eating habits.

Common childhood illness and accidents adversely affect the learning of the child. Timely immunization is one way to prevent diseases. Adequate amount of sleep is necessary for the health of the child. Parents should give due importance to hygienic living.

Parents should provide ample encouragement and opportunity for exercise.

Intellectual development is very rapid during early childhood years. The child asks too many questions which should be answered patiently by the parents. Parents should encourage child's development of language skills.

It is essential for parents to help the child in taking decisions and choosing alternatives to solve problems.

Parents should recognise the emotional needs of the child to make his life better and richer. Child's need for security should be realized by the parents. He should be accepted as an individual. He should be relieved from anxiety. He wants love and it should be made available to him. Non fulfilment of these needs may develop later problems of maladjustment.

Significant Roles of the Parents: Directly as well as indirectly, the following roles of the parents affect learning:

1. Parents as caretakers of physical needs of the children.
2. Parents as givers of security.
3. Parents as providers of love and affection.
4. Parents as role models for children to emulate
5. Parents as ideal disciplinary environment-constructive creators as well as creative.
6. Parents as developers of attitudes, skills and values.
7. Parents as providers of comfort in times of trouble.
8. Parents as admirers of children's achievements.
9. Parents as motivators and stimulators.
10. Parents as acceptors of limitations and assets of children.
11. Parents as providers of an overall stimulating environment.

The Drawbacks

Great psychological damage is caused to young children from poor family relationships. Three forms of psychological damages are caused to young children. First, the young child who develops an angry attitude towards a strict parents is likely to develop an unfavourable attitude towards all adults outside the home also.

Second, poor relationships in the family, for example, feeling of unloved and unwanted in the family may lay the foundations of an inferiority complex.

Third, unfavourable family relationships make children unhappy and keep them upset. The children remain emotionally disturbed.

Economy's Role

Undoubtedly class and socio-economic factors play a significant role in development and learning of children. The type of environment they provide to their children has a great bearing on learning.

It is very difficult to classify the society into watertight compartments. Nevertheless Indian society on the socio-economic basis can be classified as: (i) Class of people below the poverty line (ii) Lower class i.e., just above the poverty line class (iii) Lower middle class (iv) Middle class (v) Upper class (vi) VIP class (very Important Persons' class).

(i) Class of people below the poverty line constitutes nearly one-third of India's population. This class, by and large, has failed to derive benefit from educational facilities and incentives provided by the government. Almost the entire class can be placed under the category 'illiterate.' It is so much engrossed in making both ends meet that it can hardly think of providing education to its children.

(ii) The lower middle class, though conscious of the benefit of educating children, is still not able to make the maximum benefit of educational and learning opportunities and incentives.

(iii) The middle class has been able to make use of the facilities provided by the government to a considerable extent. It recognises the importance of learning and is quite keen that its children occupy respectable positions in the society. However, barring a few sections of this population, majority of its children go to local bodies/government schools which in general lack suitable buildings, equipments, libraries workshops etc. The standard of teaching-learning is on the lower side. It is true that this class has also produced great scholars, professionals and eminent persons in various fields. But the proportion is not very high.

Upper Class/VIP Class: This class makes all possible efforts to send its children to public schools of varying standards but in general higher than state-run schools. Public schools provide better schooling facilities to their students. Quite a good proportion of students educated in these schools occupy prestigious positions in different walks of life.

The community must provide a pure, simple and a well balanced environment. It must eliminate evil influences on the child. It should provide secular examples to children.

The various institutions in the community such as Panchayats, Mahila Mandals. Youth Clubs etc., should be involved in the development and learning of children.

The community and especially 'play groups' of young children exercise a considerable influence on their personality development. The activities of these play groups are highly imaginative and educative. Following are the learning and educative values of play groups in the community.

1. Children learn to cooperate.
2. Children learn to respect other's right and duties.
3. Children get opportunities for both leadership and followership training.
4. Children develop social attitudes.
5. Children get opportunities to play together and thus become conscious of the differences that exist in attitudes, values and behaviour in children of the neighbourhood.
6. Children get valuable information about their neighbourhood.

The community must ensure that the play-groups/peer groups provide suitable environment.

Attempts should be made to educate the parents to develop interest, skills and knowledge in child care.

The community and the especially the rural community must take interest in establishing educational institutions. In rural areas, it is generally expected to provide land for the school buildings.

The inter-relatedness of the community and the school must be adequately understood in our country. The community should not treat school as an institution outside the community. There should be a friendly-oriented partnership between the school and the community.

Apart from cooperating in various instructional programmes of the school, the community can offer assistance to the school in various areas like the following:

1. Electrification of the school building.
2. White washing and minor repairs of the school building.
3. Construction of compound walls.
4. Provision of sheds for cooking meals.
5. Donations of land for various purposes.
6. Painting of black-boards.
7. Supply of portraits of national leaders.
8. Supply of stationery and books to the poor students.
9. Supply of uniforms to the poor students.
10. Supply of utensils.
11. Supply of play materials.
12. Offering free services by individuals like doctors.

Social Declination

There is no doubt that a conducive environment helps to draw out the best in child-body, mind and soul. However, rural schools, in general, lack such a learning environment. Rural schools are usually housed in poor buildings. They also lack equipment and various learning facilities. Qualified and experienced teachers, when posted to rural schools, are always in the look out of transfers to urban schools. Thus students are deprived of their services.

Rural societies are conservative and traditional by and large. This fact also makes a lot of difference in the learning outcomes of students.

In the urban areas, there are several well-maintained school libraries, museums, research institutes etc. which serve as resource centres of learning. Students get a much wider exposure to new technology. Competition among institutions and students is also very keen.

All the above mentioned factors lead to wide differences in learning.

In spite of the recommendations of several education committees and commissions, we are far away from the goal of providing equal opportunities to learners. Much ground in this regard still remains to be covered.

14

Prompted Learning

As a teacher, you will be interested in how motivation influences the acquisition of skills and knowledge in a school situation. We shall look closely at the problem of learning in the classroom. Here we shall discuss some aspects of motivation that are not directly a part of the classroom situation.

"Plateaus" in Learning. Over a long period of time, the development of a motor skill, such as typewriting, working on an assembly line, or sending code messages, follows a fairly predictable pattern. At first, the individual shows a rather rapid increase in efficiency. This is followed by a period of slow improvement and then by a long period in which little or no improvement is made. When a secretary first learns to typewrite by means of the touch system, for example, her speed develops during the first year of practice from zero to perhaps 50 words per minute. The next year or so of practice may bring her speed up to 60 or 65 words per minute. After that, she will probably maintain the same level of skill for many years, with slight day-to-day fluctuation. This will be true even though she receives a certain set fee per page typed and it is to her advantage to type as rapidly as possible. We might decide that she has reached her physiological limit. However, psychologists discovered long ago that although individuals do reach a level beyond which they do not progress as long as their need remains the same, a substantial increase in need will result in progress far beyond what originally appeared to be their limit. When sufficient additional motivation arises, further improvement takes place and the individual may continue to improve for a substantial period of time.

If our typist, for example, is promised a promotion that involves prestige and money if she can attain a level of speed well beyond her present maximum, there is a good chance that she will succeed—assuming, of course, that the goal is not actually beyond her abilities. Habits of working at a speed that satisfies the individual's present motivation will not be broken until his motivation is substantially increased. He is content with his present performance even though it is well below his physiological limits. Each individual's level of performance is determined by a combination of his abilities, his level of aspiration, and the habits of work that have proved adequate to satisfy his current needs.

Of course, the ability to attain various levels of skill does vary from person to person. But regardless of our real physiological limit, we seldom come very near to attaining it. And the nearness with which we do approach it is determined by the extent of our needs.

Although we have been talking here only of simple motor skills, there is evidence that other types of learning, problem-solving, and competence in doing complex tasks, such as reading with speed and understanding, also depend on the amount of motivation furnished by our present needs.

The use of Incentives. Rewards designed to influence behaviour are often called incentives. To influence behaviour significantly, however, the reward must be needed. It must serve to satisfy some motive. In the school we offer the child interesting experiences and opportunities to satisfy his curiosity and to achieve status and self-esteem. For example, a child can have numerous incentives for reading about the pioneers. His curiosity concerning what solution they will find to each problem acts as an incentive. And he identifies himself with Daniel Boone or David Crockett and obtains interesting experiences. He is able to share his experiences with his classmates and gain their attention and approval. He gains a word of praise or a sense of security from his teacher. His reading may result in a better grade and heightened self-esteem and esteem in the eyes of his parents.

In business and industry a bonus or a promotion may be offered as a reward for extra effort. In any situation, the most successful incentives are those that appeal to one or all of the psychological motives.

Positive and Negative Incentives. Educators have stated repeatedly that praise is stronger than reproof. But before we accept such a broad generalisation, we should look closely at what is known about these common incentives.

Both praise and reproof are strong drugs. If praise is administered constantly over a period of time, it loses much of its potency. In addition, how effective it is depends a good bit on the personality of the person who administers it. We expect praise from some individuals and accept it almost as we would accept silence from another. And if we hear little but praise from everyone, we grow to value it less and less.

The same is true of reproof. If a teacher constantly berates his students, they come to expect it. In fact, if a student fails to receive his fair measure of reproof for the day, he may lose status with his fellows. And so it is in the home. A child who receives little but reproof from his parents comes to expect and accept it. Its sting becomes dulled. But give such a child an unexpected word of praise and he will grasp it as a jewel. He will treasure it as a rare source of satisfaction.

Both praise and blame, like certain drugs, lose their effectiveness as we become tolerant of them, but our tolerance varies in relation to the individual from whom we receive them. We strive for a word of praise from one person either because he rarely gives praise or because his good opinion is necessary for our security. A word of reproof from another person may fail to stir us either because we have come to expect it or because his good opinion is of little importance for our feeling of security. If praise or blame is to affect our behaviour, it must either satisfy or threaten our security, our self-esteem, our esteem in the eyes of others, or some other motive.

The varying effect that praise and blame have on different

individuals has been well demonstrated by experiments. During one learning experiment, a group of introverted children and a group of extroverted children were praised at certain times and blamed at others. The extroverted children made more improvement when they received blame than when they were praised, but the opposite was true of the introverted group. Other studies suggest that the extrovert tends to come from an environment where praise is more common than blame and that the opposite is true for the introvert. Typically, the introvert's development has been marked by strong repression whereas the extrovert has been encouraged to express himself and has often been the center of favourable attention.

Other things being equal, then, which has the more powerful effect on classroom learning—praise or blame? As you might expect, praise seems to be somewhat more powerful in actual practice. However, the evidence indicates that both serve to stimulate learning, since either one seems to produce better results than no comment whatsoever.

Praise and blame are examples of positive and negative incentives. Although individuals may react somewhat differently because of different past experiences, it is more pleasant to all of us to strive for positive rewards than it is to escape from negative threats. We strive either to improve our status or to prevent loss of our present status. Which motivation will result in greater effort depends somewhat on the nature of the individual and on the nature of the promised gain or possible loss.

Quite apart from the actual effort induced by different motivating situations, we as teachers must also be interested in the mental health of each child. Striving for advancement, particularly when it leads to success, is accompanied by a happy, pleasant feeling. Striving to prevent a threat to our present status, however, even if it is eventually successful, is accompanied by an unhappy, unpleasant feeling and by worry. The maladjustment evidenced in "nervous breakdowns" is more closely related to overworry than to overwork. Positive incentives in themselves, then, contribute more to the mental and emotional well-being of children than negative incentives do.

Motivational Product

Interests are a specific type of positive incentive. They are capable of arousing and sustaining concentrated effort. For this reason, we shall want to study them carefully. How much appeal the classroom material has to a child's interests determines to a considerable extent how hard and how long he will be willing to concentrate on it. For the most part, study fatigue is created by nothing more than disinterest or boredom.

Why Children Differ in Interests : Since children learn new things in order to satisfy physiological and psychological motives, biological factors have a strong influence on the development of their interests. If a child is large and agile, he is likely to gain self-esteem and the esteem of others from physical competition; if he is small or awkward, his security and prestige are likely to be threatened. If a child finds that experiences in the classroom nurture his security, he comes to enjoy being a student and to spend more time and effort in studious pursuits. If an adolescent girl finds that boys admire her, she is likely to enjoy dancing and similar activities in which she can receive their attention; if boys do not seek her out, she will find other activities to nurture her self-esteem.

Most interests are the product of past experiences. The goals that a child discovers to be approved by his family and his community, the experiences he has had with books, movies, companions, and teachers, and the experiments he has made in the world about him determine the direction that his interests will take.

Some differences in interests are caused by differences in chronological age. If for no reason other than the desire for social acceptability, the boy of 16 must shun some activities that are quite appropriate to the boy of eight.

Other differences in interest are related to sex. The fact that parents tend to approve one type of play activity for girls and another for boys is especially important to younger children. A girl receives favourable recognition when she spends time with dolls, plays house, or learns ballet dancing, but a boy who does the same things finds that his security and self-esteem are threatened.

Since girls, on the average, reach maturity at an earlier age than boys do, they show an earlier interest in dancing and in other activities that involve the opposite sex. Also, individual differences in physical maturation among members of the same sex have a strong effect on interests. As we have seen, some boys of 14 are sexually mature and others are immature. For both boys and girls, the attainment of sexual maturity results in new forms of motivation and in new problems. It is reflected in their choice of reading matter, conversational topics, heroes, movies, and radio and television programmes.

Actually, the specific interests that a child develops depend directly on how clearly he has been able to identify the types of activity that satisfy his motives. His desires for security, self-esteem, the esteem of others, and new experiences, and the success or failure that he meets in attempting to satisfy these desires, play a major part in determining what his interests will be. In other words, psychological motives, as well as physiological motives, are significant.

And once interests are formed, the habit motives tend to perpetuate them. A boy may retain an interest in coin-collecting, fishing, football, or photography long after they cease to satisfy the motives that they originally satisfied. Habit motives and the desire to be with friends who have the same interests may be sufficient. Or, as we trace interests throughout life, we may find that an activity remains the same but that the motives satisfied by it change greatly. For example, a boy may take up golf because it makes him feel mature and because it has social prestige; as a young man, he gains group and self-esteem from his proficiency; later he continues the game for the business contacts that come from it; and still later he follows it for reasons of health and to satisfy habit motives.

As a teacher, you will need a deep understanding of what interests are typical of both sexes at each developmental level, and of the range of interests that you can expect to find within groups of the same age and sex. Then you can translate your information into specific, practical terms, such as the games, books, movies, and songs that will be most appealing to a particular group of children.

What techniques can we use to determine specific interests? And how can we use interests in developing an effective learning situation?

Leisure-time Activities due to Interests : When children work and play under the direct supervision of adults, they have a natural tendency to display the interests they feel are expected of them. They are more interested in winning approval than they are in following their other inclinations. But in their freely chosen, leisure-time activities, they unwittingly provide us with valuable dues to what their interests really are. So you will want to take advantage of every opportunity to observe children after school hours, to talk with them about how they spend their evenings, and to enter into their social activities whenever you can do it unobtrusively and without embarrassment to the children and to yourself.

Try to find out what books they like to read, what radio and television programmes appeal to them, what movies they go to, what friends they spend their time with, what hobbies they follow, and what they do when they are with the family group. In the classroom itself you can gain insight into children's interests by encouraging them to exercise self-direction in attacking problems or in choosing assignments.

Each time you discover a new interest, remember that it has real importance in the life of the child. It represents to him a possible way of finding satisfaction for his motives and a solution to his problems. If you can manage to accommodate classroom activities to a real interest that the child himself has shown, you will succeed in creating a stimulating, effective learning situation. The secret is to enlist children's interests in the classroom rather than to oppose and reject them.

With the information you gather by observing children's leisure-time activities, you can do more than just appeal to their current interests. You can encourage them to enlarge and extend their interests in new, more rewarding directions. Since interests are the child's way of satisfying his motives, he will welcome sincere attempts to help him develop more satisfying activities. Of course when you attempt to build up new interests, you will have to be much more careful than when you appeal to interests that already exist. But once a child has discovered that a new activity provides him with satisfaction, he will readily adopt it as a new interest.

Important Advises

Never worry about creating motivation in children. Every child has a tremendous amount of motivation that he is eager to satisfy every hour of the day. If you can suggest desirable educational goals that appeal to the child's motives, and if you can give him frequent opportunities to succeed in his attempts to reach those goals, you will have harnessed one of the most powerful learning forces known.

Since frustrating problems are as essential to the learning situation as motives themselves, you will want to be careful not to remove every difficulty from the child's path. Problems are a necessary condition of learning. They must be great enough to call forth serious effort, but not so great that they lead to defeat and a retreat from important goals.

As you help children in their attempts to satisfy their motives, always remember that individual children vary in their ability to achieve. No child will strive after an impossible goal for very long. He must find his tasks challenging but not discouraging. They must be tailored to fit his individual abilities. By providing him with opportunities to succeed in winning security, self-esteem, the esteem of others, and new experiences, you will make the classroom the scene of significant learning.

Be careful about how you approach the needs and interests of the child. Your task is not so much to let each child do just what he wants to do, but rather to encourage him to strive for significant long-range goals by appealing to the needs and motives that he already possesses. In short, you will help the child to choose what he is to learn. You will not force him to do things that he finds objectionable, but you must guide him in the directions that the curriculum-maker and the school as a whole find desirable.

There is much for the child to learn, and only a short time in which to learn it. You can increase both the speed and the quality of his learning by appealing to the motives that he brings with him into the classroom.

The Method

Another question. How does learning take place? What are the conditions which favour learning? What external conditions result in improved performance by an individual? These questions are of great interest to the teachers, parents, students and the educationists. Psychologists have defined learning as any relatively permanent changes in behaviour as a result of practice or experience. It modifies or changes the behaviour of the students in terms of achieving the goals. It is the process by which the student profits from past experiences. It is an inference from behaviour and must be distinguished from it, for learning can occur without behaviour being affected. We may learn that a certain petrol-station is open twenty four hours a day without influencing our observable behaviour, unless and until we need petrol-station during the night. It is inferred that learning has occurred if in such circumstances we patronise the petrol-station concerned whereas previously we would not have done so. Thus learning is a change in behaviour potential rather than in behaviour itself. Such changes can occur for many reasons, including maturation, fatigue, injury or the effects of drugs. But the term learning is applied only to those resulting from past experience. Further, it is restricted to changes of relatively permanent nature. Once having learned to ride a bicycle or drive a car, we quite soon regain former attainments in these skills after even long periods of disuse. Long term changes in behaviour potential of this sort are to be distinguished from shorter term changes which are often the result of temporary states in the learner such as variations in motivations.

The Learning

From the above discussion, it is understood that learning is the modification of behaviour potential as a function of experience. A simpler definition, most frequently found in ordinary dictionaries, is that learning involves the acquisition of information. This is often the case, but there are a number of situations in which individuals learn without acquiring any new information. This is obvious in the development of certain motor skills where practice rather than information leads to gradual modifications in behaviour.

In addition, affective learning (learning involving emotional behaviour) does not necessarily involve the acquisition of information as it is ordinarily defined as a behaviour change due to experience including all affective motor and cognitive (intellectual) changes that do not result from other causes. For example, behaviour can change as a result of fatigue, drags or maturation; but these changes are of a transient nature resulting from genetic forces, or are induced artificially. They are not considered to involve learning.

Man learns new methods and skills to successfully do, think reason and adjust to any forthcoming problem. Learning is associated with acquisition of new behaviour or modification of old behaviour. Psychologists from their own viewpoints have defined learning in various ways. Let us discuss some important definitions given by eminent psychologists.

While a student wants to learn more and more new ideas, a teacher tries to make his teaching effective and fruitful. Similarly, a doctor is interested to know about new medicines, and an engineer wants to invent new ideas of construction. An industrialist puts into use new methods of production. A politician sticks to new methods of propaganda to attract people towards him. In the same way a housewife prepares new items of food, while children want to make themselves attractive by wearing dresses of new designs. Priests and prophets adopt new tricks to make their views popular. They manipulate methods to attract more and more persons and to have more and more followers. So it is clear from the above discussion that everybody is inclined to learn new methods for his way of life. Then a question arises spontaneously as to, how does learning take place? What is learning? What is nature and what are its principles? Now let us discuss the definitions and nature of learning.

Definition of Learning : Learning can be defined as any relatively permanent change in behaviour which occurs as a result of practice or experience. This definition has three important elements (1) learning is a change in behaviour, for better or worse. (2) It is the change that takes place through practice or experience, changes due to growth, maturation, or injury are not learning. This part of the definition distinguishes learning from innately controlled, species specific behaviour of the sort. (3) Before it can be called learning, the change must be relatively permanent, it must last a fairly long time. This rules out changes in behaviour due to motivation, fatigue, adaptation, or sensitivity of the organism.

According to Skinner, learning is not acquiring knowledge or skill by mere mechanical repetitions. It is a process in which the learner organises different elements and experiences to reach a particular goal.

In the view of Hilgard, learning refers to the change in a subject's behaviour to a given situation brought about by his repeated experiences in that situation, provided that the behaviour change cannot be explained on the basis of native response tendencies, maturation or temporary states of the subject (e.g, fatigue, drugs etc).

In the opinion of King Ley and Gray, "learning is the process by which an organism in satisfying its motivation adopts and adjusts its behaviour in order to overcome obstacles or barriers."

According to Eason, "learning includes changes in behaviour that are determined primarily by the individuals interaction with his, environment."

H. J. Klausmeireir writes, "Learning is a process whereby a change in behaviour results from some form of experience, activity, training, observation and the like change in some behaviour which results from such forces as bodily injury, disease, fatigue or use of drugs is not considered learning".

According to Cronback learning is shown by a change in behaviour as a result of experience.

Blair, Jones and Simpson are of the view that, "any change of behaviour which is a result of experience, and which causes people to face later situations differently may be called learning".

According to W. C. Morse and G. M. Wingo "Learning can be defined as changing one's potential for seeing, feeling and doing through experiences partly perceptual, partly intellectual, partly emotional and partly motor".

According to Morris L. Bigge "Learning is a change in a living individual which is not heralded by genetic inheritance, it may be a change in insights, behaviour, perception or motivation or a combination of them."

Guthrie in Psychology of Learning says learning is "The ability to learn, that is, to respond differently to a situation because of past response to the situation".

Hall opines, "the essential nature of learning process may, however, be stated quite simply. Just as the inherited equipment of reaction tendencies consists of receptor effector corrections, so the process of learning consists in the strengthening of certain of these connections as contrasted with others or in the setting up of quite new connections".

One of the shortest definitions was given by J. P. Guilford. It reads, "Learning is change in behaviour resulting from behaviour."

According to Garret, "Learning is an organization of behaviour, It is the activity by virtue of which we organise our responses with new habits".

Murphy states that "Learning is a modification of both behaviour and the way of perceiving".

Inherent Nature

Man not only learns but also trains the lower animals. For example in a circus, wild animals like tiger, elephant, and bear perform many tricks. So also a pigeon can be trained to carry letters from one place to another, and a trained dog can identify a thief. Psychologist Hays brought up a chimpanzee from his babyhood just like a human child. By providing him with special learning experiences certain changes in his behaviour were marked. As a result of his learning in his latter days he preferred more to live among human beings than among other chimpanzees. He was able to clean the dishes, polish and colour the furniture, clean the room and sharpen the pencil, etc. He was even able to attend psychological non-verbal tests with human children of his age. But in spite of all the attempts of the researchers, he could not develop his skill in language. It is because, the vocal center of animals lacks something, which human beings possess. While human beings are able to read, play, dance and gather knowledge, about various things, the animals fail to do these. The mind of human beings is a developed one and that is why they are able to master the knowledge of higher level. What learning does for a human child and how it affects his life-style is clear from the following discussions.

1. *Learning is Modification of Behaviour:* Learning produces change in behaviour. Learning is often described as the modification of behaviour. The child learns ideas, rules, customs, etc, from his surroundings in order to adjust himself with his environment and different required behaviour and predicted activities though no one teaches him to do so. Gradually this modification of behaviour becomes permanent and goes on developing and changing day by day.
2. *Learning Helps to Reach the Goal:* Learning not only brings change in behaviour but also helps one in meeting the desires of one's life. Again, goals and ambitions can be achieved only with appropriate and positive learning in a particular direction. It directly or indirectly helps the individual to reach his goal. Learning of speech, learning to laugh, cry in the case of a child, is organised deliberately. They are not accidental. Hence learning is accepted by all as an internalising process.
3. *Learning Creates Interest to know New Things:* A deep desire or thirst for knowledge is often marked in some individuals Even in case of children, it is observed that they show interest and are anxious to do new works to find out new facts and engage themselves in small and simple researches. This helps them to learn more and more.
4. *Environmental Influence brings Difference in Learning:* All children are not reared up in similar environments. A particular child is brought up in different environments during his lifetime. Hence learning process and its effects on one child may be different from that of another on the basis of their difference in environment in which their

learning experience takes place. Children coming from adverse environments such as poverty, sometimes show amazing results in learning. So also the ones coming from a proper environment sometimes show the same originality in learning. Children coming from villages and undeveloped localities, In spite of their intelligence, fail to become successful in learning due to their undeveloped environment. On the other hand, children in urban areas, In spite of their low I.Q. are successful in better learning performance. It is because their environment helps them learn better. Hence it can be said that a proper and adequate environment is very much necessary for a fruitful learning of the child. Especially the house and the school should provide the necessary stimulus for learning experience.

5. *Learning is a Problem-solving Activity:* Society is dynamic. An individual has to adjust himself with every change and he has to face many novel and unexpected situations. There are some problems that cannot be solved by means of age old customary methods. The novel situations should be met with new ideas, and at this point learning helps him. Changing problems in changing circumstances can only be solved with new forms of learning.

6. *Learning is a Matter of Habit:* From this proposition one may conclude that doing a work habitually is learning. Learning is the display of mastered personal reaction to a given situation. Man has to react in the right way to his stimulus. By habit formation, he can do away with incorrect ways of reaction formation. Secondly, learning makes habit not only to be formed in the correct way but also be organised.

7. *Learning is an Automatic Process:* Learning takes place when the child becomes active. He has to indulge himself in the process of learning. In course of performing daily activities he automatically gathers experience. And that is the process of learning. When he himself becomes aware of his requirements—mental, physical, social and emotional, etc, he becomes active. Its requirements stimulate his will and produces response. If he is easily motivated by some other factors, then learning can also take place even without a

teacher. The child learns when he feels the requirement for it. So this process is always directed to a particular goal.

8. *Learning is not Knowledge about Subjects:* Learning is not confined to the four walls of an educational institution. Reading and remembering books is also not learning. All round development of a person is learning and by learning only, one's personality matures. Studying different branches of knowledge in schools and colleges is generally termed as learning. But apart from this there are so many things such as knowledge about God, language, literature, philosophy, art, sculpture, social values, personal traits, which are also learned by human beings. So it should not be misunderstood that learning implies only reading books.
9. *Learning may be Correct or Incorrect:* Though learning is defined as modification of behaviour, the modification itself may be correct or incorrect. It may be socially acceptable or unacceptable. We learn both good behaviour and bad behaviour in our day to day experiences. But true learning warns us against bad behaviour and this is right learning.
10. *Learning Occurs both in Formal and Informal, Situations:* Process of learning starts from the birth of a child. He learns many things through social interaction with others in his environment. New habits are formed and skills mastered. Many novel ideals also occur in his own mind. New choices, new beliefs and new interests are aroused in him. Then he comes to school and learns what he is taught. He is aware of what he is learning. So all the above learning processes can be termed as formal learning. Apart from these, he also learns informally from his various other experiences. Various institutions such as family, club, gymnasium, religious place, playground, excursion, etc, render informal learning to him.
11. *Higher Learning depends upon Capacity of Individual and Complexity of Learning Material:* For successful and effective learning, so many personal factors are responsible. They are our individual capabilities. They include our memory,

interest, understanding, emotion, controlling capacity, etc. To make learning effective, the child takes the help of two processes. One is that he tries to solve some of his problems with already acquired knowledge and skills and the second is that he discovers new methods and skills to face some personal problems. In order to solve some complex problems, he needs higher and more learning.

12. *Learning is a Function of Maturation:* Learning to an extent is also a function of maturation. One cannot teach a new born baby to walk or to pick up any object with his fingers however much one may try. Before anything is learnt by a person, his sensory, motor and also the nervous system including brain must reach a certain level of maturity.

    The predetermined sequential stage of maturity of the sensory motor and nervous system of an animal is called maturation. Individuals of different species undergo different sequential patterns of development and maturation. It has been observed that unless an individual attains a particular level of maturation, he cannot learn a particular skill of learning. Different learnings require different levels of maturation. Acquisition of simple motor skills is possible in early infancy. But complex activities like reading and writing, etc, which require a developed brain has to be postponed for pre-school and early-school period.

    Important in this context is the concept of "critical period" for learning. If it has not been learnt at a particular stage of child's maturational development, it becomes difficult for him to master it at a later period. Harlow made an experiment in 1962 on monkeys regarding this. He raised some monkeys in isolation, without letting them to mix or play with other monkeys. He found that if the isolation is upto 90 days the resultant abnormal social and sexual behaviour is short-lived, but if isolation is more than that period, the abnormality persists throughout life. This made him conclude that the first 90 days is the critical period for learning of social and sexual behaviour in monkeys.

13. *Learning is Dependent on Nervous System:* Learning is also

dependent on the nervous system which includes the brain. It has been found that the animals with more complex nervous systems learn faster and acquire more complex skills than those with simpler nervous systems. An experimenter reared a chimpanzee just like a human baby soon after its birth. He also gave it special training whenever necessary. As a result of this she learnt to perform simple acts like dusting, washing dishes and painting furnitures, etc. But she could not talk because of the deficiency in the language or speech center of her brain. Thus, limitations of the brain is an important factor in the learning ability of a child or an animal.

As to human learning, the growth of cerebral cortex plays a very important role. Growth of learning ability during childhood and adolescence is directly related to maturation of the cerebral cortex. The decline of learning ability in old age is probably due to the decay of the tissues of this part of the brain.

Lashley conducted an experiment on white rats. His three important findings about learning and the brain are that learning is related to the amount of cortical tissue, available inside the brain of the subject. The greater the amount of cortical tissue, the quicker will be his learning. He proved this by taking away various percentages of cortical tissue from the brains of rats and then making them learn the maze. The second conclusion is that learning is related to the location of specific cortical tissues in the brain of the subject. He proved that the removal of specified cortical tissues led to the loss of sensitivity to visual details, removing another, to the loss of sensitivity to different odours, and so on. Thus, there are functional specialisations inside the brain. A brain has different centres for different abilities. If the subject's brain lacks a particular centre, say speech centre, he cannot learn that ability. Lashley also came to another conclusion. He found that if a particular centre in the brain of the subject, relating to some particular ability is destroyed, then it results only in temporary loss of the ability. Gradually other parts of the cerebral cortex take up the function of the destroyed centre. Hence the lost ability of the subject reappears from this. He propounded his theory of mass action, which means that cerebrum functions as mass.

14. *Learning is a Self-acting Process:* Learning is also a self-active process. Learning involves the subject. If a child has to learn, he has to be involved in the process of learning. He has to participate in his experiences and has to learn from them. There cannot be any learning without the involvement of his self. To learn, a child or a subject has not only to involve his senses but he has also to use the higher centre of his brain, which will impart pattern, meaning and significance to his sensory inputs.

The Features

We can conclude that learning is a process that provides impetus for a new behaviour or through interaction with the environment brings change in the already existing behaviour. Learning brings a permanent change in behaviour. Hence the changes in behaviour caused by regular exercise, games, habitual walks, are permanent change. The intensity of emotion may also bring change in behaviour. So it is right to conclude that human behaviour is the central point of learning process. Here behaviour does not mean physiological activities only, but inner processes like thinking, memory, power, causality and emotional reaction.

The sort of change in behaviour, which can be termed as learning may also be necessary or unnecessary. This change may occur inside the school or outside it. It may occur knowingly or unknowingly. W. R. Mescaw in his book *Educational Psychology* has given details of the characteristics of learning process. They are:

Developmental Change

Learning in case of human beings, is a matter of progressive change in behaviour. It is result of a felt need from within the organism. Unless there is a strong urge in the body to adopt a particular response and to modify its pattern, learning would not take place. Heredity and environment affect learning and the capability of the learner in a very big way. Some animals are more educable than others and similarly some individuals get more opportunities of learning than others. Learning and process of maturation are strongly related. It is the level of maturity in the individual that determines whether he would be able to make a particular response or not. More complex responses and more intricate activities cannot be acquired unless one has matured to do so. Thinking stabilizes as the level of maturity goes up. Higher intellectual activities are not possible without greater maturity. The native behaviour is less refined in comparison to the acquired one. In fact the acquired behaviour gives definite shape to the inherited behaviour, it is a sort of mere ornamental process which refines and brightens the inherited raw response. Learnt behaviour is an embellishment to the personality. Throughout one's life, not only does one learn to sit, to stand or to turn or to speak but also to dress well, to think deeply and to acquire knowledge. The home, the school, the club, etc, are the temples of learning. The child learns by himself; he also has to learn a number of response patterns in the company of his friends, parents and teachers.

Change on Permanent Basis : Learning may be defined as relatively permanent change in behaviour potential occurring as the result of past experience. It is an inference from behaviour and must be distinguished from it for learning can occur without behaviour being affected. We may learn that a certain petrol-station is open twenty four hours a day without this influencing our observable behaviour, unless and until we need petrol during the night. It is inferred that learning has occurred if in such circumstances, we patronise the petrol-station concerned whereas previously we would not have done so. Thus learning is a change in behaviour potential rather that in behaviour itself. Such changes can occur for many reasons, including maturation, fatigue, injury or the effects of drugs, but the term learning is applied only to those resulting from past experience. Further, it is restricted to changes of a relatively permanent nature. Once having learned to ride a bicycle or drive a car, we quite soon regain former attainments in these skills after even long periods of disuse. Long-term change in behaviour potential of this sort are to be distinguished from short-term changes which are often the result of temporary states in the learner such as variations in motivation. A convenient fourfold classification of learning is outlined in the remainder of this chapter.

Process of Cooperation

Learning is not an individualistic process; it is a cooperative process too. The child learns by impulse and he learns by compulsion; he learns by imitation and he learns by initiation, and he learns by adoption and he learns by assimilation. Philosophy, religion, science, architecture, etc, are the results of human learning and the capability of the human child to retain experiences. Man has developed media through which experiences are stored and transmitted from one to the other generation. Ability to retain experiences, is the key note of learning. Learning is an institutionalized and formalised affair in modern education. The child does not go to school to learn, reading and writing but he has to learn to adjust to the environment.

Learning of Creative Nature

It is a way of acting, as all true learning tasks take into account some selective responses, it is not merely the summing up of all previous knowledge and experience; it is creative synthesis of all knowledge and the experience of the learner. Hence lies the difference between animal learning and human learning. In human learning the following mental processes are involved as cited by Crow and Crow (1954)

(a) Interest and attention are directed towards a goal direction

(b) Perception of relation and interpretation

(c) Selection and recall of relevant experiences

(d) Recognition of relationships among the component experiences insight

(e) Formation of new mental pattern creation

(f) Evaluation of workability of solution-criticism

True human learning should aim at the higher level of thinking i.e., creative and critical thinking.

Learning based on Social Condition : Learning is not only individual but in a sense also social, because learning takes place in response to the social environment of the individual. A child's social interaction is of great significance to his favourable or unfavourable learning. An intelligent teacher takes note of the social climate in the classroom, the influence of peer group on a child, and so on.

Change based Learning

Transfer to a new task becomes more meaningful and advantageous to the learner when he has already discovered relationships between things and has learned to apply the principles within a given number of tasks. Learning is transferable in this way but the amount of transfer may vary. There is no wholesale transfer from one subject to another as had been supposed earlier by the theory of formal discipline. Transfer is possible between two situations, if there is identity of context, identity of procedures and identity of attitudes and ideals. In this way transfer takes place from one field of study to another and from the classroom situations to life situations. This transfer is also essential, as it leads to economy in learning.

Learning on Individual Basis

Each learner is a unique person who has his individual needs and problems, interests and attitudes, purposes and aspirations. In some, learning may be quick and fast; in others the reactions may be slow, and still in others, it may be steady and deliberate.

Purpose-based Learning

Human beings learn to achieve something, sometimes the teachers may not be aware of it at all. When the goal is more definite and explicit, the learning becomes more meaningful and effective to the learner.

Dynamic Process

Learning is a form of activity and it largely depends on the learner. It is said that no learning can take place where there is no self-activity. That is why one psychologist has said: "No one can teach you but you may learn, your teacher can direct your learning, can show you how materials are derived or related and stimulate you to study. Whether or not you learn and what you learn depends upon what you yourself do, for learning an activity".

Individual's Response

Learning is unitary as man learns as a whole being. An individual reacts as a whole person to the total learning situation rather than to one single stimulus. Since each learner responds as a whole (physically, socially and emotionally) the various motivation factors within him which affect the learner must be taken into account for effective teaching. Again, as the learner responds to the total situation, all external or environmental factors which influence his responses must also be taken note of for favourable learning. Therefore, setting the environment for learning is very important.

Learning after Maturity

Learning and maturation are interrelated. But they are distinguishable. Maturation signifies the process of growth and development. It occurs in the absence of any sort of habit, training or stimulus. On the other hand, learning is the modification of behaviour, which is the result of experience and training.

At a particular age, every child starts to sit, crawl, stand and walk. This is the result of maturation. But when the child dances, sings, plays football, drives scooter or a car and swims in the river, it is called learning. Learning is dependent on maturation to a great extent. Unless a particular stage in the process of maturation is reached, learning of any sort cannot be taken into hand. A two months old baby cannot learn dressing himself and a two year old child is not capable of typing. So maturation plays an important role in learning new skills. It prepares one physically and mentally to learn. So the relation between the two is so intimate that one is often misunderstood as the other. But they are two separate concepts and maturation fuels the organism with capability to learn.

Meaning of maturation is not the same in every sphere. Social and emotional maturation refers to ideal and law bound behaviour. It depends fully on learning. Sexual maturation presupposes physical ability and learned skills. Physical maturation denotes a stage of physical growth. Sexual maturation is generally reached in between the age 13 to 16 and physical maturation may be reached at a later stage in life. In the context of learning, maturation implies physical growth and development.

Maturation does not mean only the natural organic growth of human beings, because before and after birth the organism is affected by environmental factors. Malnutrition and infectious disease during pregnancy leaves a negative effect on the new born baby. Again afterbirth if the child is not provided with opportunities to mix with others in society, his all round growth and development is affected. From various experiments, it is proved that children confined to the four walls of home show abnormal development of personality. Growth and development of children differ due to divergent environments, in which they are brought up.

Vital Situations

The process of learning is affected by certain conditions. A knowledge of these conditions is essential for every teacher and parent, because by manipulating these conditions they can bring a required change in the behaviour of the child. Some of the important conditions are discussed below:

1. Readiness 2. Motivation 3. Interest 4. Attention 5. Drill or practice 6. Fatigue or boredom 7. Intelligence 8. Aptitude 9. Attitude 10. Emotional factors 11. Family and cultural expectations.

1. *Readiness of Learning*: When the child is not ready to learn, whatever method may be applied, he will not learn. It is applicable both for school and home. A number of students reading in the same class may be of a particular age level, but differ in readiness to learn, their readiness of experience, social and emotional stability, etc. The teacher should have a thorough knowledge about readiness in order to make his teaching effective. This helps the teacher in three ways. They are:
   (i) Firstly he can develop the skill of his teaching and become aware of the change in the readiness of students.

(ii) He can try to intensify the readiness of the students and reinforce them for it.

(iii) Students who do not show interest in study can be tackled and interest in them can be aroused by the teacher.

2. *Motivation for Learning:* Motivation is one of the most important factors in learning process. Every man should set a goal in his life. After a goal is set he is motivated to learn, because by learning only he can realise the goal. A poor student wants to earn his livelihood. So he is motivated for learning. A businessman wants to expand his business; so he is motivated to learn skills in business. But a student coming from a rich and affluent family is not so strongly motivated to learn as a student coming from a poor family. It is because he knows that without learning he can achieve his goal either by manpower or by money power. Without motivation the quality and pace of learning is hampered.

3. *Interest and Learning:* Interest is another important factor that accelerates the learning process. Different students are interested in different branches of study. So a teacher can make use of their interests and bring out the best result. During pre-childhood days, interest of the child is limited and does not last for a longer time. If now he is interested in one thing, the next moment his interest shifts to another thing. But as he grows up, his interest becomes stable and permanent. The teacher can evoke interest in students by making his teaching permanent and stimulative. This also decreases boredom, negligence and slowness of the student in his study. So he should adopt such methods as to increase the interest in the students. Only a learning with interest will enable a student to reach the goal and makes the student have interest in learning more and more.

4. *Attention of Learning:* Learning is impossible without attention. Qualitative and quantitative development of learning depends upon the quality and quantity of attention. When attention is diverted, learning is affected adversely.

5. *Place of Drill and Practice in Learning:* A simple matter is remembered easily. It needs no drilling. But in order to master complex matters, one needs drill or practice. So the teacher should bear in mind that practice makes learning perfect and act accordingly in the classroom. He should develop the practice of reading, writing, etc, in students and drill them the different materials, that they come across during learning. But drilling should not be mechanical. In mechanical drilling the students lack understanding of the object. This promotes fruitless learning.
6. *Fatigue and Boredom:* Physical and mental tiredness is known as fatigue. Disinterest in doing a work is known as boredom. Learning does not cause fatigue. If the method of teaching is faulty, the students are bored. The environment and surroundings of school also bore the students. So these factors should be taken into consideration by the teacher.
7. *Role of Intelligence in Learning:* Intelligence brings qualitative increase in learning. Difference in intelligence is clearly marked among the students in a classroom. They can be broadly divided into three categories. Some are bright, some are average and others are dull. The teacher should adopt intelligence measurement test to evaluate the level of intelligence of each and every student and group them into categories. Then his teaching should take into consideration every category of students. He should see that every teaching material reaches the least intelligent student. Generally in our educational institutions teaching is rendered for average student and so the feebleminded students are not profited from it. Again the feebleminded students are divided into three categories. They are idiot, imbecile and moron.
8. *Aptitude and Learning:* Aptitude is a natural reinforcer of learning. When interest is aroused spontaneously, it is called aptitude. Remembering is long-lasting if the learning material is backed by aptitude. On the other hand, in the absence of aptitude, the student fails to remember his learning material. So the teacher should be aware of this factor also.

9. *Attitude and Learning:* Learning is also affected by the attitude of the learner. Interest, aptitude and readiness correspond to one another. They make the learner prepared and fill him with potentialities to tackle the learning material. Attitude makes the students meet the problems with understanding, interest and smartness. If he is pressurised with much more material, he develops a negative attitude.
10. *Effect of Emotional States:* The last but not the least factor that affects the process of learning is the emotional state of the learner. If he is undergoing a pleasurable emotion, his learning is bound to be qualitatively better. On the other hand, if emotional states pressurise him and create tension in him, he develops frustration and lacks interest and readiness to learn.

Sentimental Instigation

(a) Unfulfilled requirements.
(b) Wrong attitude of parents in home.
(c) Quarrel, lack of security, inconvenience, plentitude at home.
(d) Frustration or inferiority caused by real or imaginary physical defects.
(e) Previous experience of failure in school.
(f) Neglecting behaviour by teachers and friends and avoidance by them.

11. *Role of Family and Culture in Learning*: Family and culture of the learner affects his learning to a great extent. Even his life process is affected by these two. Parent's hopes and desires count much in his life. Sometimes the parents set goals for their children. Hopes and desires of parents differ with the difference in culture and place.

    There are cultural demands, which affect the learning process. Social and educational environment reflect one's culture. So learning should be complementary to the learner's cultural demands and requirements. All such demands should be met with. For example, in a culture where democracy is a way of life, the learner should be imparted learning in consonance with democratic values.

Method of Doing and Playing

When learning is associated with playing or merry making, it becomes more effective. It arouses interest in the learner. Teaching should not be only giving lectures to the students. They become bored by that. Secondly if while learning a skill, the learner does the work with his own hands he masters it without much effort. So now the modern methods of teaching lay stress on play-way method and discard the conventional reciting-in-classroom methods. Now the classrooms have turned into playgrounds.

Diverse Facets

Learning is a process. This process depends upon a number of factors. If we categorise the factors upon which this process is based, we will find three main directions. They are

1. The internal condition of the learner - (such as capacity, motivation, age, sex, difference, experience etc.)
2. Nature of the subject to be learnt - (e.g. span or range of learning, complexity or simplicity of learning materials etc.)
3. Method of learning - (e.g. memorisation, analysis, drilling, recitation etc.)

Let us discuss these conditions of learning in detail.

1. *Role of Age in Learning:* Children fare well and better with adults. It is a general belief that learning ability decreases with increase in age. From various studies it has been proved that there is a fixed and definite age when learning ability of the child is maximum. Apart from this there is also a fixed age for better learning of literature, mathematics and science. Studies have been conducted by psychologists on the relationship between age factor and learning process. The results show that learning ability of new subjects goes on increasing till the age of 10 years. Then it remains constant till age of 20 years and after that it goes on diminishing and again becomes stable at the age of 50.

2. *Role of Sex in Learning:* Psychologist have been in the process of finding out whether there is any relationship between learning ability and sex. In some societies it has been found that children of a particular sex show more proficiency in learning than the other sex. Whether this difference is due to difference in sex or due to better facilities enjoyed by one sex over the other one, the findings are as follows:
   (i) Difference in sex does not cause any difference in their intelligence.
   (ii) While girls show more proficiency in literature, debates, songs, etc, the boys show more ability in social science, science, mathematics, etc.
   (iii) Girls are more emotional, sociable and jealous. Boys are more influential, high minded, independent-minded and self-confident.
   (iv) Girls have greater pronouncing ability, better memory and sounder sensitiveness. On the other hand, boys show good result in numerology.
   (v) Girls are interested in service, home science and literature, whereas boys show interest in scientific, technological and ideological fields.
3. *Role of Mental Stability in Learning:* Effective learning and teaching depends fully upon a factor that is known as attention. Unless the learner is attentive to the process of learning, he can learn nothing. The learner should come in contact with the learning situation practically. That is he should attend by himself. Indirect participation yields no result. If the students are told that they will be examined after three days of the learning, it is natural that a greater attention will be paid towards learning; but if they are told that they will be tested after 6 months, they may not be serious on the subject. When the students point all their potentialities on a particular subject, learning becomes more effective and memorisation is accelerated
4. *Role of Past Experience in Learning:* New learning depends upon previous learning. Learning of one material, backs the learning of another material. When a student fails in

reading, writing or doing sums in classroom it should be noted that he had a defective learning before hand. Past learning enfuels present learning and present learning enfuels the future learning process.

5. *Role of Family Background and Socio-economic Status in Learning:* Village and town atmosphere influences difference in learning efficiency remarkably. Studies have been conducted and results show that town students are more fluent orally and in verbal expressions. Their way of talking is developed and disciplined.

   The difference marked between the town and village students in the field of learning depends upon their easily available level of stimulations. There are facilities of libraries, magazines and periodicals, books, schools, museums, T. V. and social works. These stimulants tend to increase learning ability in children. Another case of difference in learning ability in children is their socio-economic status. A child reared up in a luxurious environment is bound to be different from a child brought up in a poverty stricken family. There are some other social causes also, which include social customs and traditions, casteism, feeling of success and failure and its financial consequence.

6. *Role of Experience of Success and Failure in Learning:* A feeling of inferiority and hopelessness is marked in case of students who fail in examinations. Generally children having high hopes become successful in all walks of life. So success and failure have their respective impacts on the learning process.

7. *Role of Knowledge of Promotion in Learning:* Knowledge of promotion stimulates the learner and heightens his attentions. From group experiments it has been found that the experimental group, which had the knowledge of promotion showed better result than the other groups which had no knowledge of promotion. From another experiment it has been established that further learning is impossible unless the learner knows the result of this last learning. So knowledge or result bring success in new learning. So the teacher should feel the importance of this factor.

8. *Role of Meaningfulness of Subject Matter in Learning:* It has been proved from experiments as well as observations that meaningful materials are remembered better than the meaningless materials. Meaningful material denotes those materials about which we have some previous experience. So the teacher must bear this in mind. The student should not be compelled to master unknown materials. The method of teaching should be from known to unknown.
9. *Role of Complexity of Material in Learning:* Before starting teaching, the teacher should consider whether the subject matter is simple or complex for the learner. At first a student should learn simple and easy subjects. He shows better results in this learning. Thus, when a complex subject is given to him his level of mastery decreases, but it surely adds to the development of his learning. So the teaching should be from simple to complex. On the other hand if he fails to show proficiency and his interest is hampered, he feels bored and neglects his studies. Fear complex is aroused and he displays escapist temperament.
10. *Spread of Learning Materials:* A question is often asked whether a long passage is remembered sooner or a short passage. Ebbinghaus has proved by experimenting that a long list of words takes a longer time to memorise than a short list. But it has also been proved that a bigger topic is remembered better and sooner than the shorter topic. This has been proved by psychologist Woodsworth in 1988. Hence the range of learning materials has a special role to play in the process of learning. If a longer subject is tried to be mastered as a whole from start to end., it needs much more time to remember. But if the teacher adopts the method of dividing the long subject into small divisions and learned in parts, learning is effective and quick.
11. *Role of Re-memorisation in Learning:* Re-memorisation has a strong effect on learning and memorisation. Re-memorisation is often described as mental evaluation of learnt materials. Learning the material again is known in psychology as learning by closing the book. From the

discussion below we can know how re-memorising helps memorisation process.

(a) When re-memorisation is a conscious effort and not merely a bird's eye-view, it becomes fruitful.

(b) The learner can measure his memorisation by this process. So he can be aware of his limitations and weakness in learning. He knows that he failed to remember and invents methods of remembering them again.

(c) Rememorisation creates self-confidence in the learner.

In this context drilling of a particular learned topic by the teacher is of prime importance. By drilling rememorisation takes place along with self-evaluation. But it should not be stereo-typed or mechanical. The same topic should be presented in various forms. By giving different tasks to students such as filling in the blanks, writing the summary, etc, rememorisation can be done and its effect realised.

12. *Role of Over-learning:* Overlearning sometimes brings good results. The topic which is remembered after the repetition of five times can be remembered better after the recitation of two more times. This helps the learner to produce the material more perfectly. Over-learning is something different from mere recitation or simple re-learning it again and again. Re-learning is required to memorise but over-learning makes the goal of learning felt. Drilling brings out the correct response out of the learner but over-learning confirms it.

13. *Role of Time Gap between Learning Situations:* Considering from a narrow point of view we see that the process of learning is limited to a particular period of time. A topic can be read for 7 hours at length and it can also be read by dividing it into 7 parts and each part in one hour. Which of the two methods is fruitful is a question to be answered. In school curriculum the entire syllabus is divided into parts and taught day-wise, week-wise and month-wise. Experiments prove that by giving sufficient gap between two learning situations, efficiency is increased.

14. *Difference between the Whole-method and Part-method:* In past the part method was popular and learning was based on it. But later the whole method proved to be more effective and as such this was adopted by teachers. In part method, a longer topic is learnt in parts which makes the learning mechanical and the learner goes far from the root or basic point of the subject. Correlation could not be established among the various points of discussion. They were regarded by the learner as different topics and not as the points of view of only on topic. On the other hand, efficiency increased in whole learning and learning was still more effective. And if at all a vast subject is to be divided, it should be done in such a manner so that the divisions are interrelated and interdependent. In whole-method of learning stress is laid upon the totality of the viewpoint. The success of whole-method depends upon the past experience of the learner, his temperament and complexity of material. If the subject matter is understandably interdependent and smooth, it is learnt effectively. It is observed that intelligent students prefer whole method whereas students of lower intelligence adopt part method to memorise a material.
15. *Recitation in Learning:* It has been proved that recitation at the time of reading a material makes learning more effective. It is still more helpful in the learning of spelling, vocabulary and mathematics. Learning and recitation should go hand in hand.
16. *Use of Audio-visual Aids in Learning:* It is a belief of most of the people that by merely using audio-visual aids we can bring about development in learning efficiency. But it is not correct Only showing these aids to students does not help them to learn better. There should be a complete plan as to the use of these aids. The teacher should make appropriate preparations for that. It has been proved from experiments that T. V. sets and cinema can teach students better than disqualified teachers, who do not make proper plans before using the aids. The teacher must create a suitable and stimulating environment in the classroom before using the audiovisual aids.

15

Art of Teaching

In education one of the most pressing problems is to help students develop effective methods for learning. The school demands that the child spend many hours, many days, and many years in learning the subject matter, skills, and attitudes essential for effective living in a civilised community and for active citizenship in a democracy. Then the child goes on to spend many more years learning to be a teacher, a doctor, a lawyer, or a minister. In short, nearly everyone devotes a substantial portion of his life to being a professional learner. Yet, strangely enough, few are ever taught efficient learning procedures.

Is it because nothing is known about the learning process? Not at all. We know a great deal about it. We know that efficient methods of learning can cut in half the time required by inefficient methods. And we know that the speed with which material is forgotten can be greatly reduced.

As a professional teacher, you will use your knowledge of the learning process every day—for arranging your lessons and units, for deciding what materials and activities to include in them, for determining what materials you will assign for study and how you will assign them, for deciding how and when you will help the child to review and to summarise what he has learned, and for preparing and scheduling examinations. And, though in the primary grades the child's minute-to-minute learning activities are carefully planned by his teacher, finally he must become able to learn independently. Thus you must teach each child how to learn most efficiently. You must teach him the best methods for learning how to spell words, how to develop speed and accuracy in multiplication and addition, how to learn his lines for a play, how to organise and learn the essential dates, names, and events in history, how to improve his skill in typewriting, baseball, or dancing, and how to improve his ability to read.

As you can see, you have two important professional uses for your knowledge of the learning process: (1) you will plan your classroom activities so that maximum learning takes place, and (2) you will teach the child how to learn effectively when he himself must plan his approach to the learning task.

You obtain personal as well as professional dividends from a study of effective methods for learning. You, as well as your students, will continue to learn throughout life. When you apply the principles of learning to your own study, you are likely to increase your professional competence. For example, would you expect someone to teach you to swim, to type, or to dance if he himself had never become able to swim, type, or dance? Ordinarily not. You would demand that he know more than the rules and theory of the skill. And so with a knowledge of effective methods for learning. You can best teach the child how to learn effectively and you can best use your knowledge of the learning process in building effective classroom situations if you first learn how to apply this knowledge to the learning that you must do yourself.

Fortunately, the best methods for learning are easy to master, and the time that they save us is ample payment for the few hours that we expend to become familiar with them. As with all new knowledge, though, mere mastery of efficient learning methods is not enough. We must put the effective methods into practice every day over a period of time before they will have any real effect in overcoming the inefficient learning habits that most of us have fallen into. Inefficient habits are stubborn creatures; they hate to be displaced. Luckily, the children in your classroom will not have had so many years in which to build up stubborn, inefficient habits. They will have less resistance to adopting efficient habits and will be more likely to embrace the methods that give the greatest rewards for time spent on study.

Nature

So far, we have been talking as though everyone meant just the same thing by the word "learning." True, we all have a fairly clear idea of what the term means, but, as we have discovered before, a precise definition helps us to direct our thinking more accurately. A definition is especially necessary here, since the word learning is so often used to include the effects of maturation as well as the effects of the more conscious, controllable act of learning itself. Thus, we speak of the child's "learning" to walk, but we should recognise that walking is dependent upon maturation as well as upon learning.

What we mean by "learning." Learning is the acquisition of new behaviour patterns, or the strengthening or weakening of old behaviour patterns, as the result of practice.

As we can see, learning includes a wide variety of changes in behaviour. The changes may be readily detected in the overt behaviour of the individual or they may be changes in his stock of ideas. Even a primitive, uncivilised person learns nearly all those actions that enable him to obtain food, clothing, and shelter and to communicate with his fellows. And civilised man learns in addition all those actions that make him different from a primitive man. Our methods for getting along with others, our ability to read, to write, and to use mathematical symbols, our skill in games, our health habits, our attitudes, and our control of our emotions—all are learned.

In our definition, we need to require that the changes in behaviour occur as a result of practice so that we can eliminate those changes that result from physical growth and maturation. However, we recognise that much of what we learn is learnable only after we have reached an adequate level of physical and mental maturity. And though mental or physical action—practice—is a necessary condition for learning, practice alone does not cause learning. Practice may or may not produce changes in behaviour patterns. What, then, are the important determinants of the amount of learning that will take place? Let's examine the learning process.

The Learning Process : Motives or drives are fundamental to the learning process. If we are to learn, we must first have some goal and then encounter some block that prevents us from attaining that goal. If we encounter no block—no difficulty of any kind—the chances are that we have already learned the behaviour necessary to reach the goal or that we will not learn it until our goal becomes more attractive and more demanding. The block or problem, then, rather than the number of repetitions of the experience, is the essential element in the learning situation. When we consider how little we learn from certain of our experiences, this becomes obvious. We may enter a building many times and be able to recall little concerning the doorway, steps, wall, or floor.

The child or even the adolescent may eat with his fingers and chew with his mouth open. So long as this behaviour is adequate to meet his needs, years of practice result in no improvement in his table manners. But if he becomes aware that his behaviour blocks his attainment of esteem in the eyes of his peers, and if he sees that he can regain their esteem by changing his habits, he strives hard to change and he learns rapidly.

When a child is frustrated in his attempts to reach an attractive goal, he changes. His muscular tension increases; he is less comfortable and less relaxed than he was before the block arose. He seeks a solution. Either he must destroy the block, climb over it, go around it—or find a new goal. He may simply try out one route around the block to his goal and, if that fails, try another. Or he may make intelligent use of his past experiences. If, as a direct, or accidental, result of his trial-and-error behaviour, he overcomes the block and reaches the goal, his search is ended and his muscular tension is reduced. He learns in two ways from this experience: (1) he learns how to solve his present problem, and (2) he learns a *procedure* for attacking future problems. What is there in this experience that is important to his future learning procedure? Simply this: The last attempt the child makes—the attempt immediately preceding success and the lessening of tension—is the one that he is most likely to repeat the next time tension arises, especially if either the goal or the block is similar to those he encountered in this problem.

For example, consider the baby who receives attention or food only when he cries. He soon learns to cry regularly in response to any problem that he encounters. Or suppose that a boy has a strong desire to get on the school football team. He is motivated by his need for the esteem of fellow students and also by the interesting experiences that he may enjoy. But he is blocked by his inadequate size and lack of skill in dodging, tackling, and handling the football. His past experiences and general intelligence will determine the extent to which his attempts to solve his problem are planned or random. His personality and the length of time that elapses before he sees a solution will determine the extent of his general tension. But there will be some tension and it will increase if his search for a solution fails. He has several possibilities for reducing his tension. He may choose a substitute goal, convince himself that it is worthy, and gain esteem and new experiences from it. Or he may make a direct attack on the problem. He decides that he can gain weight during the summer by eating heavily and that he can become stronger by doing heavy lifting. He gets a football, rigs up a tackling dummy, and practices the fundamental skills that are required. Then, when the football season begins, he attempts to make up for his inexperience by trying particularly hard.

If his efforts are successful, when he is faced with a similar problem in the future he is likely to adopt the same general type of attack that was successful in solving this problem. Why did he try so hard and why did he learn so many things? Because the goal appealed powerfully to many of his motives and because he met many problems as he sought to reach it.

In short, the learning process involves a motive or drive, an attractive goal, and a block to the attainment of the goal. All three aspects of the learning process are essential.

This general pattern of learning dominates the whole of human behaviour—from birth to death. It affects the personalities and adjustments of children and adults alike. It dictates how successful children will be in learning the simplest facts and the most complex skills, in school or out of school. Acts that lead to a satisfaction of needs tend to be repeated and acts that do not lead to satisfaction tend to be discarded. Although the pattern itself seems simple enough, we discover that we are dealing with what is really an extremely complex process when we try to understand and guide human behaviour, with its infinite variety of experiences, attitudes, abilities, and goals.

Solving Problems by Manipulating Ideas. When we were discussing the learning process, we used the expression "trial and error", and mentioned that learning often involves physical movement and several failures (errors) before the learner finally reaches his goal. Not all learning, however, involves such plodding, painstaking behaviour. Human beings are able to profit from past experiences. We can retain our experiences in the form of ideas. Then, when we meet familiar situations in the future, we can reach down into our store of experience and come up with appropriate ideas. And we can manipulate our ideas and in so doing find suitable solutions to a relatively new problem. Thus, learning may take place through the manipulation of ideas. The familiar pattern of motive-goal-block is still present, but we work through the process with little or no overt physical activity.

A boy may encounter the problem of obtaining an apple from a tree. He may reach for the apple, throw stones at it, climb the tree, or get a pole long enough to knock the apple from the tree. Or he may rapidly manipulate ideas involving all these possibilities without appearing to move. He may recall that he can't reach objects six feet above his head, that his thrown stone will be deflected by the lower branches of the tree, that climbing trees is hard on clothes and brings disapproval, and that his brother once retrieved his fish line from a tree by using a fishing pole. In fact, his past experiences and general ability to see relationships may allow him to see the correct solution without trying inadequate solutions.

Our first or our thousandth manipulation of ideas or attempts to motor solutions may be successful. And, through the manipulation, our ideas take new forms—we learn. Likewise, ideas manipulation and motor attempts may be, and quite likely will be, going on at the same time. Then the learning comes from a combination of the ideational and the motor attempts.

Background (Scientific)

Laboratory experiments have produced valuable data on learning and forgetting. Though most of the laboratory experiments have used relatively meaningless (nonsense) materials, the findings help us understand what takes place in the learning and forgetting of the meaningful materials of the classroom and of life. Actually, the basic difference between the meaningless materials of the laboratory and the meaningful materials of the classroom is that in the classroom we deal with situations that are similar to those we have encountered previously. That is what makes them meaningful. If we were not already familiar with it, the combination c-a-t used in the classroom and the nonsense syllable j-i-x used in the laboratory would be equally meaningless. And if we had not already had considerable experience with finding our way on country roads or city streets, the problem of learning our way about a new city would be as meaningless as the laboratory problem of learning our way through a maze.

For these reasons, a knowledge of some of the findings of the psychological laboratory can form a useful basis for a discussion of the learning of meaningful materials.

Learning Curves : Learning curves usually are drawn on a graph, with the base line divided into units of time or the number of trials required for learning. The vertical scale is divided into appropriate units of accomplishment—puzzles solved, material retained, and so on. The curve drawn against these two scales gives us a handy way of comparing, for example, accomplishment at the end of various time periods.

Learning curves that report the learning activity of one person over a relatively short time are likely to be very rough, since drastic changes may be caused by accidental distractions or temporary loss of motivation. If we want to get a stable, meaningful picture, we have to take the learning achievement of many persons (or of one person on many different tests), find the average achievement at the end of each trial or time period, and then make a graph based on these averages.

Age and Learning Ability : Is there a best age for learning? For a long time it was believed that certain ages were best for learning poetry but that other ages were better for learning, say, arithmetic or geography. Many studies have been made of learning ability and its relation to the age of the learner.

It appears that the ability to learn new and unfamiliar materials increases until about age 16 and then remains very nearly the same until the late 20's. Then there is a slight drop with each year, until at about age 70 the drop becomes rather sharp. The sharp drop occurs when senility, sometimes called second childhood, is reached. We must be cautious in interpreting this graph, however. Remember that it represents the average for a great many persons. The learning ability of some individuals, especially those who are engaged in activities that require the learning of new materials, may continue to increase far beyond the age of 16 and may not decline until much later in life than is shown to be the lot of the average person. The beginning of senility in individual cases may come at a much earlier or much later age than that indicated on the graph. In learning outside the laboratory we seldom encounter completely new materials. Consider the learning tasks that you are called upon to face. You can understand scientific concepts and you can solve problems of dealing with adults—you can learn—at a level far beyond what you could at age 16. Why is this true? Obviously it is because of what you have learned since you were 16. The situations you now meet contain far fewer new elements than they would have had if you had been forced to meet them at age 16. We have here a basic principle of education. The average child, at a rather early age, ceases to increase in sheer mental power. But if we can help him to gain an ever-increasing background of skills, knowledge, and social experiences, we prepare him to handle problems of ever-increasing complexity.

How is this curve of learning ability useful to us in the classroom? It shows us how the ability to learn new materials tends to rise from infancy to maturity. It tells us that the average

14-year-old child can learn new materials of any kind faster than the average 10-year-old can.

But obviously we cannot wait until the time of maximum learning ability before we introduce the child to the school curriculum. There is too much for him to learn, and much of the learning demanded of the 16-year-old depends directly on what he has learned years before. Certain types of learning, such as writing, playing a piano, singing, swimming, and dancing, involve motor skills as well as mental development. If the child fails to begin to learn such skills at an early age, special muscle groups may not be developed and coordinated by the time that he reaches his maximum learning ability. In addition, if he is to attain great skill in such activities, he must continue to practice for a long time after the basic learning has been achieved.

And there are other factors to consider. The young child who is interested in playing an instrument or skating will devote more time to learning these skills than will the average older person. By distributing his practice time over a number of years, he will attain greater mastery than if he had begun only after he had reached maturity. In the classroom, then, we must work with children who have not yet achieved their maximum ability to learn new materials. Yet their success after they have reached that maximum depends largely on how rich their previous learning has been.

Successful Learning

Although Motivation and learning ability are important determinants of learning efficiency, other factors also have a strong influence. Fortunately, nearly all these are factors over which we can exercise some control in the classroom.

The Value of Recall : Effortful recall is a powerful determinant of learning and retention; it pays tremendous dividends per unit of time consumed. One of the important values of a good examination is that it requires recall or an attempt to recall. Similarly, classroom discussion requires the student to recall previously learned information and to apply it to new problems. Recitation is an important method for inducing recall. The teacher uses the recitation to clarify and strengthen learning and the skillful student uses it in his independent study. Recall also takes place when the learner rehearses mentally the physical movements demanded by a game or skill. And review, though it often includes new learning, owes much of its effectiveness to the recall of information that already has been learned.

Ordinarily, recall results in a highly motivated form of additional practice with a special problem introduced—that of attempting to reconstruct a situation from our ideas alone. The educational psychologist sometimes refers to recall as "study with the book closed."

An experiment performed many years ago indicates that when the learner alternates between reading and recitation he is far more successful than when he uses all his available time for reading alone. Other investigators have reported similar findings.

Table

The Effectiveness of Time Spent in Reading Vs. Various Proportions of Time Spent in Recall During the Study of Biographical Sketches as Measured Immediately After Learning

Percentage of Time Spent in		*Scores*				
Recall	*Reading*	*Grade 8*	*Grade 6*	*Grade 5*	*Grade 4*	*Grade 3*
0	100	88	89	80	86	75
20	80	95	98	95	100	89
40	60	105	106	104	97	97
60	40	105	104	109	111	122
80	20	107	105	105	104	113
90	10	100	98	107	102	104

To make it easy for us to compare the learning that took place under each of the five methods, the experimenter computed the average score made by the pupils in each grade under all five methods and called that 100. Thus a score of 88 (average score for grade eight using no recall) is seen to be only 88 per cent as effective as the average under all methods and 88/107 as good (about 82 per cent) as the score when the pupils used 80 per cent of their time for recall.

We can see from Table that in each grade, when the children spent from 40 to 90 per cent of their study time in attempting to recall the material, they made far better scores on a test given immediately following the learning than they did when they spent all their time reading the material. The material studied by each grade was of the same general type— highly factual biographical sketches. However, the students in the upper grades had longer and more difficult sketches than did the students in the lower grades. We can see that a test following learning shows that recall was very effective indeed.

Table

The Effectiveness of Time Spent in Reading Vs. Various Proportions of Time Spent in Recall During the Study of Biographical Sketches as Measured About Four Hours After Learning

Percentage of Time Spent in		*Scores*				
Recall	*Reading*	*Grade 8*	*Grade 6*	*Grade 5*	*Grade 4*	*Grade 3*
0	100	80	74	71	79	62
20	80	96	79	81	95	76
40	60	127	113	104	100	107
60	40	131	123	122	116	123
80	20	129	119	107	107	117
90	10	121	102	115	102	114

What about the retention of such material when a test is given at a later time? Table reports the scores made by these same students on a second test given from three to four hours after the test reported in Table.

Table indicates that recitation did much more than increase the speed of learning. Materials thus learned were much better remembered than were materials learned through reading alone. The recitation, then, reduced the time needed for learning and increased the persistence of learning. Why? There are several reasons.

First, the conscious use of recall during the process of study demands that the act of reading be effortful. It prevents the reader from letting his eyes dance lightly along from word to word while he focuses his thoughts on last night's party or tomorrow's football game. It holds his attention to the business at hand. It obliges him to set specific goals and to make an immediate evaluation of his progress toward them.

Second, recall that is followed by a re-reading gives the learner a chance to check immediately on the accuracy of his learning. Correct information is confirmed and incorrect information is rejected.

Third, recall requires greater muscular activity than does reading alone. As the learner tries to repeat the material, often in his own words, he tends to use at least his throat muscles in the process.

Fourth, when the learner recalls material by himself he builds up confidence in his ability to recall it at a later time. There is less chance that panic will rob him of his learning when he tries to draw on it for an examination or a real-life situation.

Here is a particularly good example of how we can use our knowledge of the learning process both to teach children how to learn and to build effective learning situations. For example, the child should be shown (probably as early as the second or third grade) that the most effective way to study spelling is to read each word carefully with close attention to how it is spelled and then to get someone else to pronounce the words while he writes them. Or, if he cannot get someone else to do this, he can cover a word with a card and write it after a quick glance at the word. Later on, the children are taught to make liberal use of recall for learning poems or lines in a play. And in the process of work-type reading, the child is taught to read a paragraph and then to test himself over the content. The teacher, of course, can provide for recall in many ways—examinations, summaries by the child, and class discussion, to mention a few.

The Advantages of Distributed Practice : In any learning situation, the amount of study time available is limited. What is the best way to use it? If Mary has five hours a week to spend on learning a given assignment, should she spend it all at once or space it into five equal parts of one hour each, or work out some other arrangement?

This is a hard question to answer. No one solution is satisfactory for all types of learning tasks. There is evidence, however, that for most learning activities a certain amount of practice spread over a period of time is much more effective than the same amount of practice crammed into a short period of time. In learning motor skills, such as typewriting, skating/or dancing, far better results are obtained through spending a few hours each week for a number of years than by spending five times as many hours per week in one-fifth the same number of years. And the effectiveness of the more gradual learning seems to persist for a longer time after the practice has ended. However, if sufficient motivation is present, and if the child does not become tired of the task, he will obviously achieve more learning in 30 minutes than in 15.

Certainly if the learner's goal is to achieve permanent mastery of meaningful materials, he will secure better results through distributed practice than through massed practice. However, forgetting takes place rapidly after any type of learning. So if the learner's goal is merely to pass a test at some definite future date, he will obtain the best results by using the total available time shortly before the test. That is one reason why "cramming" before an examination is so popular. Cramming is the result of a short-term philosophy of learning that some students have developed and that poor teaching procedures have encouraged. So far as results measured on the test are concerned, massed practice is definitely the most economical technique. The results of the practice are fresh in the student's mind, and the student is highly motivated by the knowledge that this is the last chance he has to learn before the hour of reckoning.

In terms of permanent values, however, cramming is disastrous. The student whose aim is only to reach an immediate goal is already disposed to forget what he has learned as soon as it seems safe. As a result, he finds that the courses and examinations he encounters in the future are based on material that is less and less meaningful to him, since he fails to retain what he has learned in the past.

In planning the effective learning situation, the teacher must make numerous decisions concerning the most valuable use of classroom time. Sometimes, as in the case where a school play is to be given or a poem is to be learned, interest would be lost if the learning were spread over too long a time. But for most classroom learnings, we can distribute practice advantageously. By using frequent short examinations rather than infrequent longer ones, we can guarantee that practice will be spread over a longer period of time. And we distribute practice as well as encourage recall when we see that the child uses previous learning to attack new problems. For example, in the primary grades we teach the child to use initial sounds and endings of words as a cue to pronouncing new words. Rather than spending a long period of time in learning all these sounds, the effective teacher distributes their learning over many weeks, introducing one initial sound every day or two and seeing that the child develops his understanding of them by letting him give the initial sound and the ending of words that he does not recognise. The teacher will find that distributed practice is particularly effective when a rather large unit of material, such as the atomic weights of the various elements studied in a chemistry class or the vocabulary of a foreign language, is to be learned.

The Influence of Mental Set : An active intent to learn is much more likely to result in success than is mere passive attention. We may ride the same bus to and from school for many weeks, watching the houses along the way or even sitting beside the driver. Yet, if we were called upon to take the wheel and to follow the usual route, we would encounter difficulty. Had we been at the wheel during the first trip and forced to find our way, and had we known that we would be called upon to repeat the trip at a later time, we would have learned the route much more quickly. Similarly, if we read one book with the knowledge that we will be tested on it the next day and also a year later, and if we read another with the understanding that we will be tested on it the next day only, our memory of the material from the first book will persist for a longer time.

There is another way in which mental set affects the student's learning. Students approach their study in different ways. One decides to study a lesson for two hours; merely putting in the time becomes his primary objective. His attention focuses more on the clock than on his lesson. Another has specific purposes to accomplish during his study. He is searching for questions that may be asked on the material or he is attempting to condense the material into his own words. The mental set of the latter certainly is far more conducive to effective learning.

How we Forget : If there was no such thing as forgetting, the task of the learner and of the teacher would be simple indeed. But the problem of forgetting dominates the whole process of learning. Some forgetting even takes place during the actual learning of material. The learning curves that we talked about before are influenced by the process of forgetting. If they were not, it would be as easy to learn five new words the second five minutes of learning time as it was the first five minutes. But we find that not only must we learn new things but we must also remember, relearn, or keep from forgetting the old. Names we know today are gone next year, and the facts we knew last night have vanished before today's examination. Early studies of forgetting served to illustrate the size of the problem.

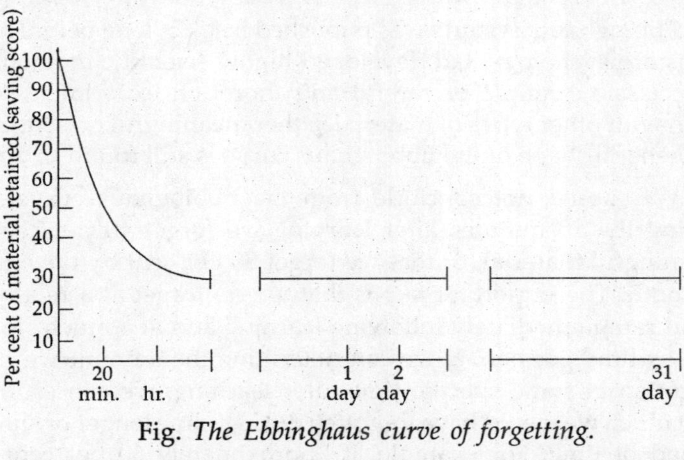

Fig. *The Ebbinghaus curve of forgetting.*

Ebbinghaus derived his curve from experiments in which he was both the observer and the learner. To simplify his task, he invented what is known as the nonsense syllable, which insists of a vowel between two consonants, such as x-o-y, j-b, or c-i-z. He arranged these syllables into lists of various lengths. He studied a list, recorded the date, hour, minute, and the number of readings that were necessary before he was able to repeat all the syllables (through spelling them out), and then laid the list aside. He followed the same procedure in learning list after list. From time to time, he tested his memory of the lists he had previously learned. Since he never learned a list beyond the level necessary to repeat it once, and since in the meantime he had learned other lists, ordinarily he could not remember any of the syllables in an earlier list until after he had re-read it at least once or twice. It began to appear that he remembered nothing! However, when he tried to relearn a list, he found that he was able to master it much more easily than he could master a list he had never learned before. This was an indication that he had not completely forgotten it.

In order to determine how much was left of his original learning, Ebbinghaus used what is called a saving score. If he required 25 readings to learn a list, and 15 to relearn it, he assumed that, he had saved the results of 10 readings, or 40 per cent of his original learning effort. In making a graph of his memory of this list, he would say that he had made a saving score of 40.

Ebbinghautrus study was published in 1885, long before most areas of psychology had developed highly scientific methods. It is a classic example of careful and thorough experimentation. Even with other types of material, either meaningful or nonsense, the general shape of the Ebbinghaus curve is still found to apply.

We should not conclude from the Ebbinghaus curve that during the 20 minutes after learning we forget 40 per cent of meaningful material, or that we forget 80 per cent by the end of a month. The important fact is that we do forget at a relatively rapid rate immediately following learning and at a much slower rate as time goes on. If we can determine the amount we have forgotten at some specific time after learning, we can estimate how much we would have forgotten during some longer or shorter period of time. For example, if approximately 60 per cent (20 minutes for Ebbinghaus' materials and methods) of meaningful material is remembered at the end of a month, we might predict that without review 42 per cent (60 minutes by the Ebbinghaus curve) will be recalled at the end of three months.

Many factors contribute to the high percentage of forgetting observed by Ebbinghaus. These factors will be discussed in greater detail under their individual headings later in the present chapter.

Why we Forget : For many years, it was customary for psychologists to say that forgetting was caused by disuse. But scientific attention to the problem, especially during recent years, indicates that disuse is far from being the cause or even a cause of forgetting.

As time passes, wood is eaten by termites, houses are consumed by fire, people grow old, and men forget. However, none of these changes are caused by the lapse of time. Granted, if termites are present they consume more wood in two years than in one. But the termites rather than time consume the wood. To attribute any of these changes to the lapse of time is to fail to recognise the true cause-and-effect relationship.

Almost all psychologists now agree that interference is the cause of nearly all our ordinary, day-to-day forgetting. Both past learnings and future learnings interfere with the memory of what we learn today. The interference is much greater between some types of material and for some methods of learning than it is for others. What conditions determine the degree to which one learned act interferes with another?

Similarity of Materials : When we were talking about Ebbinghaus, we mentioned that one reason he forgot a large proportion of the nonsense syllables he had learned was that between the time of original learning and the time of recall he studied many new lists of nonsense syllables. Materials that we learn just after or just before we learn similar materials are particularly likely to be forgotten. Suppose that on Wednesday the children in your classroom learn the poem "America." Ordinarily, you could expect them to remember most of the poem on Friday. However, if on Thursday they learn "The Star-Spangled Banner", they will remember "America" less accurately than if they had not studied the second poem. Moreover, they will remember less of the second poem than if they had not learned the first on Wednesday. Had one of the poems been humorous rather than serious, or had one been sung and the other spoken, the degree of similarity, and, consequently, the amount of interference between the two would have been reduced.

Degree of Learning : Another important factor that influences forgetting is the degree to which material has been learned. If one poem is learned thoroughly over a period of a few days, it is not likely to be forgotten when a second poem is learned. Here is a strong argument for thoroughness in learning. Thoroughly learned materials are less easily interfered with and consequently are remembered better than are partially learned materials. In addition, well-learned materials do less damage to other learning, past or future, than do poorly learned materials. And we can see why this would be true. As we become acquainted with them, two brothers, two buildings, or two poems become less similar. We become increasingly aware of the differences between them.

The Value of Review : Careful review is a valuable aid to memory, particularly when it is begun soon after the initial learning. Figure illustrates how the shape of the curve of forgetting is changed by review. Curve I (which you will recognise as the Ebbinghaus curve) shows the rapid decrease in the percentage retained during the period immediately following initial learning. Curve II shows how the curve is altered when the material is reviewed to the point where it is as well remembered as when it was first learned. Curve III represents the still slower drop that takes place after a second review.

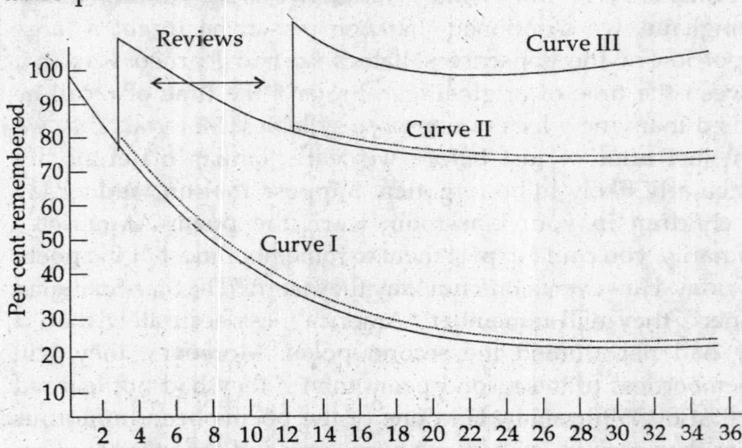

Fig. *The effect of review on the curve of foregetting.*

The first review should take place soon after learning, in order to avoid the great loss that takes place during the initial period of rapid forgetting. To be most effective, a review must be more than a second exposure to familiar material. It should provide for recall or an attempt to recall followed by an opportunity to confirm or reject what is recalled. But it goes beyond this. Although no new materials are presented, during a review the child learns many things for the first time, since he will seldom have learned all that is available during the previous exposure. In addition, new applications and understandings will be developed during the review.

The summary near the end of the class period, the review of yesterday's accomplishments before the beginning of today's problem, the examination, and the use of previous learnings to attack new problems—all are review activities that are under the teacher's control. And you will teach the child to review independently. You will teach him how to organise what he has learned and preserve it in notes and you will teach him how and when to review those notes. If you teach in the junior or senior high school, you may help the child to make a schedule of his study time. In such a schedule, time should be allowed at the end of each evening's study for a review of today's class notes and of the preparation that he has made for tomorrow's work. Also, an hour or two each week should be identified for the review of all the course notes for the semester or the year. When supervised study time is available, we schedule a regular portion of it for review and we have review lessons in our classroom whether or not we supervise the child's study. Frequently, we use such a review lesson before we begin a new unit.

Combining Sensory Experiences : Do we learn best by seeing or by hearing? The evidence is not entirely clear. There does, however, appear to be abundant evidence that the more sense organs we can use in the learning process, the better we will retain the material.

Hearing and seeing are better than either alone; and hearing, seeing, and saying the words that we hear are still better. One reason may be that when we undergo an experience through a combination of the senses it is more nearly unique and thus has fewer similarities to other learning situations. By emphasising the ways in which an experience differs, we can reduce the amount of interference with other learning experiences. For example, if a poem is to be learned, we can get different types of sensory experiences from hearing a recording of it as read by its author, from singing it individually and in a group, from reading it aloud, and from reading it silently.

The combining of sensory experiences is not limited to obtaining experiences from different senses. We can also obtain different experiences through the same sense. Motion pictures greatly extend the visual experience that a child can gain from his reading of geography, history, and literature. And he can combine his reading with many other sensory experiences. Classroom collections of insects, textiles, manufactured products of oil, iron, or coal, and visits to zoos, factories, and farms will reinforce learning through introducing touch, smell, and an entirely new visual and auditory experience.

Guided Learning : Experiments have been conducted in which students were carefully prevented from making mistakes. For example, in teaching a child to write the letters of the alphabet, we might cut stencils of the letters so that by tracing with his pencil he will always obtain perfect letters. If we are teaching a boy to jump over a bar, we might tie him to a machine that would force his legs, arms, and head through exactly the right motions of the most approved type of roll. Such guided learning might conceivably be used to teach many different motor skills. Psychologists have tried to discover whether or not it is desirable to prevent errors in this manner. The conclusions are that it is not. Although the child may learn to trace perfect letters time after time, he will not necessarily show any improvement in his ability to write freehand. We must learn about our errors and how we can avoid them as well as learn the correct responses.

Obviously, we need to have examples of excellent performance both in the learning of skills and in our social learnings. We need to see how a good jumper or basketaball player performs; we need to see graceful and correct social behaviour. But much of our learning time must be given to the recognition and elimination of our own errors—errors that are peculiar to us and that the examples seldom bring to our attention.

This is a concrete application of the principles of motivation. The problem is an essential part of the learning situation!

The Norms

We have studied why and how people learn. We have examined many conditions that are favourable to learning and retention. Can we now identify common elements in the learning situations that we have discussed? Actually, psychologists long ago attempted to do this. Certain principles or "laws" of learning have been identified. You can gain a better understanding of the learning process by studying these principles, but if you merely memorise them as pet statements, they will be valueless to you in the classroom. However, if you orient your thinking around them, and use them as points of reference, they will help you to organise your knowledge of the learning process.

The Law of Effect : When a response to a situation is accompanied or followed by a satisfied feeling, that response tends to be repeated; but when it is accompanied or followed by an unsatisfied feeling, the response tends to be eliminated.

We have seen many of the applications of this principle. Our motives demand satisfaction. And when we are able to satisfy them, we have pleasant, satisfied feeling. When we fail to satisfy them, we have an unpleasant, unsatisfied feeling. We tend to adopt—to learn—any behaviour that leads us to goals that satisfy our motives. We tend to eliminate any behaviour that fails to lead us to a desirable goal. And we tend to eliminate behaviour that results in threats or punishment.

How does this law account for the many unpleasant tasks that we learn to perform? As we have seen, human needs are extremely complex. Our actions are seldom energised by a single motive. In striving to attain large goals, we often must identify and reach smaller, more immediate goals. Although our behaviour at any time may conflict with certain of our motives, we retain this behaviour if it satisfies other more powerful motives. And although a goal that we seek may itself appear unpleasant, actually it attracts us, for it marks a point on our journey toward some very attractive goal. For example, a child may find a scolding or even a spanking rewarding if it gains for him the much more important attention that he has been denied; a boy may find the rough physical contact of football or boxing satisfying in spite of the pain; and a girl may deny herself social engagements that she craves if in so doing she attains great satisfaction from good grades, the promise of a career as a singer, or the earning of money.

The Law of Exercise : When a connection between a situation and a response is repeated, the connection is strengthened, other things being equal; but when the connection is not used over a period of time, it is weakened. (This law is sometimes called the law of "use and disuse.")

The Ebbinghaus curve of forgetting demonstrates how this law operates when the connection is not used over a period of time. The value of review, and even the fact that learning takes place with practice, illustrate how the connection is strengthened by use. Note that the law does not say that the disuse causes the forgetting. If the connection is not repeated now and then, something happens that leads to a weakening in the connection. And we know that the repetition of the connection—the practice—does not necessarily lead to improvement. But when a response is repeated time and again, it does tend to become habitual. The child who is taught to brush his teeth following each meal finally comes to brush his teeth without being told and even feels some tension if he is prevented from doing so. However, if for some reason, he does not brush his teeth for a period of time, the habit dies. If a child meets numerous social situations in a friendly and relaxed fashion, that approach finally becomes a well-established personality trait. If he withdraws from one social situation after another, that trait too becomes habitual.

The Law of Readiness : Once an attractive goal has been identified, to attain it is pleasant, to fail is annoying.

This law has special implications for us as teachers because it emphasises the importance of preparing the student to learn. If he does not have a felt need to learn—in short, if he is not ready—it is unlikely that he will learn very much. Preparing the pupil for learning is the first step in good teaching procedure. It is for this reason that many skilled teachers spend so much classroom time in presenting assignments. They set the stage, arouse curiosity, and in other ways appeal to the needs of the child. Once the child feels a readiness to learn, the teacher may need to do little more than offer occasional guidance and encouragement.

The Law of Belonging : When we are able to perceive relationships, the speed of learning and the permanence of retention are greatly increased.

The recognition of cause and effect elements, the seeing of relationships between the parts and the total, and the perceiving of familiar elements in new situations—all these factors greatly increase the speed of learning and the permanence of retention.

If the child is to make real use of the information and skills that he learns in the classroom, they must be related in some significant way to his previous learning. They must "belong" to the context of learning that he has already experienced. Isolated facts can be learned only by rote; new facts and skills are meaningful only when they appear in the company of familiar facts and skills with which the learner already feels at home.

The Learnability of Materials : In addition to the four laws of learning, there are various determinants of the learnability of materials. A knowledge of how to use these determinants to influence the behaviour of others is an important part of the stock-in-trade of the politician, the salesman, the advertiser, and the writer. And they will be of practical value to you in preparing and presenting your classroom materials. Here they are:

Duration—The longer a person is exposed to new material, the better he will learn it. Though the ten-year-old child learns less rapidly than the 14-year-old, with sufficient time he can learn very difficult skills and concepts. And though the dull child learns less rapidly than the bright child of the same age, he too can learn and learn thoroughly. Since he must have more time, however, we must give him less that is new each day.

Frequency—The more often a child encounters a given body of material the more likely he will be to remember it. Notice how this rule is used by advertisers. A supposed characteristic of a product—an advertising slogan—is repeated many times on the same radio or television programme. And then this same slogan appears on billboards and in newspapers and magazines. Politicians and propagandists use this same principle. What they wish to have believed they state again, and again, and again! When we teach a child a new technique— the use of percentage, for example—we provide him with a number of problems all involving the same principle.

Recency—The more recently a child has studied new material, the more likely he will be to remember it. The child learns to review before an examination, we review our notes just before making an oral report, the pianist reviews a selection that he is to play in tonight's concert—in each case more effort is required to have the material fresh in mind than to gain new learnings or greater skill.

Contrast—The more strongly one portion of a situation contrasts with another portion of the situation, the more likely a child is to remember it. Thus, uniqueness of a part of a situation as compared to the remainder, or of one situation as compared to other situations, is an important factor in our learning of it. We remember a situation if it is different from those we usually encounter; we remember people who are different from others in the group. A part of the value that comes from using visual and auditory aids in our classroom situations comes from the fact that they make each situation stand out as different from others.

Vividness—The greater the impact of new material on the child, the better the chance that he will learn it. In the classroom we ordinarily use a sensory impact, though in life situations the vividness may come from the extreme pleasantness or unpleasantness of the experience. The advertiser uses colour, loudness, music, and humour to give vividness to his message. The effective teacher makes learning vivid with motion pictures, recordings, coloured charts, and three-dimensional models. His students perform experiments, learn in a social setting, go on field trips, see government in action, make collections, and prepare exhibits.

One Important Qualification: These general rules of learnability hold only when other things are equal. For example, a child may remember very vivid material that he studied many months ago much better than he remembers dreary, uninteresting material that he studied, as recently as yesterday. When we say that material to which we have been exposed twice is more likely to be remembered than material to which we have been exposed but a single time, we imply that both materials possessed the same or nearly the same degree of recency, duration, vividness, and contrast.

Transfer-based Learning

How do learning experiences in the school prepare children to solve the problems they will meet in later life? How successful are human beings in transferring the material they have learned in one situation to another?

At one time it was assumed that the function of education was to provide exercise for the mind. The idea was that schooling would strengthen the mind and prepare it to meet successfully any problem that might arise. What was learned in school was considered less important than the exercise required in learning it. Solving unusual problems in arithmetic, learning to spell difficult words, and memorising selections in Latin and Greek were accepted as educationally worthwhile, not because the problems, the words, and foreign language would be valuable to the child, but because it was believed that his memory could be sharpened and his reasoning ability would be developed in the process of mastering them.

We have discovered that education is not as simple as that. A child may memorise a thousand poems, yet his memory of what he reads in his books and sees in the world about him will not be improved in the least, and he can solve thousands of difficult mathematical problems with no improvement in his ability to solve social problems.

We now recognise that the materials to be learned in the school must be selected on the basis of their ultimate worth in preparing the individual for life. And we know that to make these materials most available to the child when he needs them, we must make the situations in which the child learns as life-like as possible. To be able to solve new problems in later life, he must not only know many things, he must recognise which of those many things applies to each problem. For example, we know that if the child is to remember and use—transfer—what he learns about percentage when he later is called upon to decide what interest rate he is to pay for a so-called "easy-payment plan", he must have learned percentage and how it applies to life situations. He must be given far more than the rules to memorise and meaningless exercises to solve. We know that if he later is to become able to talk effectively to a group of his fellows, he must practice speaking in a social situation—memorisation of grammatical rules alone is inadequate.

As you can see, to provide for maximum transfer we cannot make the learnings of the classroom ends in themselves. We must select the materials, skills, and habits that we will teach the child on the basis of their value to him in meeting his life problems. We know that if they are to be retained and used, learnings must be taught in a setting that is as near as possible to the life situations that he is preparing to meet. The learnings of the classroom must have belongingness in life situations.

This places a great deal of responsibility on us as teachers. And it has resulted in tremendous changes in curriculum and general teaching procedures. For example, we now teach the child to spell only those words that he will most often use. And we teach spelling in a situation as like as possible to the life situations in which he will use it—he writes the words rather than spells them orally and he uses them in sentences, pronounces them, and knows their meaning. We take this same approach in all our teaching—we select those materials, attitudes, habits, motor and social skills, ideals, and standards of life most needed for a happy and productive life and we teach them in a social situation.

Thus our modern school curriculum includes only such learnings as have maximum value for life, and the professional teacher sees that the child learns in problem situations and not by rote.

In the present chapter we have studied the learning process itself. We have a professional need for a knowledge of the learning process as a basis for the building of effective and efficient learning situations. And we must teach the child to learn effectively when he approaches learning problems without our guidance.

The general principles will of course be the same whether the child or the teacher decides the learning procedure to be used, for always it is the child who must do the learning. But let's summarise the conditions that are most favourable to maximum learning and retention.

The problems that the child solves as he strives to reach goals are the core of the learning process, because only through meeting problems does he change his behaviour. If we can set goals that challenge the child yet appear attainable, we are assured that he will meet problems. And we teach him to set goals for himself—to make questions on the material that he studies, to outline, to take notes, and to develop special interests and to pursue them.

Recall is a powerful aid to learning. We plan our lessons and units to make maximum use of recall and we teach the child to read, check (recall), and re-read. And a mental set to learn and to remember is important. Such a set will be present when the child learns in order to achieve goals that appeal to him. We choose for learning only those things that are most likely to meet the future needs of the child. But we make sure that these same learnings satisfy present needs for new experiences, recognition, and self-esteem. We plan out-of-school assignments so that they are interesting projects to be completed rather than an hour's reading to accomplish.

We know that the primary cause of forgetting is interference and that maximum interference occurs when learning experiences are similar to one another. But when materials are well learned they are less similar to other materials than they are when poorly learned. If we use a wide variety of sensory experiences the learnings will be less similar and thus interfere less with each other. And if we consider carefully the child's ability and govern the quantity of what he learns by his ability to learn, we can encourage each child to learn thoroughly.

For maximum retention the child must see relationships—between old and new learnings and between cause and effect. We build new learnings on old and we teach the child to search for the relationships within situations and the relationships between what he knows and the new situations.

Time invested in review pays great dividends in cutting down on the speed of forgetting. We plan class activities so that review is guaranteed and we show the child how and when to review. But the ultimate test of what is learned in the school is its value to the child in later life. We recognise that not only must we choose wisely those things that he is to learn but that we must teach in a setting that is as life-like as possible.

The purpose of the present chapter has been to examine the learning process. We shall look for ways in which we can use this knowledge to build effective learning situations in classrooms.

Tenets and Theories

Many a question. What goes in the process of learning? How do we learn? How can a child learn to solve mathematical problems? How does a girl learn to cook the food or sew the clothes? The answers to which need a thorough explanation of the phenomena of learning. Psychologists have tried to perform experiments for throwing light on the phenomenon of learning and as a result have developed various learning theories. Each theory, with its systematic body of knowledge, explains the nature and process of learning. Those theories represent broad principles and techniques of learning. The set of rules and the laws of learning, having wide applicability, are drawn from these theories. In other sense, these theories can put forth various methods of learning and suggest the teacher and learner to take proper steps for the effective learning.

Modern learning theories may be classified into two broad types, namely-

(a) Stimulus response - associationist type of theories.

(b) Gestalt field or field cognition type of theories.

Determined Learning

Ivan Pavlov, a renowned psychologist of Soviet Russia won the Nobel Prize in 1909 for his work on the psychology of digestion. In his research on digestion, Pavlov used a minor surgical procedure that enabled him to collect samples of salivary fluid from the dogs that were his experimental subjects. During the course of experiment he found that the dog is not only salivating while taking food, but is also salivating at distinctly natural stimulus like sight of food, sound of the caretakers approaching with food, etc. This aroused his curiosity to conduct the experiments and ultimately propounded the conditioning theory of learning. Since Pavlov's observation is a classic example of animal learning, his experiment is called Classical Conditioning which represents learning at a very lower level. A great variety of our everyday experience are learnt through conditioning procedures. Conditioning is nothing "but the establishment of connection between a stimulus and a response which have no natural connection between them". It is learning at a very simple level, learning which we acquire mostly unconsciously. The basic principles of this learning process can be understood from the experiment of classical conditioning.

Pavlov demonstrated that a dog salivates when food is put into its mouth. This reflex of salivation is physiological and natural. But the dog can be made to salivate to any other natural stimulus say the sound of a bell, if for a few times the natural stimulus (food) is presented to the dog with the Conditioned Stimulus (CS) and Conditioned Response (CR) neutral stimulus (i.e., the sound of a bell). This salivation to the sound of a bell is unnatural and learned. Pavlov gave different names to the various type of stimuli and responses. The natural stimulus for salivation, i. e., food was called by him as Unconditioned Stimulus (US). The natural response to it, i. e., salivation while eating was called Unconditional Response (U R). The experimental stimulus which was natural before experiment is called Conditioned Stimulus (CS). Here it is the sound of the bell. The learned response (i. e., salivation) to the otherwise natural stimulus (i. e. the sound of the bell) is called Conditioned Response.

In a typical experiment on dogs Pavlov paired food and bell a few times. It was found that after a few pairings, the dog salivates even when only bell is sounded and food is not presented.

This salivation is nothing but a conditioned (i. e. learned) response to an otherwise neutral stimulus i.e. bell. Thus, we can define classical conditioning "as a process in which a neutral stimulus by pairing with a natural stimulus, acquires all the characteristics of natural stimulus".

Pavlov also found that the amount of saliva secreted in response to the stimulus gradually increases showing the strength of conditioned response. To study it properly, he collected the saliva of the dog and measured, as the trial of pairing the CS and US went on. Then he plotted the findings in a graph which is called the Conditioning Curve or Acquisition Curve.

Pavlov noted that the strength of the response gradually increases with more and more pairing of US & CS. But gradually the curve flattens that is, after certain number of trials, an increase in salivation due to a particular trial becomes less than its earlier trial, like typical learning curves, where over-learning after a point gives 'diminishing returns'. Here also, more trial after a particular point results in diminishing returns.

The theory of conditioning propounded by Pavlov is based on his views on the mechanistic approach to learning. The behaviour which is learnt must have corresponding impact on the nervous system including the brain of the organism. Frank Restle explains the impact of conditioning process on the brain of the organism in the following way, "In Pavlov's thinking, the Conditioned Stimulus (CS) would set up a weak centre of excitation in the brain and the US - UR event would involve a strong centre of activity. When one centre of excitation proceeds to the other in time, the weaker centre becomes integrated with or drawn into the stronger activity and a pathway of some sort develops in the brain. At the same time presentation of CS initiates the activity US - UR complex and the animal makes the UR The theory states that the response original made to US becomes associated with CS and what is learnt is CS - CR bond of some kind".

Innovative Approach

This various phenomena discovered by Pavlov in his experiments of classical conditioning are explained below.

1. *Higher Order Conditioning:* Pavlov found that higher order conditioning is possible. It consists of several stages of classical conditioning. In the second stage, conditioned stimulus of the first stage of conditioning (CS) is paired with a new Conditioned Stimulus (CS). The trials proceed in the following stages:

(1) US (Food)	UR (Saliva)
(2) CS+ US (Bell+ Food)	CR (Saliva)
(3) CS (Bell)	CR (Saliva)
(4) CS+ CS (Bell+ Light)	CR (Saliva)
(5) CS (Light)	CR (Saliva)

Thus, in the end, the dog will salivate to a light on the face. It might seem that higher order conditioning has no limits. But actually it has limits that is because when the CS, is paired with CS2 it is paired without US. Hence, the conditioning response to it becomes gradually extinct. Upto a point such extinction can be prevented by interspersing trials, when CS, and US are repaired. By doing this and pairing CS with another stimulus CS3 Pavlov could condition UR to CS3 but he could go no further.

2. *Contiguity:* The contiguity in time of the CS and US is very important in classical conditioning. In conditioning, the conditioned stimulus is said to be reinforced by the unconditioned stimulus. To be reinforced, CS is to be continuous in time with U-S. But contiguity in time is a very vague term. How much is the inter-stimulus interval? (Inter-Stimulus interval is the interval between the onset of the CS, and onset of the US). The inner stimulus intervals varies with the learner and also the response which is being conditioned.

   However, in general, short inter stimulus interval ranging from 5 to 30 seconds are optimum.

3. *Background Conditioning:* Another point worth noting in this context is backward conditioning where Unconditioned Stimulus (US) is given before the Conditioned Stimulus. Pavlov found that it is not possible. But psychologists have proved later on that such conditioning is possible in case of human beings.

4. *Extinction, Spontaneous Recovery and Reconditioning:* If the CS (Sound of the bell is repeated several times not being followed by the US (food), it means that there is nothing followed by the US (food). It means that there is no pairing, and consequently no reinforcement. Then what does happen? The dog starts secreting less of saliva with each presentation of the CS without the US until a point comes when it stops the secretion totally. This process is known as extinction of the learned response of secreting, saliva to the CS (bell). If the experimenter stops this experiment at this point, he will conclude that extinction is the erasure of the learning obtained by conditioning. But actually it is not that extinction is the process of inhibition or the response acquired is conditioning. It is new learning superimposed on the old without destroying the latter. This is proved from the phenomenon of spontaneous recovery and reconditioning.

   It has been found that after the extinction of the Conditioned Response, if the animal is given some rest and then given trial by presenting it with CS (bell), it will again salivate to the bell, though not much. This proves that a Conditioned Response is called 'Spontaneous Recovery' and it proves that the old conditioning was not totally extinct after all. That in extinction, tne original conditioned response does not become extinguished, is proved by reconditioning. Pavlov proved that conditioning after extinction, is much more rapid than the original conditioning.

5. Stimulus Generalisation: Pavlov discovered that when the dog has learnt to salivate to the bell, it will also salivate to the all other sounds similar to the bell. This is stimulus generalisation. Many human responses and learnings are

acquired through this process of stimulus generalisation. While explaining this phenomenon Pavlov wrote that when the brain gets excited its effect also radiates to the surrounding parts and points, because of the excitement of the surrounding parts, the other associate areas of the brain gets into activity and therefore other objects having similar characteristics and attributes also serve as conditioned stimuli. Pavlov called this phenomenon as "eradication of excitation", an important aspect of any learning process. Pavlov discovered that this is also possible. According to him, the animal can be positive conditioned to high tone sound and negatively conditioned to low tone. If the high tone is decreased with reinforcement and the low tone is increased without reinforcement, the dog can differentiate very small differences in pitch. But the difference between pitches should not be too fine, i.e. should not be less than a limit. If that occurs, the dog runs into temper-barks, bites, jumps, etc, which was called by Pavlov as 'Experimental Neurosis'. He thought in being positively conditioned to highest one, there is cerebral excitation in the brain, while negatively conditioned low tone produces cerebral inhibition. When the difference between the two tones is very fine, there is a clash between two excitations and inhibition joined simultaneously which results in experimental neurosis. Later on, Pavlov developed his theories of psychosis and neurosis based on this concept.

6. *Motivational Factors:* Pavlov found that the strength or ease with which the conditioning will be done also depends upon motivational factors like hunger, sex, etc. If the response of the animal is related to some organic needs, conditioning will be better.

Following the general procedure already described, Pavlov and his friends conditioned the salivary response of the dog to a variety of stimuli—visual, auditory, olfactory and cutaneous. Vladimir Mechterer, another, Russian psychologist also conducted classical conditioning experiments with so called "Protective reflex". In this experiment simulation is received inspite of the subject's reaction. The sequence of stimuli bell and electric shock remain, regardless of what the subject does. Gradually the subject learns to withdraw his paw, hand or finger, even when only the erstwhile stimulus (bell) is given. Thus, the bell becomes the conditioned stimulus and withdrawal in response to its conditioned response.

Contributions of Pavlov : Pavlov brought a revolution in the field of study of learning process. His distinct contribution to psychology showed how a part of the environment can control a subject's response, though normally should have no connection with it. He experimentally proved in an objective way how learning can be acquired. He considered the process of conditioning as sufficient to explain all forms of learning.

As he puts it "different kinds of habits based on training, education and discipline of any sort are nothing but a long chain of conditioned reflexes." Later on psychologists belonging to behaviour school used this concept of conditioning to explain all forms of learning. His emphasis on the objective behaviour of the subject rather than on its mental process were later followed by behaviourists like Watson to develop their theories of behaviourism and learning.

Instances of Human-beings : There is ample evidence of classical conditioning occuring in human subjects. A possible example in everyday observation is the situation of a child meeting a doctor quite undisturbed before the first inoculation, but crying at the sight of him before the second. More, systematically, Watson and Rayner established a fear of white rats in a nine month old infant named Albert. The child originally had no fear of these animals and would play with them quite happily, but he was frightened by loud noises. On a number of occasions the experimenters sounded a gong as Albert was handling a rat, after which they presented the rat alone again and found that he responded to it with crying and other signs of fear. Classical conditioning has even been reported in human foetus.

Theory's Relevance

The phenomenon of conditioning does not limit itself to such laboratory experiments only. The day to day learning at home, school, etc, consists of plenty of examples where the child learns through conditioning.

Fear, love and hatred towards the subjects are created through conditioning. A mathematics teacher, with his defective methods of teaching or improper behaviour may be disliked by students or by a particular student. He, without caring to know the basic reason, always rebukes and punishes him while returning him the checked home-assignments. Gradually, the child begins to fear home-assignments of any sort. He also develops a distaste and hatred towards the subject of mathematics.

On the contrary, the sympathetic treatment given by the teacher and his interesting and effective methodology can bring a desirable impact on the students through the process of conditioning. They develop a positive attitude towards the subject and love their teacher as well as the subject.

The use of audio-visual aids in the teaching-learning process involves conditioning theory in making the students learn so many things. The child gets an idea of a particular object or phenomenon through this aid. For example, the teacher shows him the picture of a cat, along with the written word 'cat'. The teacher speaks out 'cat' and asks the student to say "cat" everytime when the picture is presented. After sometime the picture of the cat is not presented, only the written word 'cat' is shown. But the child responds to it by saying 'cat. He associates the written word 'cat' with the picture of the cat and the sound of the word.

In developing desirable habits, interests, attitudes, sense of application in the children, etc, the conditioning process may help the teacher and parents a lot. Not only it helps the development of proper behaviour in them but also, is helpful in removing many bad habits — unhealthy attitudes, superstition, fear and phobias — through deconditioning. A child who fears a particular object can be made to seek pleasure from it. Another child who thinks it is a dangerous sign if a cat crosses his way, can be made to give up his misbelief. In this way, the conditioning theory throws light on so many aspects of learning and helps the teacher and parents in their task.

Trial and Error-based Theory

E. L. Thorndike (1874 - 1949) was the first American S. R. psychologist who conducted a series of experiments on learning with animals. The theory of learning propounded by him on the basis of data from these experiments, is known as "the Trial and Error Learning" or "The Intelligence" published in 1898.

Thorndike experiments with lower animals have thrown much light on the learning processes. In one of his experiments, Thorndike confined a hungry cat to a cage closed by door which could be opened by a latch. Food was kept outside the door so that it could be within the sight of the animal. The cat tried to come out of the cage by biting, crawling, scratching, etc. After 160 seconds, it succeeded in pushing the latch accidentally, and came out. Thorndike repeated this experiment several times. On the 24th attempt the cat took only seven seconds to come out. Similar experiments were conducted on rats, monkeys, rabbits, etc. Thorndike termed this method as 'trial and error' or 'hit and miss' method because prior to the learning of a task, the animal made many trials before it hit the right response. The preliminary responses were full of errors. Thorndike concluded the following from the above experiments:

(a) The animal in the learning situation resorted to random activity.

(b) As the learning situation proceeded there was gradual reduction of useless movements.

(c) After a number of trials the animals learnt to use the release mechanism without resorting to any useless movements.

(d) In learning the animal's improvement was regular.

Thorndike concluded that when confronted with a problem situation, the animal, in the earlier stages makes a series of actions and movements to achieve the goal. A large number of these movements are exploratory in nature. They are unnecessary and, to the observer, they seem to be just blind efforts, random in nature. Gradually, with the repeated trial the unsuccessful actions are diminished and the successful actions are increased manifold. Some contend that this type of learning is essentially and usually miscalled 'trial and error learning'. It should be called learning by 'selection of the successful variant', for it is by the selection of the right way rather than by the elimination of the wrong one that new response are learnt. The wrong one is usually eliminated because it cannot exist in the presence of the right one. Yet in hundreds of human activities, 'trial and error' method works successfully and it is considered as one of the most significant aspects of learning. Learning to play golf, to ride bicycle, to do typing, to drive a car, to skate, to swim, to write, to play a musical instrument, to model with clay, to paddle a canoe, and thousands of other human activities involve the process of trial and error. In learning sports skills, this method plays an extremely important role. Novices try a number of methods of kicking, hitting, throwing, catching, etc, before they succeed in doing so correctly. In everyday life, we make trial with many garments before we select one which fits well, many colours in painting before the right colour is found, even though we have enough knowledge and experience.

A few important concepts involved in this theory need a little more consideration. First, by trial and error method; learning is not instant, it is gradual and a function of time. Those expecting immediate results would generally criticise it. If the individual is given sufficient time for exploration, learning will proceed satisfactory. Second, the goal of activity in progress must be clear and be in sight of the learner. A clear goal or purpose invokes a more vigorous response from the learner who tries to achieve it as fast as possible. Third, the learner must be given an opportunity to understand the situation as a whole and not in fragments. Every component of a skill must be shown and presented as a the 'whole'. The piecemeal presentation of the situation creates stumbling blocks in the way of learning proper response. Fourth, the earlier stage of learning is the stage of exploration which necessitates wastage of effort and energy because the individual himself is to 'find out' the 'successful variant' unaided He is not guided, he is like a stranger who has to find his own way through the thick of the situation. Fifth, some precondition (s) must exist in the organism to receive the stimulus and try to respond. For example, a satisfied cat would not make efforts to reach food.

Lastly, in all types of learning, trial and error is an essential element. If trial and error is rationally analysed, it is found to be an essential ingredient of our natural behaviour rather than a consciously-devised method! It is a descriptive process of behaviour. Establishment of stimulus-response bond, satisfaction or annoyance and practice are basic factors involved in trial and error.

Laws of Learning

The law of effect which is Thorndike's primary law of learning takes place according to three basic laws. They are the Law of Effect, the Law of Exercise and the Law of Readiness.

1. *The Law of Effect:* The Law of Effect is Thorndike's primary law of learning. It stresses the importance of effect or consequence learning i.e. on the strengths or weakness of the connections between the stimulus and response. It says, "when a modifiable connection between a situation and response is made and is accompanied or followed by a satisfying state of affairs, that connection's strength is increased. When made, and accompanied or followed by an annoying state of affairs, its strength is decreased". Though the terms 'satisfying' and 'annoying' have subjective connotations, Thorndike tries to define them objectively. He says, " By a satisfying state of affairs is meant one which the animal does nothing to avoid, often doing things which renew it. By annoying state of affairs is meant one which the animal does nothing to preserve, often doing things which puts an end to it. Responses which are rewarded are firmly established and become more probable for recurrence. On the other hand, annoying responses, that is, responses which are meted out with punishment, are unlearnt and become less probable for recurrence. Thus, the Law of Effect of Thorndike is just another name for what the psychologists call the law of rewards and punishment. The cat inside the puzzle box is rewarded in the form of food, when it makes correct response.

   Therefore, it learns that response. Other random responses which are not thus rewarded are not learnt by it.

2. *The Law of Exercise:* This law explains the role of practice or repetition in learning. It states, "when any activity is repeated a number of times, there is a tendency for that activity to be firmly established and easily-learnt, while the activity seldom repeated becomes difficult for learning". This law has two parts. The first part is the law of use which states that if a situation is followed by a particular response, then a bond (S-R connection) is established. This bond between the stimulus and the response becomes strengthened by repetition or exercise. The second part is the law of disuse which states that when a given situation is rarely followed by a particular response, the bond between the stimulus and the response becomes weakened.

   Under this Law of Exercise, there are various sub-laws, like the law of frequency, the law of recency, the law of vividness of intensity. By frequency is meant the frequency of repetition of the particular response to a particular stimulus or situation. The sub-law of frequency states that a bond which has been recently established is less prone to error. The sub-law of vividness that signifies the active and interested exercise strengthens the bond more than mere mechanical exercise.

   Thorndike established a connection between the law of effect and the law of exercise by observing that the satisfying response is more often repeated and consequently becomes more permanently established.

3. *The Law of Readiness:* The Law of Readiness of Thorndike states, "when a bond is ready to act, gives satisfication and not to act gives annoyance. When a bond which is not ready to act, is made to act annoyance is caused. The readiness and lack of readiness of the bond is the result of condition of the nervous system. The neurons of the nervous system, which are responsible for conduction of nerve impulses, are called the 'condition units'. The condition (readiness or lack of readiness) of the nervous system is ultimately dependent upon those of the 'conduction units'. All the conduction units are not always

in readiness to receive and conduct nerve impulses, which are the result of stimuli acting upon the nervous system. They are not always in readiness to omit responses to the stimuli. When any conduction unit is in readiness to conduct, for it, to do so, is satisfying and not to do so, is annoying."

The readiness or lack of readiness in nervous system to participate in the establishment of a bond is dependent on various factors like maturation, attitude and the past experience of the learner.

Concept of Sub-laws

(1) *Law of Contiguity:* This denotes that situation which occurs together either simultaneously or in close succession tends towards receiving one another since one situation has association with many other situations or objects. It is also known as Law of Association. The temple of Sri Jagannath Dev reminds us of Puri, Nilamadhaba, King Indradumna, Gundicha Rani, Anangabhima Deva, Kanchi Abijan etc., because of their contiguity and association. Contiguity is one of the important factors in associational learning theories. Associationists believe that although reward will aid association to proceed more rapidly and will perhaps, strengthen the connection, association will occur, regardless of reward, if the stimulus and the responses are contiguous. The greater the affinity between the stimulus and the responses, the faster would the learning proceed. Learning of poetry i.e. memorizing a poem is easier than cramming prose because the words in the former are rightly and oppositely associated with one another which is not the case with prose.

(2) *Law of Multiple Response to the Same External Situation:* Here the connection is that the individual makes several responses and not one to the same situation or the external stimulus. A chance word or observation, sets off a train of thoughts which runs for a long time. Some external stimulus seems to be necessary in the beginning but in a series of the further internal or external activity i.e. one

reaction leads to a number of further reactions in sequence. There are, then multiple responses to a single stimulus. In this process, the desirable responses may be selected and practised and the undesirable ones eliminated. The higher the animal is in the hierarchy of the evolutionary scale, the greater the number and the variety of responses. This hints at the variability of human behaviour. This law is also called concomitant or Attendant Learning. During an athletic class, the learner not only learns the activity pattern but also how his coach explains the procedures, how he dresses up; what techniques, what peculiar word or sentences he used to make teaching more effective. All these factors ultimately decide whether the learner would give response wholly or partially. By this way the habit of concentrating on the activity of paying attention, initiative, etc, may be cultivated. This means that one learns many things in one single situation.

(3) *Law of Attitude, Set or Disposition:* What response shall an individual make to a given stimulus depends upon his attitude or his disposition at that time. Further satisfaction or annoyance would also depend on this factor. The attitudes are acquired from the previous experience, and the state of affairs of the individual at that time. An inexperienced and a seasoned athletic differs in his attitude towards a particular learning situation. The former is well set mentally to practise drills, skills, etc. The latter is well disposed to take to the whole game. Thorndike says that a well-fed cat goes to sleep in the cage while a hungry one would strive to get out of it and reach for food. In the same way, the mental and the physical disposition of the individual at that time determines as to what extent, he would respond to the new stimulus.

(4) *Law of Partial Activity:* "A part, or an element or an aspect of a situation may be prepotent in causing response, and may have responses bound more or less exclusively to it regardless of some or all of its accompaniments". A student who had solved a number of puzzles or gone through a number of intelligence tests "gets on to the thing" more

quickly than the one who has not had similar experiences. Similarly, the situation in the sports field also demands the distinction to be made between the raw hand and the one who knows something. The latter would look for more complex activities while the former remains stuck up with simpler ones.

(5) *Law of Associative Shifting:* This is a 'conditioned' response. A response may be shifted from one situation to another which is presented at the same time. In the process of motor skill acquisition, the situation is gradually transferred from element to element until the whole complex skill becomes clear. Conditioning is so universal that it might truly be said that the teacher can get any response of which a student is capable and is associated with any situation to which he is sensitive.

(6) *Law of Belongings:* According to this sub-law, if the connection between the stimulus and the response is natural, learning would be more effective. Motor skills based on natural activities of running, jumping, throwing, etc, are learnt faster. Artificial activities are difficult to learn. For example, it is harder to try running backwards with the same arm foot coordination.

(7) *Law of Intensity of Stimulus:* Learning depends much on the intensity or strength of the stimulus. The stronger the stimulus, the stronger will the response be. For example, a player who is getting an opportunity of participation in the national or international tournament, will practice hard and more seriously. Most often the strength of a stimulus is intensified by using extrinsic and intrinsic devices of motivation.

(8) *Law of Primacy:* This denotes that the situations which are presented at the outset, elicit a more lasting response. That is why it is said that the first impression is the best impression. Teacher's first day appearance, his turn-out, his speech, the condition of the playground, the equipment, etc, go to make the fast impression on the students. This ultimately will determine the quantum of satisfaction or dissatisfaction which a learner derives therefrom At the

end of a serious activity-practise class, the physical education teachers are advised to provide a recreative game so that the students forget the primary painful experiences of forced skill-practice.

(9) *Law of Recency:* Experiences received recently are revived easily and very often such experiences are more vivid than others. They can be recalled without much effort than those occuring in the middle of the activity. If first impression is the best impression, best impression is the last impression. If at the end of the class, the last act is satisfying, the impression will linger on in the minds of the students.

(10) *The Law of Assimilation and Analogy:* This law states that when the learner is faced with a new situation for which he has no natural or learned response, the response he makes, will be that found useful in a similar situation in the past. In other words, the law states that the responses to new situations and problems are made on the basis of the past experience.

***Laws of Thorndike* :** At first, Thorndike called his bond theory of learning as blind and mechanical. But subsequently, he modified his theory to such an extent that it could hardly be termed as blind mechanical. The modification of his laws of effect and exercise were necessitated in the light of further experimental evidence. In 1929, he admitted before the International Congress of Psychology that his law of exercise and effect needed revision. Then, soon after that, he published his revised laws.

(1) *Revision of Law of Exercise:* He revised this law as a result of his experiment on human learning. According to the revision, the law of exercise is not considered as an independent law. Mere repetition of a response or practice is not enough. Repetition or practice brings improvement, when other factors like rewards are present. Connection gets strengthened when recurrence is rewarded. Simple recurrence does not strengthen the connection.

(2) *Revision of the Law of Effect:* He also revised his law of effect. The original law of effect had given equal importance to the effects of rewards and punishment. But later on

Thorndike discovered that the effects of rewards and punishment do not weaken to that extent.

(3) *The Principle of Polarity:* He also introduced a new concept called the principle of polarity which means that "connections act more easily in the directions in which they are formed than in the opposite direction."

(4) *The Concept of Spread of Effects:* Another concept introduced by him is the concept of spread of effects. This concept suggests that the effect of reward and punishment is not confined to a particular connection but it has a "spread". It also affects-adjacent connections which are there, both before and after the rewarded connection.

(5) *The Concept of Belongingness:* He also introduced the concept of belongingness into his learning theory. A connection is more easily learnt if the response belongs to a situation i.e. fits perfectly into the situation. This concept merely states that an appropriate and useful response to a situation is more easily learnt than in appropriate one.

(6) *The Concept of Motivation:* Another important revision of his learning theory is the admission that motivations are very important for learning. Motives like hunger, sex, thirst, etc, determine which are to be avoided. They also provide the basis for repetition and confirmation of the responses already made.

The Assessment

Thorndike is the first S-R theorist. He placed much importance upon the need for experimental evidence and objective verification in psychology. According to W. F. Hill "Thorndike was no less a pioneer of objective psychology than Watson. Indeed his original contributions were quite likely more important than Watson".

Hill also hails him as "the first real reinforcement psychologist" as "he incorporated within the objective psychology the law of effect". The theory of reward and punishment was very clearly explained by him for the first time in the history of psychology. He explains that acts that are rewarded tend to recur and acts not reinforced or punished tend to become less probable of recurrence.

His law of effect has also called attention to the importance of motivation, belongingness, etc, in learning.

His theory of learning propounded very important laws in relation to learning process. It has much implication for the teachers and the students. For example the law of exercise stresses the need for practice for better learning. The law of disuse explains the process of forgetting. The law of attitude or disposition brings out the importance of the attitude of the learner on his learning capacity. The law of assimilation or analogy brings out the principle of transfer of learning.

Varied Defects

But the learning of theory of Thorndike has certain shortcomings also. First, his contention that learning is only a connection between the situation and response is not true. His argument is that the cat only learnt physiological movements, cannot be accepted as true. A cat that has learnt to pull the loop will, on the next trial go to the place where the loop was, even though it has been removed to another place. But when it discovers its new locations, it will no longer go to the former place. Thus the cat has certainly got acquainted with the cage, the outlet, the locations and the use of release mechanism. It has not learnt only physiological movements or connections. Rather it has learnt the cognitive map of the problem environment and also its solution. Secondly, the law of exercise of Thorndike is too mechanical. It does not take into account factors of learning. Thorndike should have known that mere repetition without understanding does not improve learning. However the latter revision of the law made by Thorndike nullifies much of the criticisms against it. Thirdly, Thorndike explains the law of readiness with reference to connections between neurons. The law of readiness is useless, unless it refers to mental readiness. He also does not explain this law clearly. That is why some psychologists interpret this law as natural readiness. Fourthly the law of effect cannot be explained without reference to mind. Guthrie disproves this theory. He suggests, what is learnt is what is connected not what is rewarded. Tolman's theory of latent learning proves that the law of effect is not an essential law, as learning can also take place without reward.

Educational Relevance

Thorndike's theory of trial and error has enough educational significance. It tries to explain the process of learning, carefully on the basis of actual experiments performed not only on the animal's but on human learning also, which to a greater extent, follow the path of trial and error. A child while confronted with a mathematical problem, tries so many possibilities of its solution, before he arrives at the correct one. Even the discoveries and inventions in the various fields of knowledge are the results of trial and error process.

For example, let us take the discovery made by Archimedes in the form of his well-known principle. He was confronted with a problem given by his emperor. There was a drive that he will be beheaded if he could not get the solutions to the problem. There was a block as he could not think of any solution. The problem was difficult. He went on experimenting and made a number of attempts (trials) for the solution of his problem. One day while taking his bath, he got chance success in one of his attempts and this led to the formation of the law of floating bodies.

But the excessive use of the method, trial and error, without caring for the development of understanding should not be encouraged in any circumstances. We cannot reduce the human learning as mechanical and blind-folded as advocated by this theory. It must be supported by reason, understanding and insight. Trials and practice coupled with insight, will make the process of learning more effective than either of the methods adopted alone.

As far as the Thorndikes laws of learning are concerned, it goes without saying that Thorndike has done a valuable service to the field of learning and teaching by providing these laws. These laws state the following things in general.

(1) In the process of teaching and learning the main task of the teacher is to see what things he likes to be remembered or forgotten by his students. After this, he must try to strengthen the bonds or connections between the stimuli and responses of those things, which are to be remembered,

through repetition, drill and reward. The connection should be weakened through disuse and annoying results.

(2) The child must be made ready to learn. His interest, attitude and mental preparation is essential for the smooth sailing in the teaching learning process.

(3) It is also emphasized that the past experiences and learning give an adequate base for the new learning. Therefore the teacher should try to make use of the previous knowledge and experience of the students. The child must, also, be encouraged to see similarities and dissimilarities between the different kinds of responses to stimuli and with the help of something in one situation to the other similar situation.

(4) The child should be encouraged to do his work independently. He must try the various solutions of the problem before arriving at the correct one. But every care should be taken to see that he may not waste his time and energy. He should not be allowed to repeat his mistakes and proceed blindly without using his reasoning and thinking powers and utilize the past learning experiences.

In short, Thorndike's theory and laws of learning have contributed a lot to educational theory and practice. It has made learning purposeful and goal-directed and has brought motivation to the forefront. It has also given impetus to the work of practice, drill and repetition and realized the psychological importance of rewards and praise in the process of teaching and learning.

Learning-based Insight

The term psychology has been defined in different ways. Particularly three definitions have been predominant: Psychology as the science of mind, of consciousness and of behaviour. Psychologists who advocate learning by insight accept the last definition of psychology as the science of behaviour. This group of psychologists are known as gestaltists. The gestaltists lay more emphasis on insight or understanding in the learning process.

Kohler, a German psychologist, is the exponent of this theory. He conducted a number of experiments on higher animals like chimpanzees, monkeys, etc. After a long observation, he came to certain conclusions which later on became the mainstay of cognitive theories. Kohler believed that no discussion on learning, without reference to 'insight' could be complete in anyway. Learning could not take place in the absence of insight'. By 'insight' he meant inner-sight i.e., seeing or penetrating deep into problematic situations. Insight, he said, involves 'foresight' as opposed to 'hind-sight' in trial and error theory. The crux of trial and error learning is the 'after thought' whereas in learning by insight "the problematic situation is reviewed as a whole, and the solution at once comes vividly before the mind in the form of foresight'. The right solutions is foreseen before the action is initiated. That is to say that in trial and error theory, thinking succeeds action while in learning by insight thinking precedes action. In the former case, the learner is bound to try a number of responses before selecting the correct-one, while in the latter case, the 'trial' is made internally at mental level so that at the end only correct response occurs.

Experiment-based Learning

To prove the above thesis, Kohler conducted certain experiments on such animals which are higher in the biological hierarchy. In one of his classical experiments, he put a chimpanzee in a cage with iron bars and kept food (bananas) at some distance from the cage so that the food could be pulled into the cage by the chimpanzee by using the bamboo sticks lying near the cage. At first the chimpanzee, to reach the foodstuff, made frantic efforts and showed hectic activity. Then it sat in a corner just brooding over the whole situation. With a sudden start, it took one stick and tried to reach the food but failed. He then took another stick fixed it into the broader-end of the other and ultimately pulled the food into the cage with the lengthened stick.

From numerous experiments of this sort, Kohler concluded that when 'insight' is gained into the entire situation, the animal abruptly gets hold of the correct response to be given. However, this kind of learning requires understanding of the situation as a whole. The goal of the activity must be clear to begin with and the learner must posses the power of 'generalisation', along with that of 'differentiation'. Lower animals posses neither power of generalization nor of differentiation; they cannot retain experiences nor store knowledge; their behaviour is a mass of thropisms and reflexes. Whether they have 'foresight' except the instinctive danger-signaling mechanisms, is a matter of guess.

In a contrived learning situation, the problems are so structured that the significant features are perceived in proper relationship, with distraction or confusing features and aspects being subordinated or kept in the background. The use of 'insight' leads to the solution of problem. Children especially young ones, cannot perceive the problematic situation as a whole, without guidance from parents and teachers. In school, the teacher has to play the role of a guide, helping the child to perceive the situation as a whole so that the use of insight is frequent and direct. Unless the learner is capable of putting the problem situation in proper perspective, the use of insight becomes redundant.

Instances More and More : Insight may be particularly important in human learning. We have all had the experience of quite suddenly seeing the solution to a problem after a period of puzzlement, and it then seems so obvious that we cannot understand why we had any difficulty. Often such sudden insight appears to be triggered off by some new perception-seeing an object, hearing a remark, or remembering something which gives us a fresh perspective on the situation. The process appears to involve recombination of past experiences and understanding of the relationships or principles underlying the solution, features which have been demonstrated experimentally with human subjects.

Wertheimer, before presenting one of his problems, taught his subjects how to find the area of a rectangle. They were told the product of two adjacent sides formula, and were also shown why this formula works by dividing a rectangle into squares and demonstrating that the area is the number of squares in a row times the number of rows. Wertheimer then asked his subjects to find the area of a parallelogram. Some replied that they could not do this without being told how. Others blindly applied the formula for the area of a rectangle. But some understood how to use their knowledge about areas of rectangles in finding the area of a parallelogram. One five and a half year old boy, for example, cut off one end of the parallelogram and fitted it against the other end to make a rectangle. This sort of solution involves a restructuring of the problem and an understanding of how existing knowledge can be used to solve it. From this type of inquiry Wertheimer concluded that children should be taught to understand how problems are solved rather than to apply rote learned solutions.

Mandatory Features

Now it should be clear that this was not just a random response. It makes more sense to say that the chimpanzee had insight-he perceived the box as something that can be climbed upon in order to seize something high. What happened does not look much like the gradual elimination of errors and the gradual strengthening of a correct response hit upon by chance. Once the insight has been attained, the problem is mastered. It can be solved immediately the next time. After the principle is understood, quite a few changes in the situation can be made without causing any difficulty. Then it matters little whether the lure is banana or orange, or just where the box is located, or its shape or size, (of course, there are limits to how big the changes can be without causing trouble). In other words, learning generalizes (or transfers) widely, once the principle is understood. This is one of the important characteristics of insight in learning

Kohler also found that some chimpanzees were able to solve more complicated problems, like stacking boxes so as to get bananas placed even higher or fitting two sticks together to make them long enough to reach food placed outside their cage. Typically the solution came rather suddenly, usually, after a quiet period in which the chimp looked over the situation.

In the Gestalt view, we solve a problem in this way. We think of various hunches (hypotheses) about what to do. Practically never do we fumble blindly, although some of our hunches may be very poor ones. What we try helps us to know which hunches will not work. It is as though we are testing our hunches, although we usually are not very systematic in doing so. Merely by thinking, we may perceive some possibilities and their probable effects without our doing anything overtly. Finally, either all at once or piecemeal, we get insight into the principle. We can use it to solve not only this problem but many others like it.

Certain factors may make it easier or harder to get insight into a problem. For one thing, past experience with similar problems may be helpful. A person with an engineering background, for example, is more likely to get insight into an engineering problem than someone without such a background.

It can also make a difference whether or not the various parts of the problem are handicapped in that the mechanism is largely hidden. Therefore, the insight into the relationship between pulling the string and the opening of the door is not possible. That is why his learning must be a fumbling, trial and error process.

Another factor having bearing on insight is strong preconceptions. We can feel so strongly that the solution lies in a particular direction that we are blind to other possibilities. All our efforts go into the wrong ideas. For instance, so long as we think that the way to get a stuck door open is to force it, then all that we can think about is how to bring enough force to bear on it. We might end with an ingenious arrangement of jacks and levers that finally break the door down, when unlocking it would have done the job! Even in our stupidity, however, our behaviour is not random or automatic. The lesson for all of us is clear; we should not get stuck on a premature hunch but should look over the problem in order to get a variety of hunches. Then we shall be less likely to waste our time in a blind alley.

Learning based on Trial and Error

There are some fundamental difference between Thorndike's Trial and Error-learning and Gestalt's insightful learning. Firstly in Thorndike's experiment the lever to open the door of the cage is out of sight of the subject. So the subject can't see it. Hence it is difficult on the part of the cat to understand the situation and apply its insight to solve the problem. According to Gestalt Theory the role of understanding and organisation of perceptual process is the most important in learning process. A problematic condition should be studied as a whole in the start and then it should be divided into interrelated parts. Then the situation is reorganised into a whole. This leads to the solution of a problem. All learning processes progress in such a manner. In short, perceptual comprehension is essential in learning process. In the process of perception it is marked that the perceiver completes the incomplete task by himself and considers the figure as a whole. It is clearly understood from the experiment of Kohler. The chimpanzee in the cage after some unsuccessful trials used two sticks by putting one in another to get the banana. Here the distance between the place of chimpanzee in the cage and the position of banana was judged by him and it used the two sticks to reach his goal. This became possible by the cognition and insight of the chimpanzee. So there lies the main difference between the trial and error learning and the insightful learning.

Trial and Error Learning	*Insightful Learning*
1. Dependent upon effort and labour.	1. Dependent on nature's gift.
2. Available to all.	2. Available to only higher animals.
3. Stress on physiological efficiency.	3. Stress on psychological efficiency.
4. Based on sensory-motor coordination.	4. Based on perception.
5. Goal directed activity.	5. More work done by sub-conscious brain.
6. No transfer of training takes place.	6. No transfer of training takes place.

Educational Relevance

This theory brings the following important facts into limelight:

1. The whole is greater than the parts and therefore, the situation should be viewed as a whole.

2. The use of blind fumbling and mechanical trial and error should be minimised. The learner should try to see relevant relationships and act intelligently.
3. The purpose or motive plays the central role in the learning process.

Based on the appeal of this theory, teachers are required to pay attention to the following aspects.

(i) Subject matter (learning material) should be presented in Gestalt form. While teaching the topic 'parts of a flowering plant' the initial start should not be made by presenting the different parts. The plant or flower as a whole should be represented before them and later on the parts should be emphasized. The problem of mathematics requiring solution should be presented as a whole; it should be tried for the solution.

(ii) In the organisation of the syllabus and planning of the curriculum, the Gestalt principle should be given due consideration. A particular subject should not be treated as the mere collection of isolated facts or topics. It should be closely integrated into a whole. Similarly the curriculum, comprising of different subjects and activities should reflect unity and cohesiveness.

(iii) This theory has brought 'motivation' to the forefront by assigning purpose and motive, the central role in learning process. The child should be motivated by arousing his interest and curiosity and he should be acquainted well with the specific aims and purposes of his learning.

(iv) The greater contribution of the insight theory of learning is that it has made learning an intelligent task requiring mental abilities instead of blind fumbling and automatic responses to specific stimuli. It has called a halt to the age old mechanical memorization, drill and practice work which lacks in basic understanding and use of thinking and creative mental powers.

It emphasizes that the learner must be given opportunities for using his mental abilities. Instead of telling him how to do a work or solve a problem, he should be placed in the position of an independent inquirer and discoverer. He should himself collect the information and discover the knowledge. The teacher should not engage himself in spoon-feeding but help the children in acquiring knowledge and skill through their own attempts by using their mental powers. Scientific and progressive methods like. heuristic method, analytic and problem solving, which advocate learning by insight, should be kept in vogue.

Concept of Motivation

In psychology, motivation is one of the most fascinating and important areas. If we can understand the motives of a child, we can understand and even predict his behaviour. Why is this true? Because motives are the dynamic force that energises behaviour. It is motivation that compels the child to act. And motives are persistent—they keep him acting until he finds satisfactions for them. Not only do motives keep him acting, they direct his actions toward specific goals.

As you can see, you have a professional need for understanding motivation. You will want to master both the theory (the 'why') of motivation and the methods (the 'how') through which you can use motives to guide behaviour and to promote learning.

There are certain basic motives or needs that every person—child and adult—strives to satisfy. So long as our present behaviour and knowledge are adequate to satisfy all our needs, we do not change our behaviour or acquire new knowledge. We modify our attitudes, interests, and personalities, and we acquire new knowledge, only when our present behaviour and knowledge do not satisfy our motives. The only things that appeal to us, the only goals that we desire to attain, are those that will help us to satisfy some strongly felt motive.

To learn something new, then, there must be (1) a *goal* that attracts us and (2) some *obstacle* that keeps us from attaining that goal. For if no obstacles stood in our way, our present behaviour and knowledge would take us directly to our goals and we would have no need to learn.

We learn only when there is no other way for us to reach the goals that our unsatisfied motives create. When we feel a need for learning, for example, it is because we are convinced that we can satisfy some motive only by acquiring learning. This felt need is a far more important element in the effective learning situation than is the simple physical presence of materials to be learned.

Let's look at why we learn from another angle. You want to be a successful teacher. That is a goal that appeals to many of your psychological needs. You want the esteem of your pupils, their parents, your fellow teachers, and your supervisor. And you want to feel a pride in your own professional skill. In addition, you want to be secure in your position as a teacher. Thus, professional skill and knowledge become very real goals to you. Are there any problems that must be solved before you attain these goals? You can see that there are numerous problems. Somehow you must learn a great deal about boys and girls as well as about general teaching methods and materials. You suspect that to reach your goals you must learn about the motives of children and how you can appeal to these motives.

Have you ever noticed how much a child learns when he sets out to raise a calf or a pig, to plant a garden, or to build a radio, a soap-box automobile, a telegraph set, a telescope, or a club house? Although few of the conditions are present that we like to think are essential to an effective learning situation, he learns more on his own than he does when he attacks some of our well-planned classroom problems. When he feels a strong enough need, the child reads instructions that under ordinary circumstances are far beyond his reading level, and he obtains information from his elders without any forcing on their part. No record of attendance is required—no routine of examination is needed to keep him at the task. Yet in our clean, well-lighted, and well-equipped classrooms, we find that we must force information on this same child, and we find it difficult to teach him to solve tasks that appear far simpler than the extracurricular and freely chosen learning activities that he handles with ease.

Why is this true? Why does a child who must collect money for newspapers learn to make change correctly? Why does a child find it easy to remember what movie is playing at any theater at any time? Why does he have no trouble learning how to travel from one part of a large city to another and yet encounter extreme difficulty in learning to follow the simplest directions for cleaning his room or preparing a theme?

The answers to these questions lie in the fundamental needs of children. We can provide children with every opportunity to learn, but, if they feel little or no need to learn what we want them to, their learning will be slow and meager. Since need arises only when motives demand satisfaction, we must try to identify the basic motives that affect both children and adults.

Because a study of the 'why' of human behaviour contributes so much to our understanding of effective learning situations, we shall devote this whole chapter to motivation. We shall look at the specific effects that motivation has on classroom learning. In a sense, then, this chapter will introduce you to the remaining chapters, and will help you integrate the materials you have studied in the preceding chapters. In this chapter we shall study *why children learn* in both the classroom and in life outside the school.

Motives themselves do not vary greatly from person to person. Differences in behaviour from one person to another result primarily from differences in the obstacles they encounter as they seek to satisfy their motives. So first let us examine the motivational forces that form the central core of human nature— the rules that govern the learning of all; and second let us look at the problems that make one child or one adult different from another.

Motives of Human Beings

Motives are the drives that energise all behaviour. Every learned act that we perform—simple or complex—and the manner in which we perform it are the results of our attempts to satisfy motives. The child's learning, both in the classroom and in informal activities, and the personality traits that he exhibits are but symptoms of his strivings to satisfy his motives.

The motives that energise human behaviour can be divided into three broad groups: (1) physiological motives, (2) psychological motives, and (3) habit motives.

Physiological Motives : These are the motives that insure the preservation of life for the individual and for the human race. They include hunger, sex, fatigue, elimination of body wastes, thirst, avoidance of pain, and the desire to maintain a proper bodily temperature. These motives are present in all animal life, but in man their method of expression becomes so interwoven with his learned social customs that it is exceedingly difficult to isolate them. The same pattern of behaviour may be aroused at different times by different motives, and any single pattern of behaviour is likely to be caused by numerous interacting motives. Our methods for satisfying our physiological motives are often intimately related to psychological motives and habit motives.

Psychological Motives : Psychological motives (sometimes called 'ego' motives) are extremely important determinants of human behaviour. In lower animals these motives are of little importance, but in man they often exert a stronger pressure than the more basic physiological drives. The cave man's direct approach to the problems of securing food or winning a mate has long since been modified by the forces of law and social custom.

Our desire to maintain and bolster our self-esteem and our feeling of esteem in the eyes of others and our needs for security and for new experiences, are the important psychological motives. Many different terms have been used in referring to these motives. Some psychologists, for example, believe that man has a psychological need to conform and to master. But we can consider conformity and mastery as parts of man's basic drive for security and esteem.

Situations involving a conflict between psychological motives and physiological motives give us some idea of how strong psychological motives really are. Probably no physiological motive is stronger than the desire to live. But we know that men in battle have volunteered to hold a position protecting others even when they knew that they were going to almost certain death. Self-preservation could motivate them in but one direction—retreat. Yet some military units have been able to build a tradition so strong that every man will volunteer for any mission, regardless of its danger. All the physiological motives urge them toward self-preservation, but the psychological motives alone are powerful enough to make them comply with the tradition.

Why are psychological motives so powerful? One reason is that we can seldom satisfy them completely. We may enhance our security, but we are never secure in a final and complete sense. Our feelings of security can be nurtured but never satiated. And so it is with self-esteem and our feeling of esteem in the eyes of others. We work and strive for ever greater conquests. As soon as we have attained one goal, we set up a new, more difficult one. There are probably few men who, once they have been elected governor or senator, do not dream of extending their authority and prestige over the whole nation. And kings and dictators have often thought longingly of ruling the whole world. Physiological motives, on the other hand, can be completely satisfied—at least temporarily. And in our culture the goals that satisfy our physiological motives are more easily attained than are the goals that fulfil our psychological needs.

Most of the behaviour problems that you encounter will result from threats to the child's feeling of security, self-esteem, or the regard of others. These threats occur in the home, on the playground, and in the classroom. A problem exists for the child whenever he is blocked in his attempts to satisfy his psychological motives. He has a constant need for security and esteem that he actively seeks to satisfy. As a skillful teacher, you will want to construct problem situations that offer the child an opportunity to satisfy his psychological drives. Because these motives are so powerful, attempts to satisfy them lead to the most effective learning.

Habit Motives : A habit once it is well established, furnishes its own source of motivation. Originally, it may have been formed in an attempt to satisfy needs based on a physiological or psychological motive. We learn to comb our hair or brush our teeth because it increases our security, self-esteem, or esteem in the eyes of others. However, once the habit is established we retain it. It acts as a motive in its own right long after the original source of motivation has become satisfied in other ways. Smoking, chewing gum or tobacco, cleanliness, following a certain route to school, posture, pitch of the voice in speaking, and application to the job at hand are other examples of such habits.

Life's Problems

In many respects, the problems that we meet in life are even more important than our motives, because it is the problems that compel us to change our behaviour—that make us learn. The psychologist often refers to these problems as frustrations, and to the tense feeling that arises when problems are encountered as a feeling of frustration. Figure 1 shows us the three general types of frustration that can block our motives.

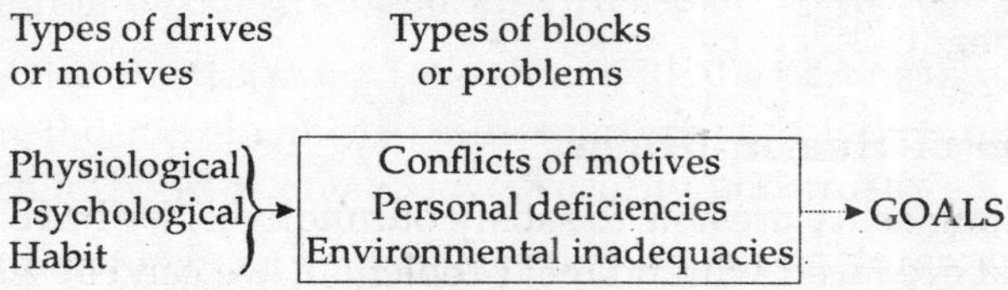

Fig. The motivations and frustrations in human behaviour.

Conflict between Motives : As you have often been told, "You cannot eat your cake and have it too." You have to resolve the conflict between two or more motives. You want to save your money for future needs, but a new suit of clothes or an evening at a night club seems desirable too. You want to attend school during the summer to prepare yourself for a better position, but travel or a summer at a resort offers more opportunity for new experiences. The child in the classroom wants to win your approval, but he finds that in order to do so he must earn the disapproval of some of his fellow students.

Personal Deficiencies : Personal deficiencies make up a second general class of frustrations. Because of insufficient size, strength, or agility, a child is unable to compete successfully with his fellows in rough-and-tumble play. Because of some lack of attractiveness, such as being too large or having a poor complexion, a girl is rejected by members of either her own or the opposite sex; because of insufficient intellectual ability, a child fails to attain success in the classroom; because he has suffered the loss of an arm or a leg, or is afflicted by muscular paralysis or some other disability, a child may lose both security and self-esteem.

Environmental Inadequacies : Our third class of frustrations includes those that arise from a deficiency in the environment. A sailor is unable to obtain fresh drinking water. An explorer cannot find enough game to live on. A boy cannot secure spending money or clothing that meets the standards set by his fellows. A girl is ashamed of her clothes, her home, or the neighbourhood in which she lives. Frequently the home, the school, and the peer group make social, intellectual, or emotional demands on the child that he is unable to meet. A personal defect that would be insignificant in one environment poses an insoluble problem in another. The race, nationality, and religion of the child become serious problems in one group and highly acceptable characteristics in another.

Reaction of Human Beings

As long as we are able to satisfy our motives, we have no real need and are faced with no real problem. If we can eat when we are hungry, drink when we are thirsty, receive the praise of our fellows, feel secure in our job and family, and brush our teeth if we are in the habit of so doing, we are scarcely aware of the potential power of our motives.

But when we are unable to satisfy our motives immediately, our contentment vanishes and we become tense. Mentally or physically, we spring into motion. Motion is typical of all animals in problem situations. We may learn to suppress physical motion by finding that mental activity is more likely to lead us to a solution of our problems, but the tendency to move remains with us. This tendency appears to arise from a heightened muscular tension that is typical of our behaviour whenever we encounter a problem that we cannot solve immediately. This type of reaction has had survival value through the long period of animal and human development. If our ancestors had felt contented and relaxed when they grew hungry, they would have starved and we would not have been born. If they had become sleepy when their motives were frustrated, they would have failed to avoid pain or to seek warmth. In short, the restlessness, aggression, and wakefulness that we experience when we are frustrated are natural responses, and, at least until recent times, have contributed to the preservation of the individual and the survival of the species.

As we move about in our search for a solution, our behaviour may be based on trial and error, or it may progress through a planned series of attempts to investigate the various possibilities for solving the problem.

But we can plan and carry out an intelligent campaign only if the present obstacle resembles one that we have overcome in the past. Our physical tension mounts and our search for a solution becomes more random when we feel that we are faced with a problem that is really insurmountable. The tension may lead to digestive disturbances and to acts of aggression toward individuals or other objects in our environment. Problem-solving behaviour is a highly active process.

This pattern is typical of human behaviour. The problems that stand between us and the satisfaction of our needs compel us to search actively for solutions. If a high-school girl feels that she needs a new party dress, she may be willing to take a job to earn extra money even though she has to sacrifice sleep and recreation. In the classroom, this same need for social approval may compel a child to sacrifice play time so that he can keep up with his classmates in spelling or algebra.

Personality is shaped by the problems encountered and by the individual's solution to those problems. If the girl who felt the need for a new party dress had chosen instead to pinch money from her mothers purse, or if the school child had copied from his neighbour's paper, and if these actions had resulted in general satisfaction, each child would have taken a serious step toward developing an unsavory personality. Thus motives are the life force, but the problems encountered shape life's course.

Fortunately, our civilisation forbids the use of physical force to compel children to learn. The teacher is not permitted to block physiological motives intentionally in order to force a child to master a mathematical problem or the parts of speech. Instead, we rely almost exclusively on psychological motives and on habit motives to encourage learning in the classroom.

And these are important motivational forces. The child needs the approval of both his teacher and his classmates. He wants to receive good marks to show to his parents and to convince himself of his own adequacy. By guiding and rewarding his curiosity, which is primarily a desire for new experiences, we can encourage him to move on from one valuable learning experience to another.

The habits of work and attention that we help the child to develop will carry him through many tasks for which he feels no immediate need. Once developed, correct habits of learning are perpetuated by two very strong forces: (1) the motivational value possessed by all habits and (2) the efficiency and ease of effort that they carry with them.

A general principle of behaviour is that the individual tends to eliminate unnecessary motion. As he practices a task, he becomes more efficient. For example, if a child attempts to find information in a book, he flounders about. But after he is taught to use the index, he goes directly to the proper place and finds what he wants. With practice, he forms the habit of using the index and, since this leads him most directly to his goal, he has an added reason for retaining his habit. We must consider this factor of efficiency when we seek to break habits that have become well established. If we have learned to operate the typewriter by the hunt-and-peck system, we are not likely to change to the more effective touch system without considerable motivation and instruction. To make a change would interfere with our existing habits and would result, at least for a time, in a loss in efficiency. However, once we do make the change and grow competent under the new method, our efficiency supplements the force of our new habit to guarantee that we will maintain it. Thus, though it is difficult to discard old habits of work and to adopt new ones, if we can once find better methods and practice them for a time, they will be retained.

The Relative Value of Various Goals : In a sense, striving toward goals is nothing more than an attempt to satisfy motives that have been blocked by obstacles or problems. Once we have reached our goal, we tell ourselves, the tension created by our present failure to overcome our problems will be reduced.

The effort that we expend to achieve a given goal is determined by a number of factors, some of which are more powerful than the importance of the goal itself. We strive harder for a small satisfaction that we can attain now than for a much larger goal that we can attain only at the end of a long period of time. A dime held near to the eye appears to be larger than the sun; a small reward attainable now may loom larger, and may induce more effort, than a great reward that can be obtained only in the indefinite future. When we set out on a 20-mile hike, the thought of arriving at our destination hours later furnishes us with little immediate satisfaction. Instead, we pick out a tree or a hill a mile or so away and then watch as our footsteps make the distance dwindle.

And so the child strives far harder for a gold star or a word of praise that he can get this morning or this afternoon than he does for a Ph. D. that will not be within his reach for twenty years. But notice that the higher his level of intellectual development, the longer he is willing to wait for rewards. The mature student is quite content to work for goals that are in the far-distant future. He is able to break his major goals down into the smaller steps of a book read, a paper completed, a few pages written, or a semester of study accomplished.

But immature students have not yet learned that the only way to reach important goals is by moving forward a step at a time. As a matter of fact, since their experience is so limited, they may not even be aware of the existence of distant goals. So one of your big jobs in working with these pupils is to break down the large but relatively unattainable goals of life into small, attainable goals. At the end of each small unit of accomplishment, you will want to provide opportunities for reward through a sense of accomplishment, through a satisfaction of curiosity, or through a feeling of teacher or group approval. The child cannot work for a mastery of arithmetic simply because he may need it when he becomes an engineer many years later. Each small step in the long-range plan must prove rewarding to his curiosity, his security, his self-esteem, his esteem in the eyes of others, or to some other motive.

Only by making sure that every unit of work will satisfy some need of every child, can we create a good learning situation. Pupils are more likely to strive toward vital goals when they themselves feel that the goals are important than when they are prodded by a taskmaster.

When the school provides for the satisfaction of needs, pupil motivation soars to the same high level that exists in out-of-school, informal, child-directed learning situations. What is more, the learning is directed toward a planned end. To the values of out-of-school learning, we add adult assistance and planning, the facilities of the library, well-lighted classrooms, and carefully chosen laboratory equipment.

But here is where our thinking about education so often goes astray. True—the tasks to be performed must fulfill a felt need of the child. But this alone is not enough. The tasks must also point toward definite and wisely chosen goals that possess social utility and that prepare the child to meet future problems of life. The school must be child-centered, but the child must not be deserted by the teacher and the curriculum maker and left to chart his course unassisted. Since he cannot appreciate how great his future need will be for certain-skills and knowledge, he is entitled to the very best guidance that educational experts can offer him. It will be your duty, as a teacher, to see that the child's activity takes him in a desirable direction and at the same time fulfills needs that he feels at the moment. As you grow in experience, you will discover that goals with high social utility can be made as rewarding to the needs of the child as goals with little or no utility.

Levels of Aspiration : Different persons aspire to different levels of attainment. If we are to make an accurate estimate of how valuable a goal is to a specific child, we must think not only of how important it seems to us as adults, or of how soon the child can attain it, but also of how attractive it seems to the child. Goals that seem to us to have the same apparent size and to be the same distance from attainment may differ greatly in attractiveness from child to child. One reason is that individual children have individual needs. Some children are most in need of security, others of self-esteem, and still others of new experiences. These needs arise from the life problems that the child is encountering at the moment and from the level of aspiration that has been determined by himself, his family, and his associates.

His race, his religion, his family, his teachers, and his friends have taught him what values to place on various goals. One family places a high value on scholarship and assumes that its children will do well in school and will enter a profession. A child from such a family will need high marks to maintain his security, self-esteem, and esteem in the eyes of others. Another family places a higher value upon material possessions and urges its children to get a good job as soon as possible. The members of a minority group who have had few educational and cultural opportunities may expect relatively little from their offspring, whereas the members of another group may expect a great deal. One religious group may place high value on conformity to moral codes; persons who do not belong to any religious group may emphasise the importance of attaining a large share of worldly goods. A child's friends may be interested in music, art, and books, or in baseball and fishing. All these and many other aspects of the child's experience and of his present environment help to determine how attractive various goals will seem to him.

If the child sets up goals that are in proportion to his abilities he will probably succeed in reaching them. But if his goals are so high and his abilities so low that his efforts are not rewarded, he will be forced either to set a lower goal for himself or to choose quite different goals—goals that may even be socially unacceptable.

You will want to help each pupil to set his levels of aspiration low enough to guarantee some measure of success as he strives toward them, yet high enough to produce enough frustration to call forth effort and to stimulate learning. The level of aspiration is one determinant of how much frustration he will encounter. Since we find little or no motivation without frustration, and since no learning occurs without both motivation and frustration, the level of aspiration must not be too low. On the other hand, if the goal seems unattainable, the child may be driven into despair, unhappiness, random activity and aggression. Ideally, the goal should be attainable but high enough to be difficult. Such a goal fosters high motivation and stimulates the child to make logical exploratory efforts.

How the "personality" Determines Values : Each of us behaves with some degree of consistency and stability. Our individual pattern of behaviour is controlled by our habits, by our levels of aspiration, and by our past experiences in achieving success or suffering failure. This pattern is a major portion of what we call "personality."

Though we usually think of our personality as affecting others, its effect upon our own behaviour is no less important. One person—through habit, level of aspiration, and successful experiences in the past—places a high value on honesty; another seeks immediate successes without regard for the methods that he must employ to attain them. One child must aim for the praise of parents and teachers; another for the attention of his peer group. And still another must find his successes and excitement in a dream world. One adolescent may feel the need of having a camera, a coin collection, or the security and prestige of a good job; another needs a fast car or flashy clothes.

Thus, when you make an assignment, show a film, or give a demonstration, each pupil views this classroom experience from an entirely different vantage point from that of every other pupil—each seeks different goals. In reading a story, one child's past experiences and levels of aspiration make him identify himself with the hero, another with the heroine, and still another with the villain. One child gains his greatest pleasure from the wealth or physical traits of the hero (or the villain), another from his romantic successes or power over others.

16

Teaching Methods

For purposes of study, it is convenient for us to isolate the aspects of the learning process. But we must remember that knowledge about the learning process is not an end in itself. Our real goal is to learn how to apply our knowledge so that children will learn in the most effective way possible.

The old saying that teachers are born and not made no longer holds true. As a modern, well-trained teacher, you must first have learned what and how to teach each child. You must know the material that you are to teach, the nature of the child, and the best methods of instruction. True, much of what makes you able to learn to teach and to enjoy teaching has come from your original nature and from the environmental forces that you encountered before you entered the teacher-training programme. But without training, regardless of your interests ability, and personality, you could not possibly perform at the level expected of the professional teacher in today's schools.

Since most prospective teachers lack experience in dealing with children, let us see how we can apply our knowledge of educational psychology to the actual business of classroom teaching. Let us attempt to identify some of the problems of directing classroom learning and see what application we can find for our knowledge of the learning process.

1. We know that in an hour's time a child may learn much or he may learn little. What makes a learning situation effective?
2. We know that the learnings that take place in the classroom are not ends in themselves. How can we guide learning toward educationally worthwhile goals?
3. We know that it is the child rather than the teacher who must do the learning. How can we so guide the learning situation that the child maintains an active attack on his learning problems?
4. We know that children in the same school grade differ widely in ability. How can we make adjustments for differences in learning ability?
5. We know that in spite of our best efforts, we cannot make every minute's work so fascinating for every child that learning will proceed automatically toward educational goals. How can we gain and preserve the leadership that we must have if we are to offer the necessary guidance of the classroom learnings?
6. We know that to learn the child must solve problems. How can we help him to develop work habits and problem-solving skills that will result in economy, persistence, and effectiveness in solving problems of increasing complexity?
7. We know that forgetting is ever an enemy of what has been learned. How can we provide for maximum retention?
8. We know that we must use minute-to-minute and day-to-day learning situations for the mastery of a large body of essential materials and skills. Can we find a general teaching procedure that will make maximum use of what is known concerning how children learn most effectively?
9. We know that not only must classroom learning be remembered but it must be made applicable to the problems that the child will meet in life. What criteria can we use for selecting the classroom learnings?

Let's take these professional problems one at a time and seek satisfactory solutions.

What is an effective learning situation? The answer to our

first question is relatively simple. But to answer the eight other questions that we have listed, we must first identify the conditions of effective learning.

An effective learning situation is one in which the child strongly desires solutions for problems that block him from satisfying one or more of his motives. His need for security, self-esteem, the esteem of others, and new experiences are always present in the classroom. If he can see opportunities to satisfy these needs, if he must learn in order to do so, and if the learning is within his ability, the chances are great that he will learn effectively. But if the problem situation presents a threat to the child's security, or a loss in his self-esteem or esteem in the eyes of others, or if it fails to offer him new experiences, it will not lead to effective learning, no matter how many times the child is forced to read a certain passage, to repeat a certain answer, or to copy certain set of exercises.

Thus, in the effective learning situation the child is actively striving to solve problems. As teachers, we must achieve this condition and more. We must guide his activity toward educationally sound goals. How can we accomplish this?

Educational Ends

From the standpoint of providing a felt need to learn, the most important characteristic of the classroom is that it is a social situation. There is a social interaction between the child and his teacher and between the child and his peers—he strongly desires the esteem of both. The classroom provides also a vast opportunity for new and interesting experiences. And, working with friends and a well-adjusted teacher on mutually interesting problems, the child should find security there. In addition, the classroom can satisfy certain of the child's habit motives. There is ample motivational force available for energising the learnings of the classroom. How can we direct this force? How can the classroom experiences be made rewarding to each child?

We know that for effective learning, the child must be trying to reach goals that are important to him. It is not enough that we see that the learnings he attains will be important to him in the future. They must be important now. How can we make goals that will be important, now?

The ability to write an effective business letter, the ability to talk convincingly to fellow adults, the ability to keep personal accounts accurately will be tremendously important to the child when he becomes an adult. But they will not be important to the child unless progress toward them results in recognition, self-esteem, new experiences, and security now.

The child can become extremely active in digging information from reference books, in writing a poem or a theme, in working an experiment in chemistry, or in preparing a talk. And he thus learns a great deal that will be useful to him as an adult. But he will be extremely active only if these activities satisfy present needs. He may need the reference material, for example, to defend a position that he has taken. He may need the poem or theme because it will give him the approval of peers, parents, or teachers. The experiment in chemistry may be a fascinating new experience. And he may have to give the talk in front of his fellow students. A boy raises a pig and keeps careful records of its costs not because of his future need for this knowledge but because of present rewards; a girl bakes a cake and makes an attractive dress not because she will some day be a homemaker but because she wants to wear the dress or receive praise for her skill in making it.

This, then, is the secret of directing effective learning toward educational goals. You are always aware of the long-range objectives toward which you guide the child—but you offer the child immediately attainable ones. Although you evaluate effective learning in terms of educational goals, you recognise that the child strives toward personal goals. And each child in your classroom will attack problems that temporarily block his attainment of personal needs.

An effective learning situation is not enough. You must guide the child's activity toward goals that are educationally worth while and you must help the child to maintain an active attack on the problems that stand between him and his goals.

Sorting the Problems

Why must you know how to guide the child to an active attack on his problems? Will he not strive actively to solve problems if his goals are important and attainable? Actually, the maintenance of the child's attack on problems is one of your most important professional tasks. You may know that the goals are extremely worthwhile but the child himself must be led to see how they can satisfy his needs. You may know that the goals that are being set are attainable, but without your guidance the child may not see that they are. And without guidance the child's attack may be sidetracked. Each child will require redirection from time to time if he is to persist in solving his problems.

Let's see how we can help the child to maintain an active attack on his problems without guiding and restricting his efforts to such an extent that his learning becomes ineffective.

To say that learning is an active process does not mean that you as the teacher should busy yourself in pouring out information every minute of the day. In fact, the more active you are in solving problems before they are felt by the child and in illustrating ideas before the child has had a chance to search for applications, the more passive the child is likely to be.

The amount of mental activity in which a pupil engages seems to be closely related to how often the teacher is content to remain silent. Teacher glibness, or words for words sake, almost certainly interferes with the learning process. Even the most able student needs time to ingest ideas and information. The illustrations and applications that occur to the child as a result of his own thinking are far more valuable than the flood of information emanating from an over-fluent instructor.

You know from your own experience that one student may get a great deal from listening to the lectures of an able teacher, whereas another may get little or nothing. The reason is that the first student is stimulated to think by what he hears. He goes beyond what is said, recalls examples, forms hypotheses, and sees relationships. But the second, fearful of missing a single fact, tries to remember every word. For the first one, every sentence creates a problem; the other merely tries to hang on from one sentence to the next—the only problem he meets is that of trying to remember everything he hears. The immature student is incapable of creating his own problems as he listens to the teacher's discussion. You must take the time and the trouble to suggest problems to him that will challenge his interest.

But how do you take the group of children that sit in your class (or run noisily about the room) on the opening day of the semester and lead them to identify attractive goals? How do you transfer the general activity into the activity that is essential to effective learning? How do you use the child's own needs to maintain an active attack on classroom problems?

For one thing, you will utilise the child's desire for your esteem. You will want to learn the names of the students in the classroom as soon as possible. You will want to find out about their abilities. Take time for a friendly word with each child and show an interest in him. Students are eager to serve and feel more like members of the team when they are asked to contribute their energies and talents. Encouraging each child to share in classroom responsibilities builds rapport and cooperation. Your interest and trust may help transform a potential problem child into a stable, confident citizen.

And you use the child's own needs to hold his attention to the task at hand. Every child wants to win the esteem of his peers. This force, properly channeled, can be of great value to you in creating an effective learning situation.

If most of the students find a task rewarding, and if they are anxious to carry it through to completion, group pressure alone is usually enough to hold down disrupting forces. Many leaders have succeeded by not pushing to the front and not attacking a problem until the interested group was aware of the problem's existence. Instead, they wait until the problem becomes so troublesome that the group actively demands a solution. By seeming to ignore the problem until others demanded that it be solved, and only then leading the group to the attack, they have been able to establish strong and effective leadership.

One of the important motives of the child is the desire for new and interesting experiences. Children resent boredom and do not learn well when they are bored. Although we find it difficult to make each day an exciting new adventure to each child, there are numerous ways in which we can prevent classroom learning from becoming monotonous. A change of pace or a change of activity helps prevent boredom. Particularly among younger children we must vary the mood and the activity frequently. We can use different problems during the same work period or we can try different approaches to the same problem. For example, one part of the period may be given over to individual work, another part to a discussion by the class as a whole, and another part to work in small informal committees. The use of a wide variety of materials—motion pictures, recordings, maps, and models—insures an effective change of pace. Your own appearance and actions can be an element in preventing boredom and promoting active learning—try to speak in an interesting rather than a monotonous voice, wear clothing with some colour, inject humour into the learning situations.

As you work with children you will find that you can suggest methods for attacking specific problems rather than giving them the solutions. You become sensitive to signs of inattention or of departure from the problem at hand. You give individual help where it is needed, but you do not stop an active attack even though you feel certain that it is not the most direct approach to a solution. You will find that some children require much more guidance than others. You will discover that for some children the larger problems must be broken into smaller problems.

Ability Difference

We know that some children lack the ability to progress at the rate we expect of children of their age. But unless they can maintain their self-respect and feel pleased with their progress, they will not learn as rapidly as they can and they will seek satisfactions for their needs in other activities. How can you adjust the learning problems so that each child finds success in the classroom?

First, you must be sure that each child is allowed to complete one task before he begins another. This is particularly important to the child of lower ability, since unless he can complete a task he gains a feeling of failure rather than success from having attempted it. His ability does not allow him to keep several tasks in mind at the same time. You must be sure that each task you lead him to attempt is in keeping with his potentialities for successful completion. The learning that a child acquires from carrying out successfully a relatively small, but carefully chosen, portion of the course work is far more permanent than the learning achieved by muddling through the entire work of the course in a vague and haphazard fashion.

Children sometimes complete the work of a grade so unsatisfactorily that they are required to repeat it. Almost without exception, at the end of his second time around, the repeater has achieved little more mastery than he achieved the first time. If he does show any improvement, the chances are that it is the result of his year's growth in mental maturity rather than of any benefits derived from the previous inadequate exposure to the materials. How can this problem be met in the classroom? Is there any way of adjusting the content of the course to the student who is simply incapable of mastering the entire programme that has been prescribed?

Ideally, the teacher should be able to plan the class work so that some children can master the most necessary skills and the most important knowledge while more able children go on to more advanced activities in keeping with their abilities. At present, however, the organisation of our schools makes such adjustments difficult. But it is a worthy objective. An intelligent adjustment of course content results in far greater permanence of learning than does our present procedure of exposing all members of the class to the same amount of material. It is impossible, of course, for the teacher to do this job by himself. He needs sincere help from curriculum-makers and textbook writers.

However, there are ways in which the skillful teacher can adjust for individual differences in ability and at the same time keep the class together within the broad limits of the course. For example, as soon as you have become acquainted with the ability of each member of the class (through personal conferences, test data, and a study of the child's past record), you can adjust your assignments to fit the child's needs. In a social studies class, you might suggest that one sixth-grade child should investigate the types of animals found in Brazil by reading about them in a supplementary fourth-grade text, and suggest to another that he study the differences in government between Brazil and the United States by using supplementary references of eighth-or ninth-grade difficulty. When you use differential assignments of this sort, you will get the best results by encouraging each child to volunteer for the projects that are of special interest to him. Be careful to call upon each child to present his own findings and be sure that each child is rewarded in examinations for achieving at the level of which he is capable. By rewarding each child and by holding him responsible for his learning, you encourage him to form desirable work habits. But if you hold him responsible for concepts and materials that are beyond his ability to master, you will force him into confusion and discouragement.

The differential assignment gives the pupil of low ability a chance to make a real contribution to the class attack on a general problem. In your planning, do not be content simply to provide reading materials that are written at different levels of difficulty but that contain the same information. That is not enough. Instead, encourage the class as a whole to attack the same large problem and encourage each member of the class to contribute different facts and ideas to its solution.

Our knowledge of individual differences in ability makes one fact clear: Good teaching does not decrease individual differences, either in background of knowledge, mental growth, or special skills. In any one year of instruction, the bright child, if he is really challenged, may grow as much as one and a half to two years in mental ability, reading ability, and general educational achievement. The dull child, even with maximum opportunity and the best of teaching, can scarcely be expected to grow even one year for each year of instruction. Your job as a teacher, then, is not to try to improve on the child's mental equipment, but rather to help him make the best possible use of what he has.

There are numerous ways for seeing that each child finds success in learning to the best of his ability. For example, the child must be successful on the examinations that he takes. One way for making this possible is to examine only on core skills and facts and to use other methods of appraisal and reward for the special contributions of the more able child.

You must use care in pitching your level of instruction so that all children will have an opportunity to learn. Materials presented to the entire class must be understandable by even the most retarded child. You must not allow yourself to be so carried away by the gleaming faces and understanding nods of the bright children that you leave the average or dull child completely confused. Yet if you direct all instruction at the retarded child you fail to offer the bright child the stimulation that he needs.

What is the solution? Obviously you must devote a large portion of instructional time to helping each child identify the problems that he can solve and to furnishing him with the guidance he needs. And the oral instructions or information that you direct to a group of children must be understandable by every child in the group. Material that you present orally as well as material that you assign in books must be chosen with due regard for the ability of the child to understand.

Classroom Leadership

As a classroom teacher, you must furnish leadership. The kind of leadership that you furnish will be a most important determinant of the effectiveness of the learning situation. You could decide to be autocratic—you could seek to decide the minute-by-minute activity of each pupil. You could tell your pupils how you want everything done and, if you had the strength and persistence, you might thus achieve what is sometimes called a well-disciplined classroom. But you would not have an effective learning situation. You would drive your pupils to conform to your wishes by threat of failure and fear of punishment. Your pupils would be working to escape goads rather than working toward goals. For effective learning, the child's attention must be focused on goals that he needs to attain.

There is a second possible type of leadership. You could decide to allow your pupils to take all responsibility, to make all decisions, to set all standards of behaviour, to determine what, when, and how to study. Your role could be no more important than that of any individual pupil—in fact, you could strive to be one of the pupils. This type of leadership is known as *laissez faire*, or "let-alone". If you were to behave in this way, you might have activity in your classroom but it would not lead to active learning, except occasionally and by chance. You would not be offering the guidance that is expected of the professional teacher.

Fortunately, there is a third type of leadership—democratic

leadership—which has come to be accepted as the only type of leadership that the professional teacher may offer. It maintains an active attack on educationally worthwhile problems. You help the child to find appealing goals and to identify the problems that he must solve to attain them. Your leadership involves an element of salesmanship. You know that the child has certain needs. You offer him opportunities for satisfying these needs through learning in the classroom. Your skill in doing this will determine how actively the child will attack his problem and how effectively he will learn.

The leadership that you furnish should not stifle the development of pupil leadership or block pupil responsibility. But, particularly during the opening weeks of work with a group, you must be present promptly at the time class is to begin and you must be ready to assume leadership. If you fail in this responsibility, you will find that other leadership will emerge before you realise it, and the class may be held in undesirable directions. The easiest way to make your leadership acceptable to the pupils is to have a plan for beginning work and for setting the stage for an effective learning situation.

In leading your pupils to attack problems you do not direct the behaviour of your class so much as you furnish an example. Your own behaviour sets the pattern for student behaviour. The fact that you are a mature person to whom the community has delegated authority means that your influence— for good or bad—will be great. You can abuse your authority and abandon your leadership by exhibiting inconsistent or childish behaviour. You can strengthen your leadership by behaving with maturity and stability.

In short, your must show by your own attitude that you expect to set the pattern of behaviour in the classroom. If you expect the class to start promptly, you yourself must start promptly. Instead of shouting over the din of conflicting voices, you wait for order and quiet before you begin. A quiet voice promotes quietness, but a loud voice is a challenge to the pupils to outshout you. By making full use of class time through such techniques as having papers arranged by rows before distributing them and having individuals designated to get materials rather than allowing group congestion, you create an atmosphere in which getting down to business seems the natural way of behaving.

"Discipline" is not an imposed state. Rather, it develops from the desire of the individual child to conform to the behaviour of the group and from his discovery of socially acceptable ways for attaining self-esteem, the esteem of others, new experiences, and security.

If you are successful in setting standards of expected behaviour and in creating an effective learning situation for each child, you will automatically have a classroom with excellent "discipline." Instead of an unbroken, frightened silence, you will have a state of activity in which children feel free to attack felt problems. It will be a goal-directed rather than a goad-directed situation.

Ideally, as time goes on you will want to act more as a spectator than as an overt leader. But you can assume that role only after every child has met a problem that he is actively attempting to solve. Until this situation has developed, you must maintain direct contact with all the members of the group, or at least with those who are not yet able to identify goals beyond the problems at hand.

Thus you first help the class to get the general group goals identified. Each pupil sees for himself how achieving them will satisfy his needs. You start out from a situation that has familiar elements for every child. Perhaps you are to begin the social studies work with a study of the pioneer—his problems and how he met them. You start with something that is familiar to all members of the class. You may ask the students to consider the area around their own homes. What did it look like in pioneer times—no buildings, no streets or roads, no towns. How would a pioneer obtain food, clothing and shelter? During a short discussion it becomes apparent that different students can contribute to different phases of the problem. One may have a grandmother who was a pioneer, another knows of a log cabin still standing, another wants to know how a pioneer obtained soap, wove cloth, or made leather. Another is interested in hunting and wants to know about the firearms of the pioneer. Still another may have an idea that plants furnished medicine, flavouring, and dye. Individual differences, leadership, committees, and individual projects begin to break out from this first group approach.

It will require weeks of effort to build an atmosphere of satisfaction and interest in the work; you can destroy this atmosphere in a few moments by delivering a reprimand intended for one or two persons to the whole group. If a few are tardy, noisy, careless, rude, or otherwise not reaching acceptable standards, this must not be made a cause for threatening the esteem, interest, and security of all. The skillful teacher pulls out the best for comment and sets up attractive goals to lead, but he seldom feels that it is desirable to drive.

Potential Mechanism

Every teacher, no matter what his special interest, is responsible for helping pupils develop efficient study habits and techniques. Children must be taught how to read, for example, not only so that they can gain knowledge from reading but also so that they can integrate their new knowledge with what they already know. They must be encouraged to challenge and to evaluate what they read. We are interested here in how the development of these techniques leads to the creation of an effective learning situation.

When a child enters the classroom, we cannot assume that he knows how to study effectively The study habits that he develops under your influence will be determined by the kind of assignment and examination you give, and by the way in which you guide class discussions. If you emphasise detailed, isolated facts, for example, the student will follow your lead and build his study habits around the same emphasis. If you emphasise broad relationships and underlying values, he will adjust his study habits accordingly.

In many courses, it is necessary for students to develop special study habits and skills. If students are to be expected to obtain information from charts and graphs, for example, you will want to be sure that each child knows how to read them with understanding. Or you may want to provide practice in using the library and special study aids, such as chapter questions, the index, and the glossary.

In a science class, a good procedure is to choose a portion of the new assignment and to ask the students to read a certain paragraph in it. Then you might ask one of the students a question to test his knowledge of the new material, or you might ask him to propose some questions that will test understanding of the paragraph. You may want to proceed well into the assignment, paragraph by paragraph, following the same procedure.

You will certainly want to explain the effectiveness of recall as a study procedure and provide frequent class exercises that require the use of recall in the supervised study of the course materials.

How much material a child reads before he stops to recall will depend upon the difficulty of the material and the number of ideas it contains. In mathematics, the study unit may be only a single sentence, in chemistry a paragraph, and in the social sciences two or three paragraphs. Encourage each child to spend a few minutes in recall at the end of each large study unit and to check on the completeness of his recall before he proceeds.

Since a well-formed habit furnishes its own source of motivation, the formation of good learning habits should be one of your primary aims. Training in the development of these habits should start with the earliest tasks and should continue for as long as the child remains in school. The child who frequently experiences the satisfaction that accompanies the successful completion of his tasks soon comes to value that feeling and is reluctant to leave a task unfinished.

Effective study techniques, then, are teachable, and they are an important part of the equipment of the efficient learner.

Highest Retention

When we studied human learning, one of our major discoveries was that review has a tremendous effect on retention. Forgetting is cut to a minimum when review is correctly scheduled and carried out. Review is particularly powerful in aiding us to remember clearly for a long period of time. But we know that we cannot expect the child to review properly until he understands the value of review and has established efficient habits of reviewing. You will be responsible for using instructional procedures that promote and encourage review. There are many ways in which you can do this.

Recalling yesterday's material to set the stage for today's class, summarising the lesson and the unit, introducing new problems that require the use of previously learned materials and procedures, and the written examination are all effective review techniques. Their greatest value, however, is the long-range effect they have on the learner: When the child learns to expect reviews and is rewarded for reviewing, he develops the habit of reviewing.

When you begin your teaching, you may find that you are proceeding far too rapidly to new materials and skills without providing sufficient time for the development, elaboration, illustration, and review of each important concept along the way. Almost all new teachers have that experience. You may be tempted to cover the entire course in a week or two, and to be satisfied that your explanations and instructions are so clear that each child must understand the material. In your eagerness, you may forget that teaching is much more than just dispensing information and answers, and that you cannot transfer understandings directly from your mind to the mind of the child. You cannot guide him directly to goals. He himself must meet problems and find applications. The child needs time to accept and to review the information and understandings that you yourself have taken years to acquire.

You will need to be especially careful to avoid these faults if you were a brilliant student yourself. If you found the curriculum of the elementary and secondary schools easy to master, you may become impatient with students who are less capable than you were. This is a regrettable tendency, because your high intelligence and broad scholastic background should help rather than hinder you in guiding the average and below-average child to solve his learning problems.

The Review of Yesterday's Learnings. To be certain that the children have the material they learned yesterday under control and ready to take its place with what they are to learn today, you will need to devote some time to review at the beginning of each class meeting. Your technique in conducting this review will determine whether or not each child is to participate actively in it. A particularly poor technique, one that you will want to avoid, is to call on a good student to summarise yesterday's work.

Certainly this saves time, but it accomplishes even less than if you were to give the summary yourself. As soon as you have announced which child is to recite, the review ceases to be a problem for the other children. Once they discover that only the most capable students are always called on, they simply retire from the review session. As a result, only the students who have already proved their ability actually profit from the reviews.

A far sounder procedure is to direct your questions to the class in general and to allow time enough for each member to formulate his reply. In this way, everyone reviews before anyone recites. You may want to give a weaker student the opportunity to make the first contribution, and then encourage the stronger students to furnish additional points. By emphasising and confirming what each pupil gets right in his contribution, you reward him for his effort. You can usually assume that any errors will be corrected by the pupils who contribute later. This general procedure for conducting review encourages each child to form the habit of reviewing. He learns to recall yesterday's material as he enters the classroom and as he prepares the day's new assignment.

This emphasis on class review does not mean that formal drill in response to questions about facts, dates, and names has again become an approved educational practice. Emphasis on review is simply a modern application of the discovery that learnings are soon lost unless we place them in new frameworks, apply them to new problems, recall them, and make them ready to serve as a basis for new learnings.

As you gain experience, you will come to recognise how important it is to devote a large portion of your instructional time to nailing down, reviewing, and integrating the principles, understandings, and skills that are of crucial importance. Even when you present new materials, you will find review valuable. The old rule of presenting the new in terms of the old has not become outmoded in teaching practice. If facts or principles are worth learning, they are certainly worth reviewing.

The Summary as a Review. You must be sure, then, that new knowledge is built upon and becomes integrated with what is already known. You will want to emphasise the relationship between new material and present knowledge. To insure that this relationship is meaningful, try to encourage the pupils to supply appropriate applications and illustrations, instead of handing them out yourself. Near the end of the class period, take time to summarise today's learnings. Tomorrow's assignment should come logically from the problems identified in today's summary. The summary and its culmination in the assignment are extremely important parts of effective teaching technique. The summary lesson at the end of each unit provides a further opportunity for reviewing the progress that has been made and for identifying new problems. It gives the children a chance to make a logical transition to the new unit by tying together the material that they have learned and the problems that they are yet to solve.

The Examination as a Review : The examination itself has an important function in review. The child is motivated to review before the examination. He reviews while he is taking the examination, and he reviews when the examination is later discussed in class. We shall talk more about the use of the examination as a learning device and as a method of appraising the child's progress. Here we are interested in how the examination implements review.

When we know that we must actually demonstrate our grasp of materials, we are motivated to learn them. It might seem that merely knowing that material will be useful at some later time should provide sufficient incentive for learning it. Sometimes that is enough, but not always. The effectiveness of incentives depends in part on how soon they can be realised. Knowing that we will be rewarded tomorrow for having new material under control is a greater incentive than simply knowing that the material may be useful some time in the future. For this reason, short, frequent examinations have a greater motivational effect than do longer but less frequent examinations.

Some General Principles of Review : A few new facts and principles, well understood, are of more permanent value than many facts and principles inadequately understood. The amount of new material that a child can learn each day increases as he grows in mental age and as his background of information develops. Thus, in the lower grades children must spend far less time learning new materials and far more time reviewing and integrating what they have already learned than must children in the upper grades.

As a professional teacher, you will realise that working out the correct solution is less important to a child than is the experience that he gains in facing the problem. And so it is with review itself. As each student reviews, his new knowledge is revitalised and integrated with his past learnings. The act of review is much more than simply getting back to the level of learning that had been achieved before forgetting took place. It leads to new understandings and to new relationships. It reveals to the student exciting generalisations that are infinitely more permanent and useful to him than are isolated facts and ideas.

Concept of Organised Classwork

We have tried to identify the factors that are important in creating an effective learning situation that moves toward educational goals. Let us now examine the important professional problem of directing the minute-to-minute effective learning situations toward broad week-to-week and year-to-year objectives. What approach have teachers found most effective in planning for a day-to-day progress toward the broad course objectives?

Many years ago, Johann Friederich Herbart (1776-1841) listed five formal steps that he considered basic to good teaching procedure. These steps, little modified except for changes in name and a reduction in formality, have persisted to the present time as the psychological basis for directing effective learning. They are: preparation, presentation, association, systematisation, and application. Let us see how these steps are related to what we know about the learning process.

Preparation : Preparation (or exploration and assignment, as it is called by some writers) consists principally of arousing in the child an eagerness to learn. The child's awareness of a problem, and his belief that he can satisfy certain needs by solving it, are the primary requirements of an effective learning situation. His need may be simply a desire for new experiences (sometimes called curiosity), or he may want to win the esteem of his fellow students or of his teacher. As you introduce each new unit and make each day's assignment, you can suggest to the child how the coming activities will help him to satisfy his needs. Making assignments is not a matter of doling out jobs. Rather, it is an opportunity to set up attractive goals and to suggest ways in which they can be reached. Children learn very little unless they feel the need to solve a problem. Assigning a certain number of pages to be read fails to pose any real problem, except that of finding the necessary time. And it fails to satisfy and need, except the need to avoid censure for failure to carry it out.

Properly used, the assignment gives us a golden opportunity to bring into play the psychological motives of each child. It leads directly to the development of a need and an eagerness to learn. It brings problems into focus and it suggests to the child ways in which he can satisfy his needs. It gives direction to his work. It is here that we can provide for individual differences in ability and guide each child toward the path that he is best able to travel. It is here that the child develops his mental set to learn and to remember.

One of the results of a carefully planned assignment is that the child voluntarily assumes responsibility for his learning. If his interest is great enough, you will need to do little more than guide him from time to time when his efforts lead him into a particularly difficult phase of the assignment.

How much time should be spent in making the assignment depends on several factors: the type of subject matter, whether you are introducing a new unit or just giving day-to-day direction, and the maturity of the pupils. Few teachers can be accused of spending too much time in making assignments. The tendency is to spend far too little time.

Ideally, the next day's assignment should grow out of the summary of the day's accomplishment. It follows the summary and usually precedes the period of supervised study. Since it does come near the end of the class period, many teachers fall into the habit of treating it casually, forgetting that preparation is the first and most important step in learning. We must be constantly on guard not to become so engrossed in the work at hand that we fail to build a need for the work to be done before the class meets again. At the beginning of a new unit of work, for example, an entire class period can profitably be devoted to making the assignment. With experience, you will learn how much time is needed for making the daily assignments. In any event, making assignments must not be a dictatorial act. The more successful you are in building a need for learning, the more democratic the learning process becomes.

Presentation : There is a wide variety of methods for presenting the materials that the pupils need in overcoming the problems and in reaching the goals identified during the assignment. You will make a detailed study of these methods in other professional courses. Here we can say simply that the specific methods used will depend somewhat on the subject and on the age and abilities of the pupils.

In literature and the social studies, for example, much of the presentation of the material that the child needs for solving his problems is individualised. The child reads materials that are appropriate to his abilities. In the natural sciences, presentation often takes place in the laboratory. In mathematics, you yourself may present the necessary background material, or you may encourage the pupils to "discover" it by themselves under your guidance. No matter what technique you use, presentation must never degenerate into a mechanical handing out of information. Although you are anxious to guide the child to effective means of solving his problems and reaching his goal, so far as possible the actual exploration should be conducted by the child himself.

The actual solutions that the child discovers as he searches for materials that will solve, his problems may be far less important than the skills that he gains in learning how to solve problems. You will find that questions such as "Where can we find out about this?" or "How can we divide this job up so that some of us can do one part of it and some can do another?" are far more effective than are direct suggestions on where the solutions can be found or an apportioning of individual parts of the job by you.

With many types of problems you may want to suggest that the class should form committees to take over specific parts of the project. It may be that the materials or ideas for meeting certain types of problems should come from resources outside the classroom. This may be accomplished by letting the children write letters, visit city officials, make trips to libraries or museums, or arrange for field trips for the purpose of collecting information or observing conditions. Whatever method is used (laboratory, class discussion, reading, visual aids, field trips, or committees) the direction and choice often can come from the students, under your guidance. Allowing each child to contribute to the solution of the group's problems can lead automatically to an adjustment for individual differences in ability, background, and interest and to a tremendous energising of the activity.

Association : This step has been called assimilation by some modern writers and comparison and abstraction by others. To a large extent, it consists of seeing that the mastery of the new materials grows out of the previous mastery of similar materials and problems. The new learning must take place as a building on and an integrating with the old.

In studying government, the child learns first about his own city or country government, and then proceeds to state and national government. In studying geography, he begins with the rivers, climate, and raw materials of the region with which he is familiar, and then goes on to the features of broader regions with which he is less familiar. He moves from the known to the unknown. He approaches the problems faced by other groups of people or by other nations, either during his own time or at other times, through his knowledge of current problems. History, geography, and sociology must have their roots in the daily lives of the pupils. Facts about the culture of other peoples (the food they eat, the clothing they wear, and the houses they build) take on meaning when they are studied in relation to the problems posed by climate, soil, raw materials, plant and animal life, and transportation routes. Since these factors influence our own living habits, they provide a meaningful approach to the habits of others. By understanding that cultural patterns are the expression of human needs, the child is able to comprehend the behaviour of whole groups and nations of people in terms of his own felt needs and problems.

A failure to provide for significant association in the learning experience encourages children to be satisfied with pat verbalisms at the expense of true understanding. Facts are necessary, of course, since they must precede application. But unless the child is able to utilise facts in actual situations, they are of little value to him. If the child's school experience is to be valuable to him in later life, he must develop the ability to apply the facts he learns in school to other situations. By providing for meaningful association at every phase of the learning process, you can guarantee that the facts he learns will take on meaning in ever-widening contexts.

Systematisation : This step, which has been called organisation by some modern writers and generalisation by others, is closely interwoven with presentation and association. Since children are limited in experience and background knowledge, especially in the early grades, it is your responsibility to suggest to them how the new facts they encounter fit into orderly patterns of knowledge. Fortunately, the tendency to generalise is inherent in all human beings; it is one mark of intelligent behaviour. If the infant lacked this tendency, he would never learn to avoid touching all hot stoves after he had touched one. As he matures, he must learn to extend his powers of generalising to less vivid experiences, to abstract facts and concepts. He must gradually become aware that all knowledge is part of an organised system.

Through learning to generalise his knowledge, the child learns to take the well-learned elements of one situation and recognise where they belong when he encounters them in a new situation. Generalisation is a key to the transfer of training from one problem situation to the solution of another.

At an elementary level, the child discovers that methods for determining the square inches in the rectangles that are pictured in his arithmetic book can be applied also to computing the square feet in the playground or the size of a surface that is to be painted. At a higher level, he recognises that the Golden Rule can be applied as a guide in his relations with others.

Application : In this step, the pupil uses the knowledge that he has gained from a particular study unit in some concrete situation. He uses his organised knowledge of punctuation, for example, in writing themes. But if you want to make sure that he can generalise his new knowledge, you will see that he continues to apply it in all the writing he does after he has learned the specific elements of punctuation. The more often we apply the materials we have learned, the deeper our general understanding of them becomes and the longer we retain them.

Application satisfies the motivation that the pupil experienced during the assignment period. It gives him a feeling of security and self-esteem. The pleasant feeling that accompanies successful application serves to fix the new learning securely in his mind, ready to be used again when it is needed.

Transfer at Wide Level

Now we come to our final problem. We know that classroom learning must prepare the child for life's needs. Though technically the curriculum-maker specifies what should be learned by the children in your classes, you yourself determine what is learned by each child. How can you appraise the relative values of the possible learnings of the classroom? How can you guarantee that what should be learned, is learned?

Incidental vs. Planned Learning : The child learns much in the classroom that has not been listed in our lesson plans or included in our written course of study. He may notice the colour of the room, and the presence or even the purpose of items of instructional equipment left in the room by another class. He may learn how to live with his classmates with the least amount of unpleasantness, and he may learn to make allowances for the day-to-day variations in the teacher's mood. However, most of these so-called incidental learnings occur only if some problem arises in his mind about the colour of the room, the use of a piece of equipment, or getting along with his classmates or with his teacher. He acquires little that is not needed for the solution of actual problems. For example, you may have lived in your present neighbourhood for some time and yet cannot recall the location of the nearest fire alarm box, whether or not there is a telephone pole near a certain corner, or the number of steps on your front porch.

Certainly frequency of an experience does not guarantee that a child will learn. Unless weaknesses in his writing become a problem for him, a child can write a hundred letters or themes and show no improvement. Even if you help him to develop good work habits they soon deteriorate unless his good habits make the work easier or in some other way are rewarding to him. If poor habits meet his needs as well as good ones and if there is no demand that he attain a certain degree of efficiency, poor habits remain. In short, mere presence of opportunity to learn does not guarantee learning.

We recognise, then, that no important fact or principle may be entrusted to incidental learning alone and that all the really important skills, ideals, and attitudes must be taught by every teacher regardless of his subject-matter specialty. But the child can gain much from so-called incidental learnings if you take full advantage of your opportunities. Although certain specific learnings are a part of a social studies class, for example, at the same time you can teach, incidentally, oral and written English, spelling, and effective habits of learning. And in the English class as you teach oral and written expression you can help the child to develop emotionally and socially. But you must be conscious of these incidental goals. You cannot expect the learnings to occur automatically.

For this reason, whether you teach in the elementary or in the secondary school, you must be aware of what each subject that the child studies can contribute to his total curriculum. In addition to knowing the specific goals of your subject, you must know the general goals of education and the specific goals that each other teacher strives to reach. The personal and educational development of boys and girls—not the mere teaching of English, sciences, mathematics, art, or music—is your major professional responsibility.

Social Utility : You will be responsible for the teaching of a broad area of subject matter and skills. Some of the pupils in your class will have the ability to achieve nearly all the learnings that are set as objectives for your class. But there are others who can achieve but a small portion. We know that a few learnings well mastered are much more valuable than an inadequate exposure to many learnings. What criteria can you use for selecting that portion of the curriculum that is most important to the child? Let's examine the criteria that are used by the curriculum-maker when he builds the total course of study for a grade or subject-matter area.

The most common criterion of the curriculum-builder is that of social utility. He seeks to determine whether a certain bit of information, a concept, or a skill has sufficient value that it should be learned by every child, by most children, by only the most able children, or by no child. The curriculum-maker recognises that the accumulated knowledge of our society is so vast that each individual masters but a comparatively small portion of it. We must select those items of knowledge most necessary to the life of the child in a social world.

Each child must be given the best possible preparation for meeting the problems of later life. He must prepare for a vocation, for citizenship, and for satisfying leisure-time activity.

If you teach in the high school, you should be enthusiastic about what your specialty contributes to the total educational growth of each child. If you are a social-studies teacher you will see that the problems of the world and the necessity for training in good citizenship make preparation in the social studies extremely important. If you teach science, you will have spent many years in getting acquainted with the wonders and values of that field and you will be convinced of the value of your contribution. If you teach English, you will know that excellence in written and oral English has wide practical and cultural value and that far too little time is available for its development. Whatever you teach—physical education and health, art, music, mathematics, and languages, or any other portion of the curriculum—you will see that children need the knowledge and skills that you can offer them. But you must not allow this enthusiasm to prevent you from coordinating your effort with the efforts of those who teach different subjects.

There is little doubt that each child could be a better citizen if he could possess the knowledge that is held by the professor of social science or at least by the college major in that field. There is little doubt that science is important. Its importance has been demonstrated both in the winning of wars and the development of a peacetime world. Ability in oral and written expression and an appreciation of good literature contribute much to the success and happiness of the individual. There is no doubt that without health all other learning avails us but little and that art and music are strong contributors to the peace and happiness of the

Awasthy, G.C. : *Broadcasting in India*, Allied Publishers Private Ltd., Bombay, 1965

Bloom, B.S. : *Taxonomy of Educational Objectives: The Classification of Educational Goals. Handbook Cognitive Domain and Affective Domain*, Oxford, New York, 1965.

Beiggs L.S. : *Educational Psychology*, Fitteburgh American Institute for Research, 1966.

Brown, J.W. Lewis, R.B. & Hercleread. A.V. : *Instruction: Materials and Methods*, Mc Graw Hill Book Co., New York, 1964.

Chauhan, S.S. : *A Textbook of Programmed Instruction*, Sterling Publishers, New Delhi.

Das, R.C. : *Educational Psychology*, Sterling Publishers, New Delhi.

Gagne, R.M. : *The Conditions of Learning*, Holt Binsort and Winston, New York, 1965.

Haban, Charles, F. : *Movies that Teach*, New York, Dryden Press, 1945.

Hancock, Alan : *Planning for Educational Psychology*, Longmans, London, 1977.

Kulkarni, S.S. : *Teaching Learning Process: A Systems Analysis*, UNESCO Regional Office for Education in Asia, Bangkok, 1975.

Kaul, B.N. & Others : *Studies in Distance Education*, Association of Indian Universities, IGNOU, New Delhi, 1983.

Lowman, J. : *Mastering Techniques of Teaching*, Prentice Hall India, New Delhi, 1987.

individual. The only legitimate question that can be raised in any issue of this kind concerns the best use that we can make of our limited time for education and the limited abilities of even the superior students.

Particularly if you teach in the elementary grades where you have control of the child's time for most of the day, you must not allow yourself to concentrate on any one subject-matter field to the neglect of other fields simply because of your own personal interests. Too often a teacher who has a particularly strong interest in natural science, social science, art, languages, or music devotes a large portion of the available time to one of these areas while reading, arithmetic, spelling, writing, and other necessary skills receive too little emphasis. When this happens the child fails to get the preparation for life that he needs. We see examples of this in the secondary school also. Suppose that you are convinced that a knowledge of early American history is extremely important and interesting yet you are assigned to teach a class in local government. And suppose that you disregard the name and purpose of the course and emphasise American history, with the result that the children never gain an adequate knowledge of local government. What happens when, at a later period, a portion of their curriculum is devoted to a study of American history? As you can see, material they already know will be repeated and your students will have missed completely the knowledge of local government that they should have obtained.

Thus, since there is a limited period of time and even the better students can learn but a few new things each day, the decision on what to teach cannot be made on the basis of which elements of knowledge have or may have value. The decision must be made on the basis of which combination has most value

Matheson, Alastair. *The Communication Materials and Methods*, Mc Graw Hill Book Company, New Delhi, 1964.

Mohanty, J. : *Educational Broadcasting: Radio & Television in Education*, Sterling Publishers, New Delhi, 1984.

———, *Educational Administration, Management & School Organisation*, Meneka Prakashan, Sambalpur, 1996.

———, *Indian Education in the Emerging Society*, Sterling Publishers, New Delhi, 1982.

Menon, Narayan : *The Communication Revolution*, National Book Trust, New Delhi, 1976.

Mukhopadhyay, M. : *Educational Technology Year Book*, 1988, AIAET, New Delhi, 1989.

Munn, Norman L. : *The Fundamentals of Human Adjustment*, Houghter Miffin Co., Boston, 1965.

Ottaway A.K.C. : *Education and Psychology*, Routldge and Kegan Paul, London, 1962.

Rahman, S.A. : *Study in Educational Television*, Royal Pub., Orissa, 1972.

Rewntreu, Desk : *Educational Technology in Curriculum Development*, Harper and Row Publishers, London, 1990.

Sampath, K. : *Introduction to Educational Psychology*, Sterling, New Delhi, 1981.

Schramm, Wilbur : *The Process and Effects of Mass Communication*, Uni of Illinois, Urbane.

———, *Programmes Instruction: Today and Tomorrow*, The Funds of Advancement of Education, New York, 1962.

Sharma, G.D. & Ahmed, S.R. : *Methodologies of Teaching in Colleges*, UNESCO UGC & NIEPA, New Delhi, 1994.

Singh, Bakshish : *Correspondence Education in India*, National Council for Correspondence Education, India, 1978.

Vedanayagam, G. : *Teaching Technology for College Teachers*, Sterling Publishers, New Delhi, 1989.

The most common criterion of the curriculum-builder is that of social utility. He seeks to determine whether a certain bit of information, a concept, or a skill has sufficient value that it should be learned by every child, by most children, by only the most able children, or by no child. The curriculum-maker recognises that the accumulated knowledge of our society is so vast that each individual masters but a comparatively small portion of it. We must select those items of knowledge most necessary to the life of the child in a social world.

Each child must be given the best possible preparation for meeting the problems of later life. He must prepare for a vocation, for citizenship, and for satisfying leisure-time activity.

If you teach in the high school, you should be enthusiastic about what your specialty contributes to the total educational growth of each child. If you are a social-studies teacher you will see that the problems of the world and the necessity for training in good citizenship make preparation in the social studies extremely important. If you teach science, you will have spent many years in getting acquainted with the wonders and values of that field and you will be convinced of the value of your contribution. If you teach English, you will know that excellence in written and oral English has wide practical and cultural value and that far too little time is available for its development. Whatever you teach—physical education and health, art, music, mathematics, and languages, or any other portion of the curriculum—you will see that children need the knowledge and skills that you can offer them. But you must not allow this enthusiasm to prevent you from coordinating your effort with the efforts of those who teach different subjects.

There is little doubt that each child could be a better citizen if he could possess the knowledge that is held by the professor of social science or at least by the college major in that field. There is little doubt that science is important. Its importance has been demonstrated both in the winning of wars and the development of a peacetime world. Ability in oral and written expression and an appreciation of good literature contribute much to the success and happiness of the individual. There is no doubt that without health all other learning avails us but little and that art and music are strong contributors to the peace and happiness of the individual. The only legitimate question that can be raised in any issue of this kind concerns the best use that we can make of our limited time for education and the limited abilities of even the superior students.

Particularly if you teach in the elementary grades where you have control of the child's time for most of the day, you must not allow yourself to concentrate on any one subject-matter field to the neglect of other fields simply because of your own personal interests. Too often a teacher who has a particularly strong interest in natural science, social science, art, languages, or music devotes a large portion of the available time to one of these areas while reading, arithmetic, spelling, writing, and other necessary skills receive too little emphasis. When this happens the child fails to get the preparation for life that he needs. We see examples of this in the secondary school also. Suppose that you are convinced that a knowledge of early American history is extremely important and interesting yet you are assigned to teach a class in local government. And suppose that you disregard the name and purpose of the course and emphasise American history, with the result that the children never gain an adequate knowledge of local government. What happens when, at a later period, a portion of their curriculum is devoted to a study of American history? As you can see, material they already know will be repeated and your students will have missed completely the knowledge of local government that they should have obtained.

Thus, since there is a limited period of time and even the better students can learn but a few new things each day, the decision on what to teach cannot be made on the basis of which elements of knowledge have or may have value. The decision must be made on the basis of which combination has most value in meeting the social, economic, and personal needs of the child.

Although the creation of an effective learning situation is a basic professional task of the teacher, your responsibility cannot stop there. Just any learning will not do. Learning must have a purpose. It must be organised toward the child's present and future life needs. Learning problems must be chosen in accordance with each child's abilities and life goals. We must apply our knowledge of the principles of learning and motivation as we guide the learning of each child in the classroom.

Index

❑❑❑